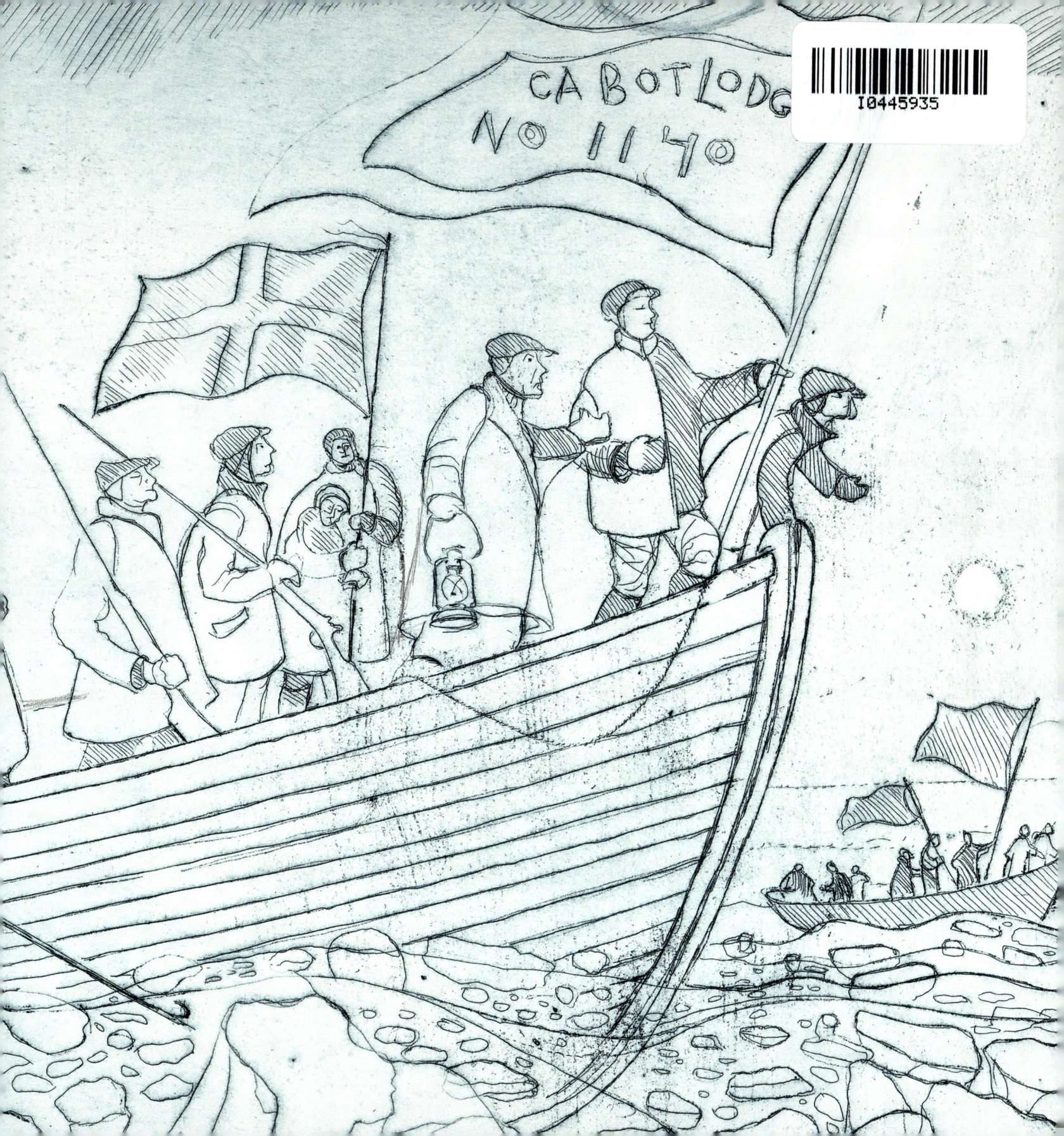

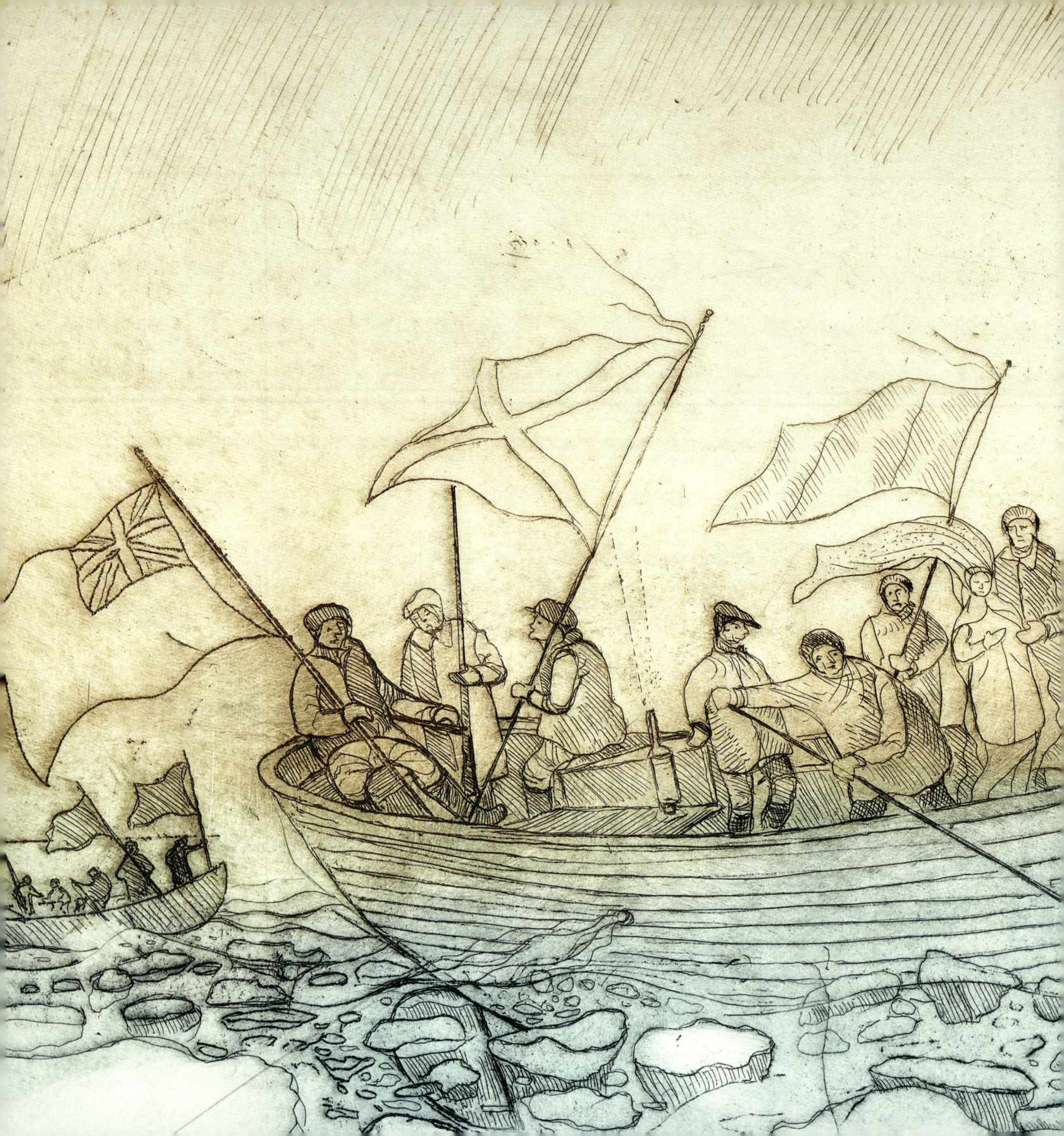

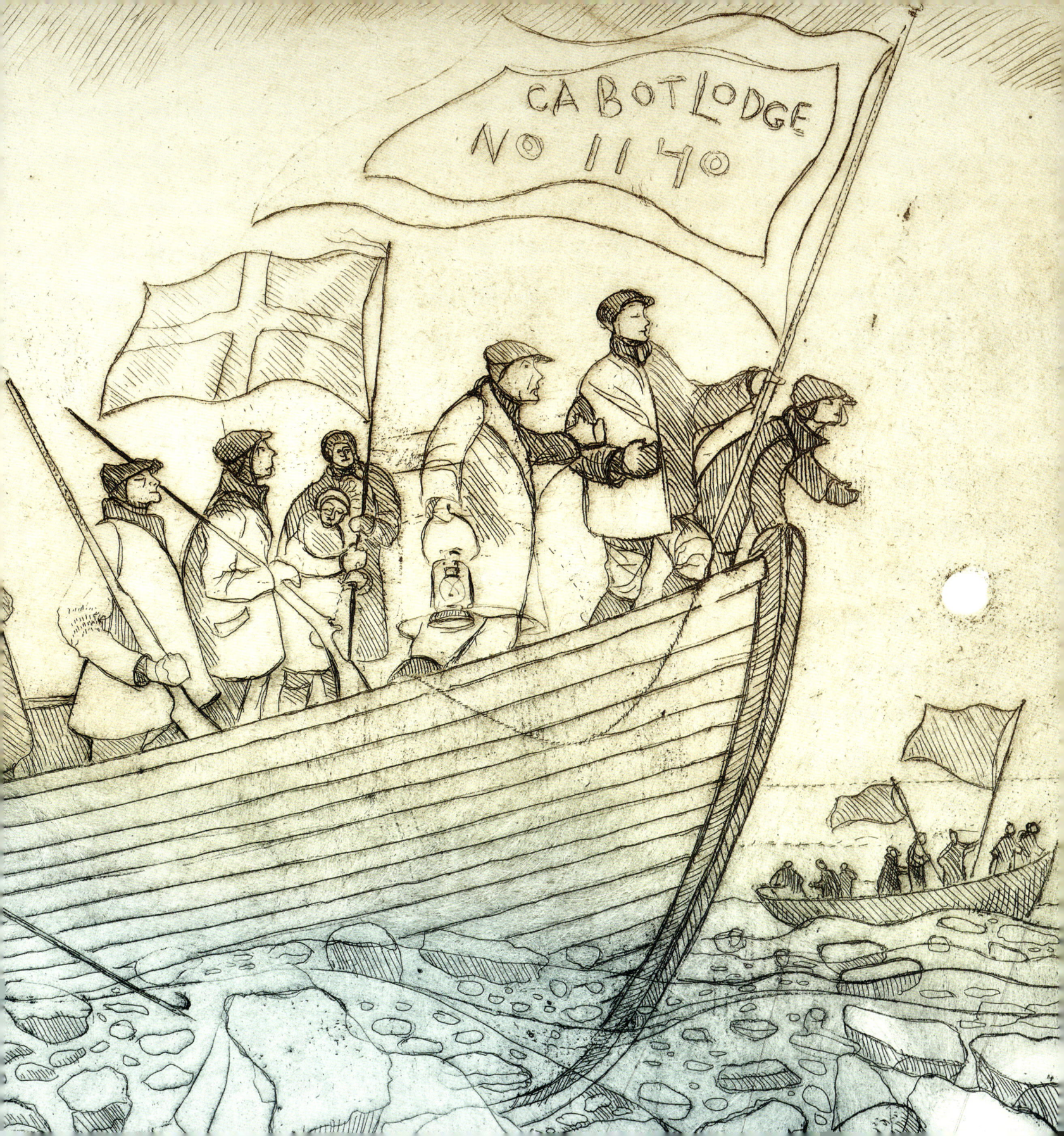

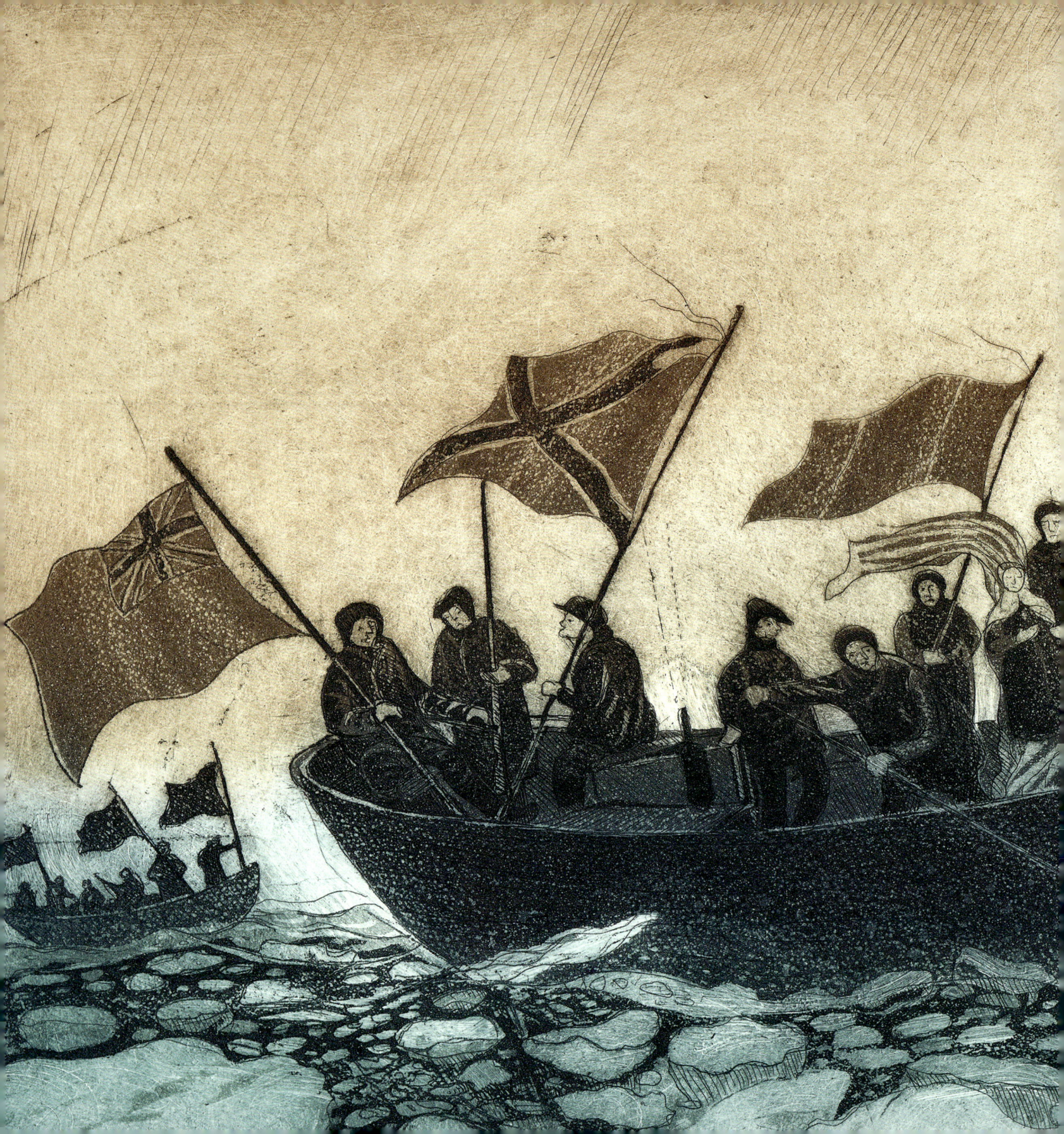

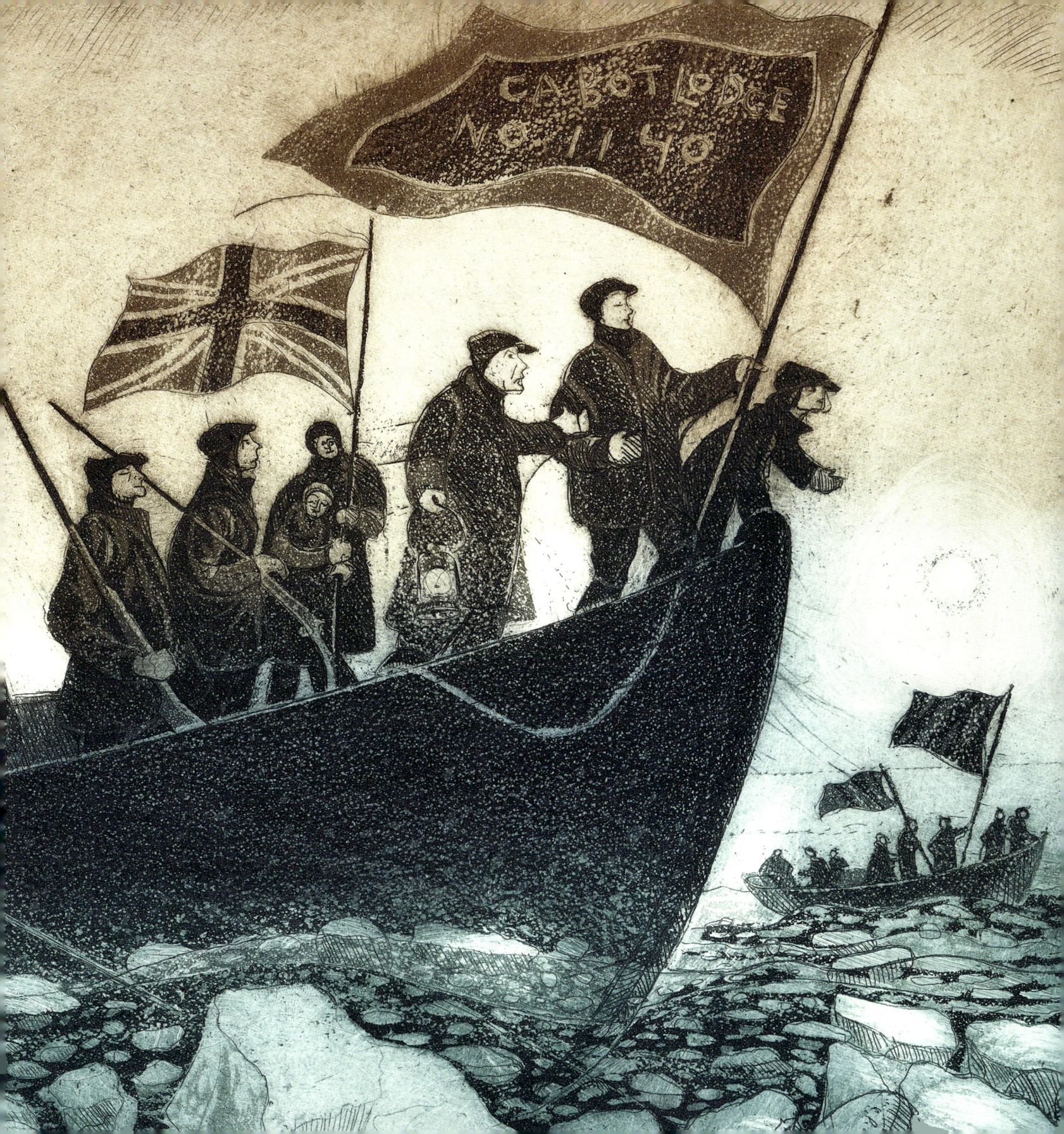

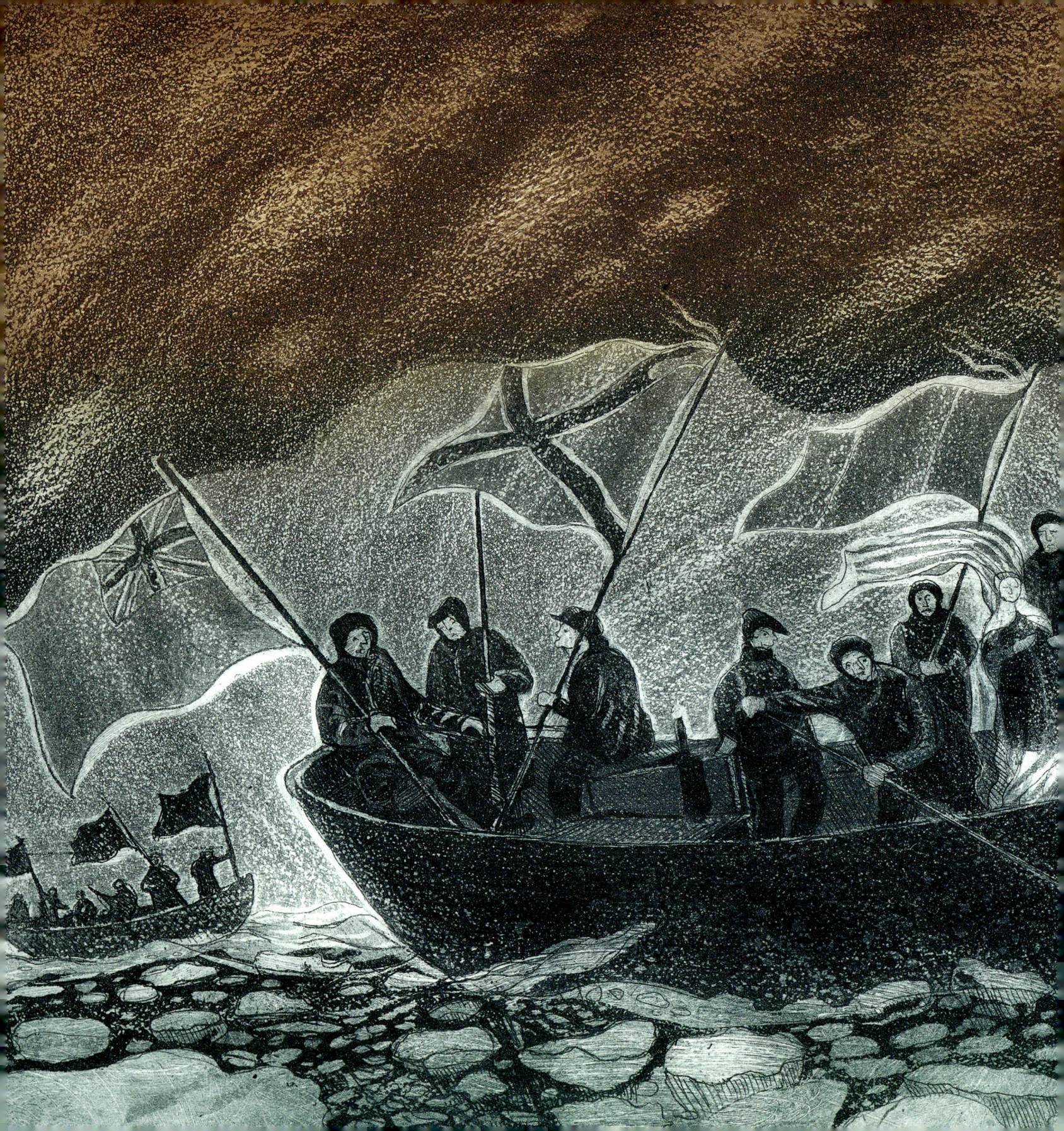

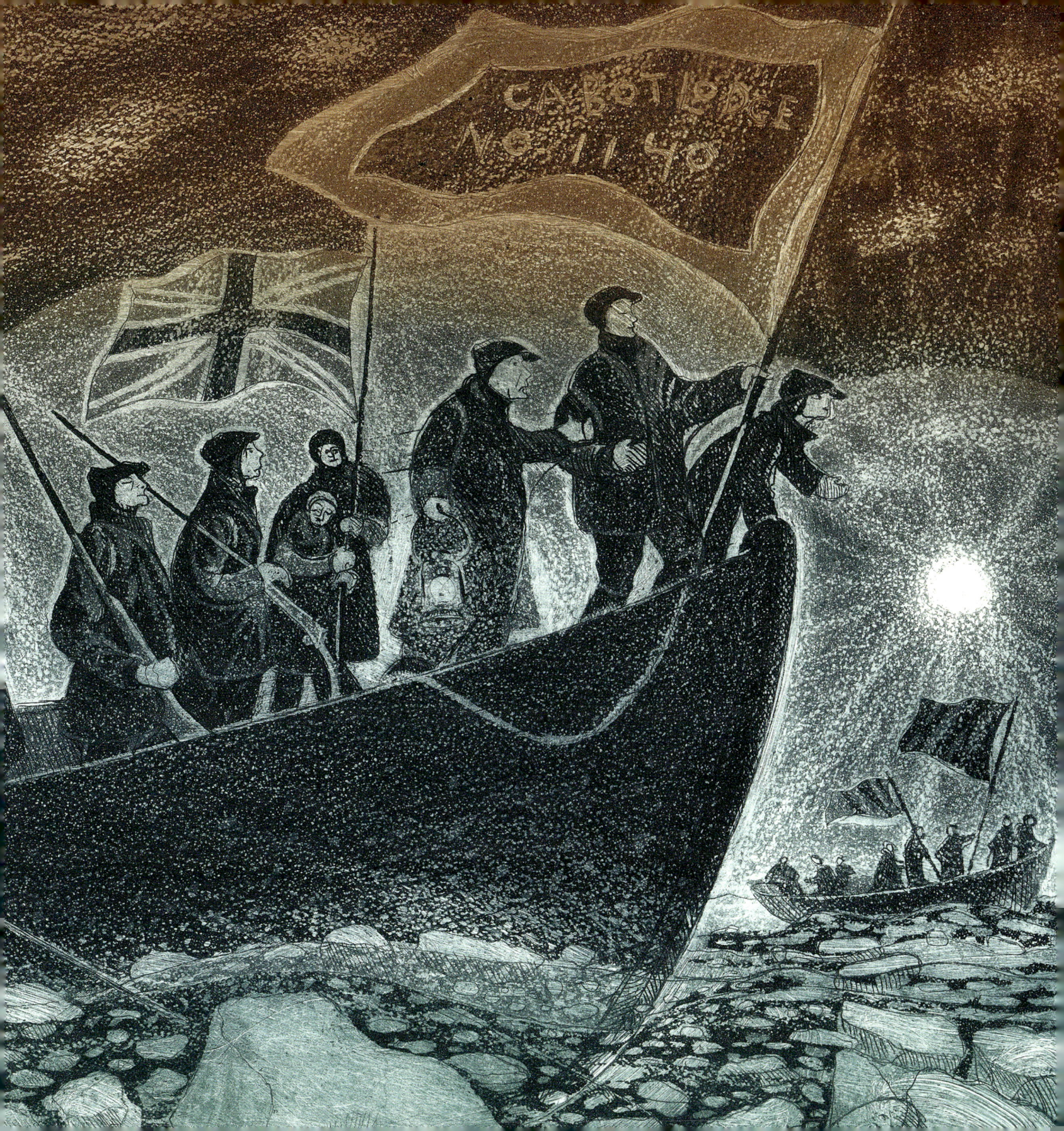

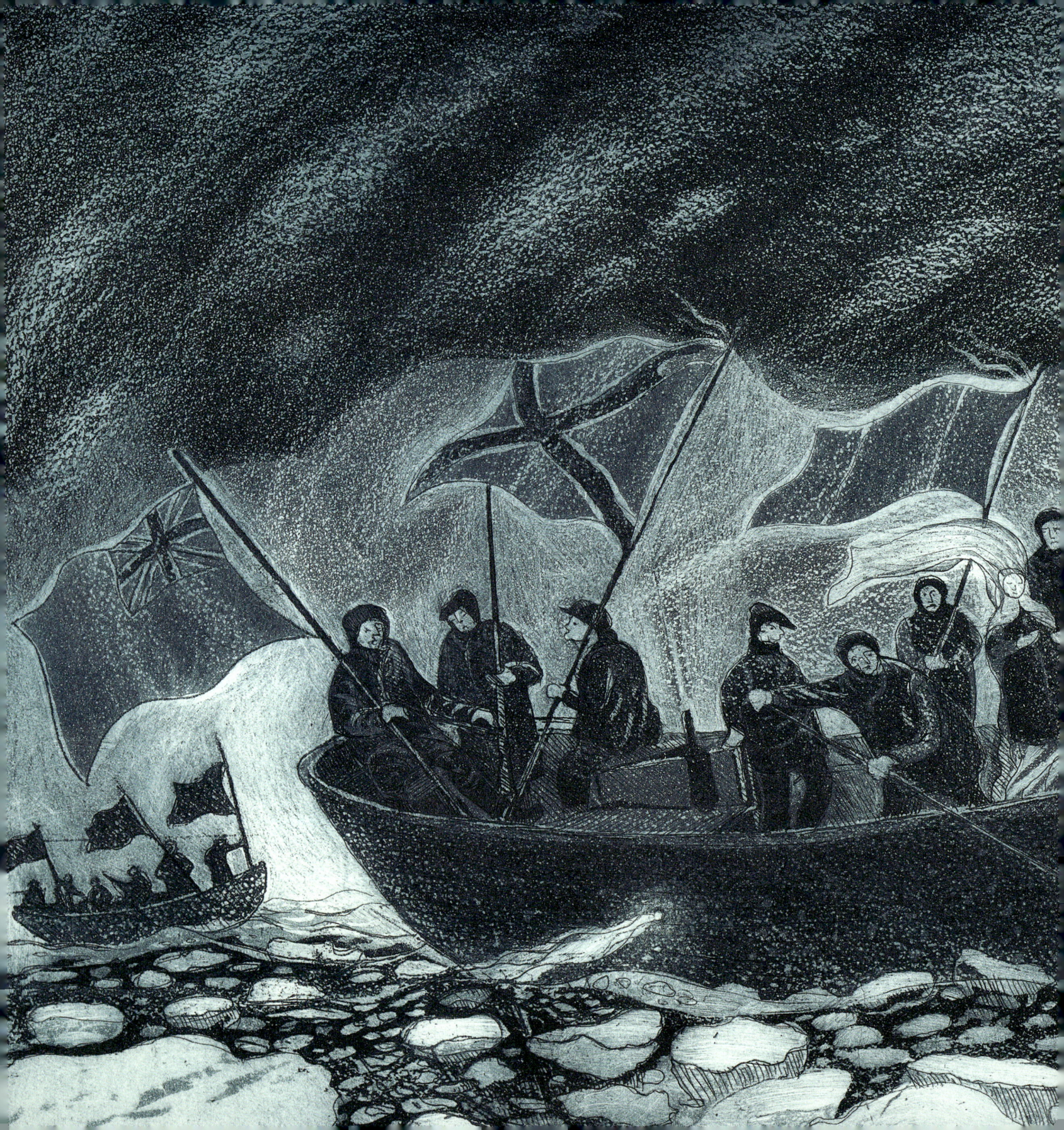

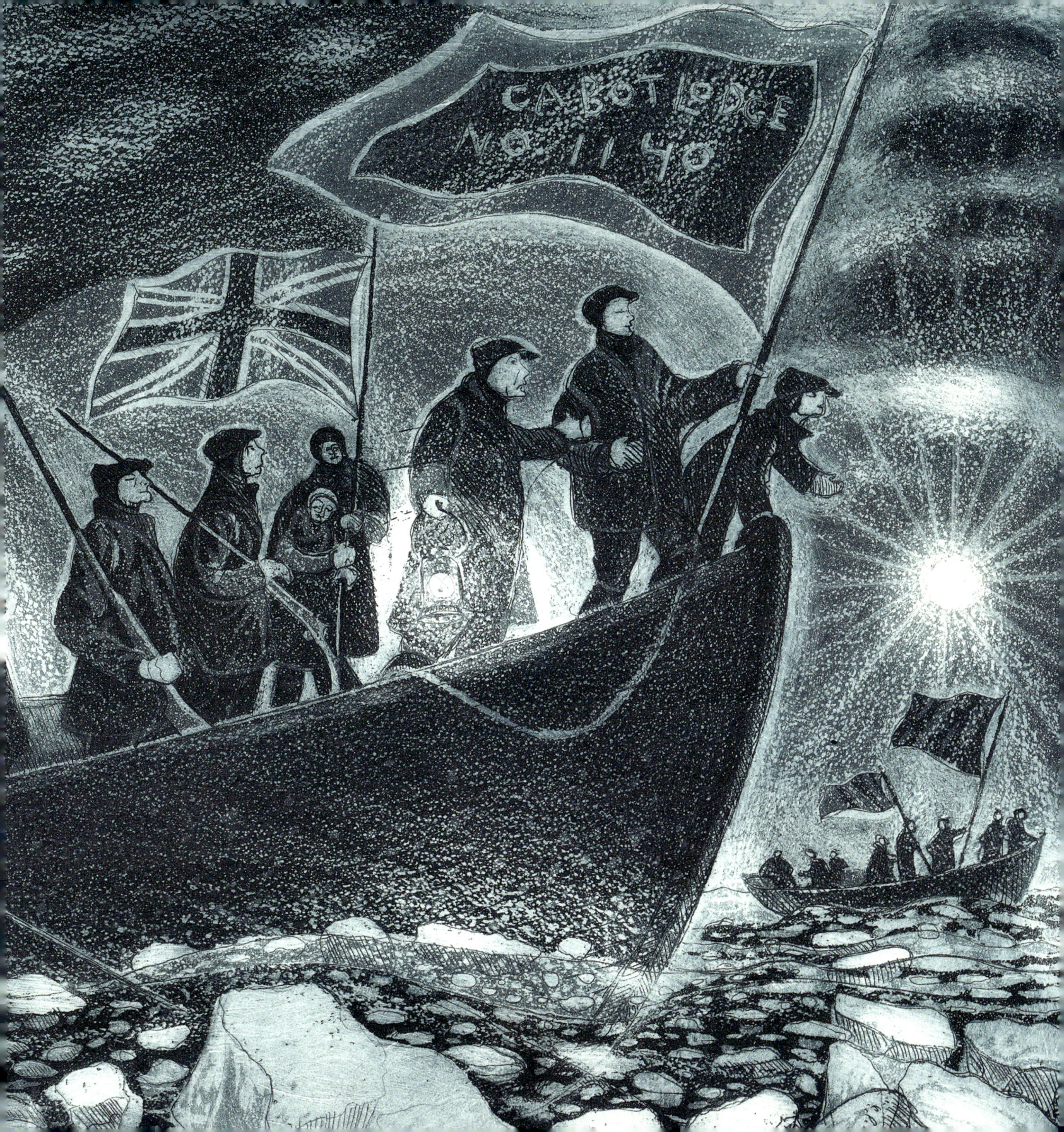

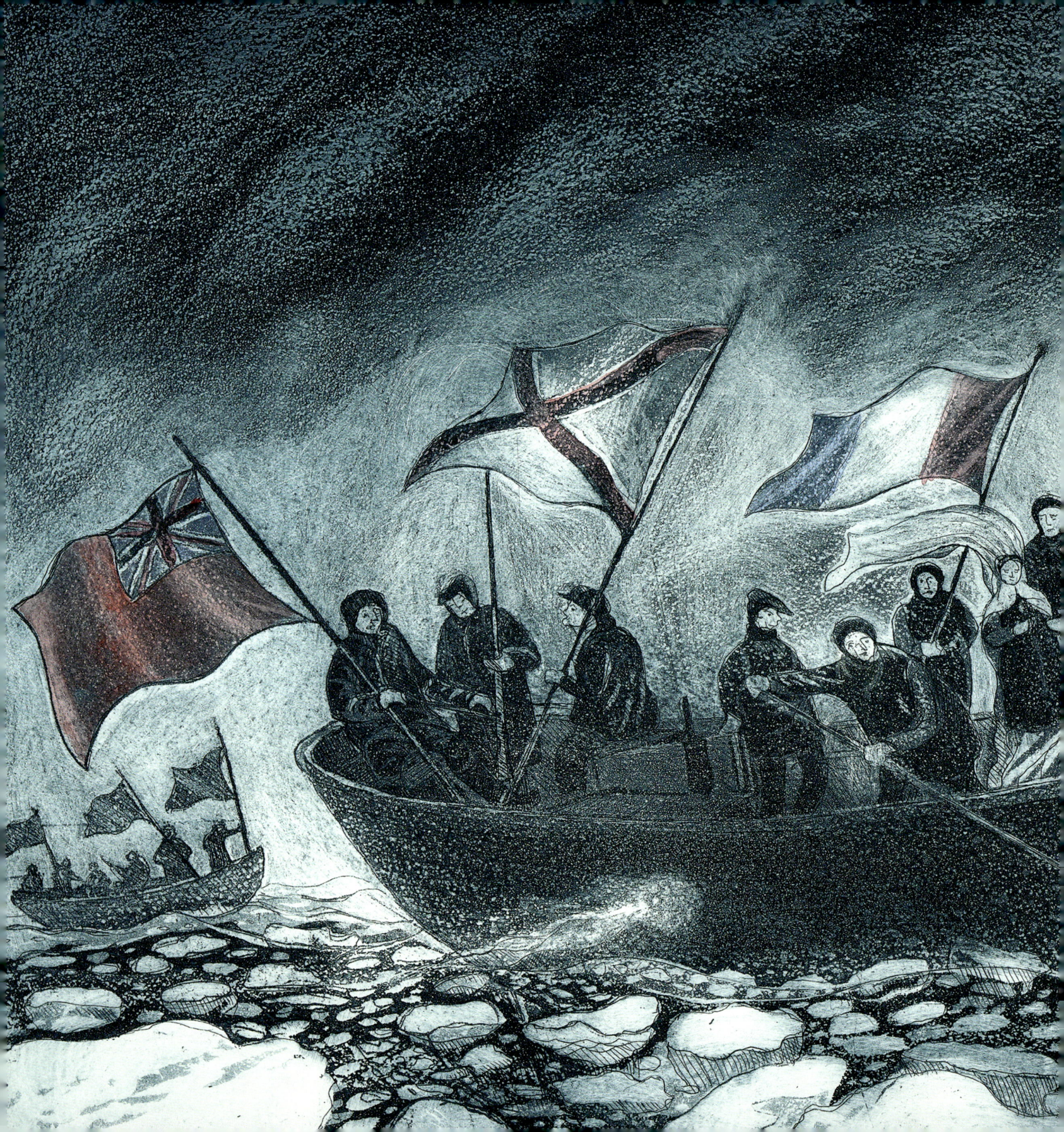

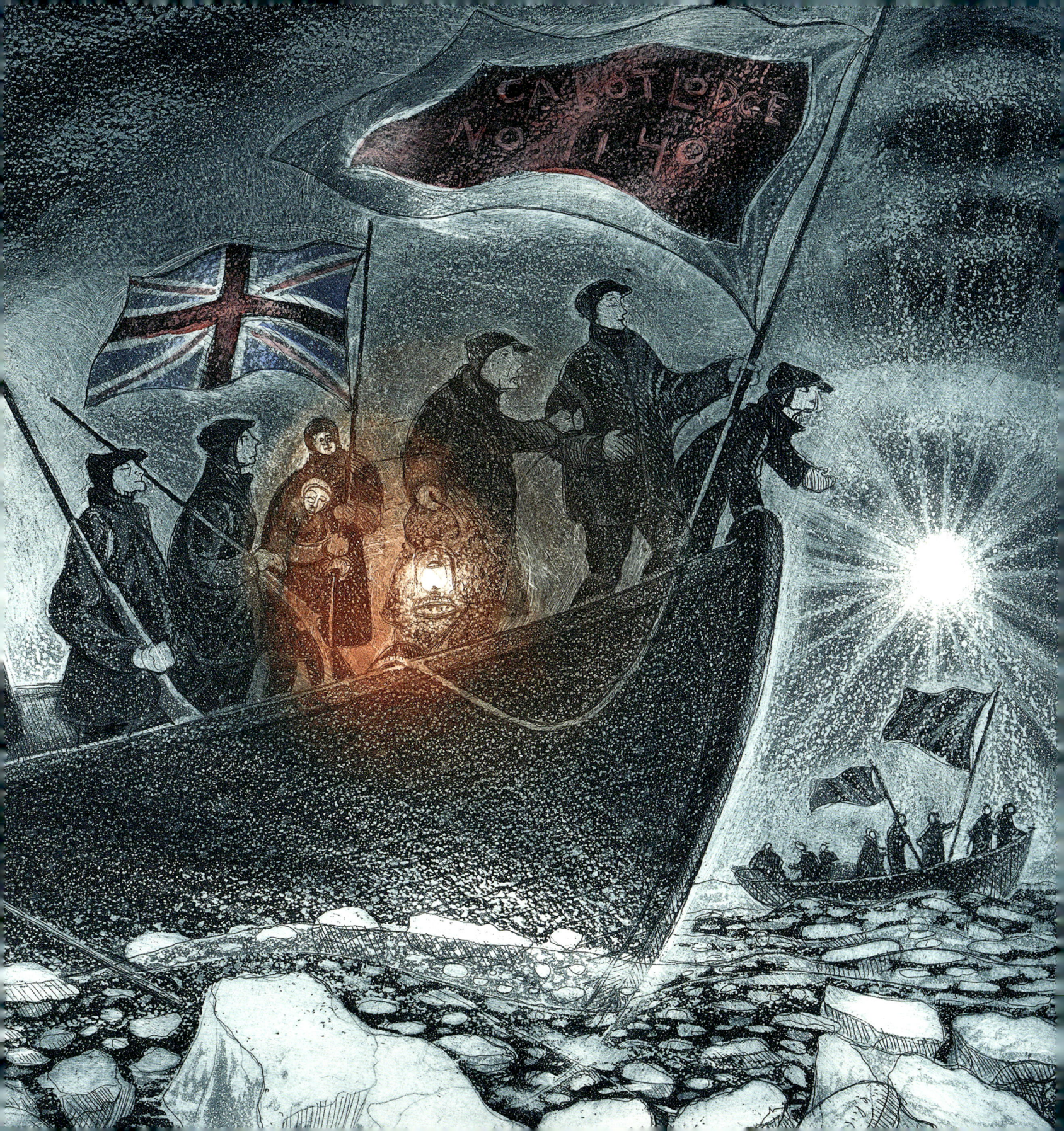

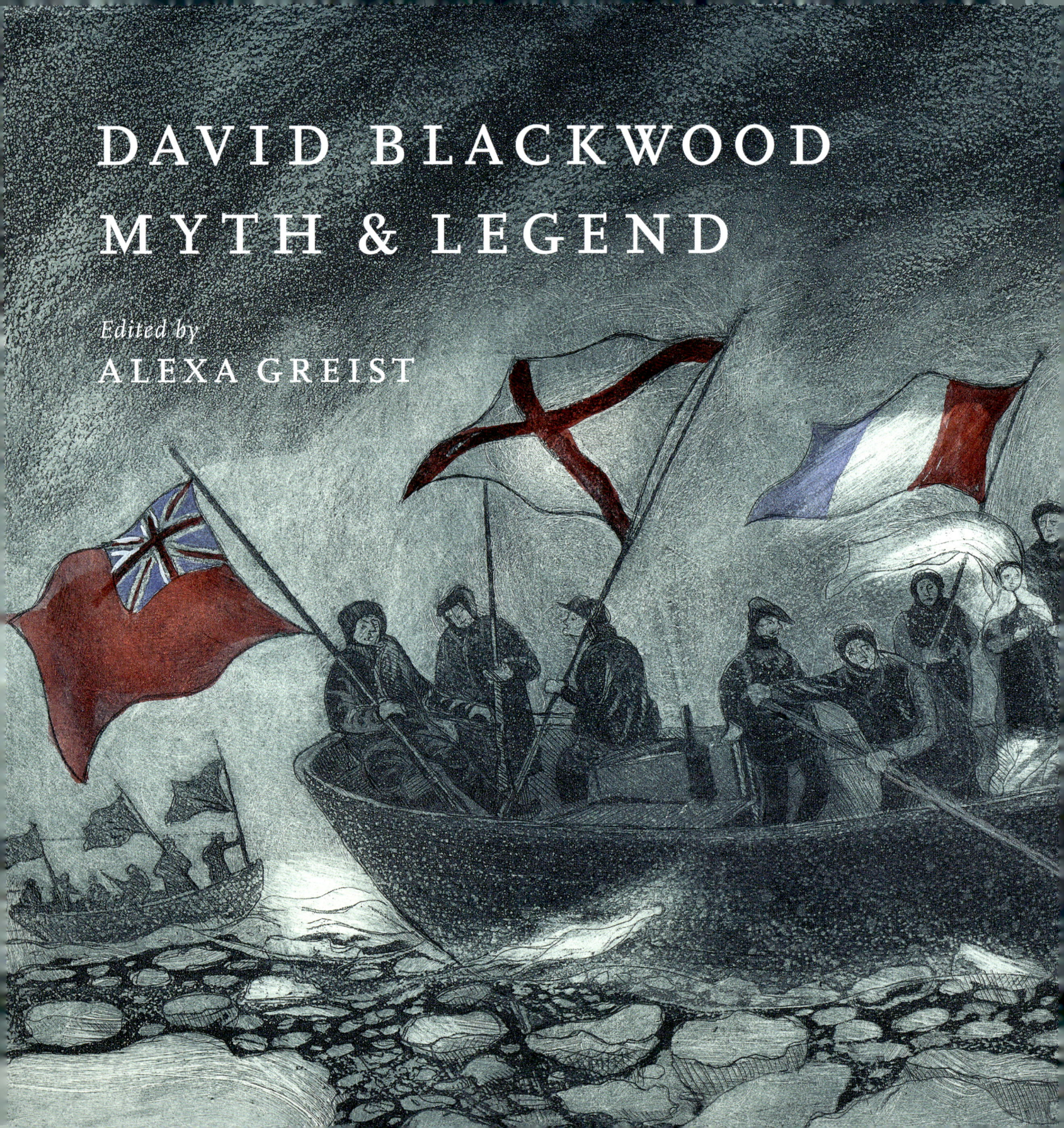

DAVID BLACKWOOD
MYTH & LEGEND

Edited by
ALEXA GREIST

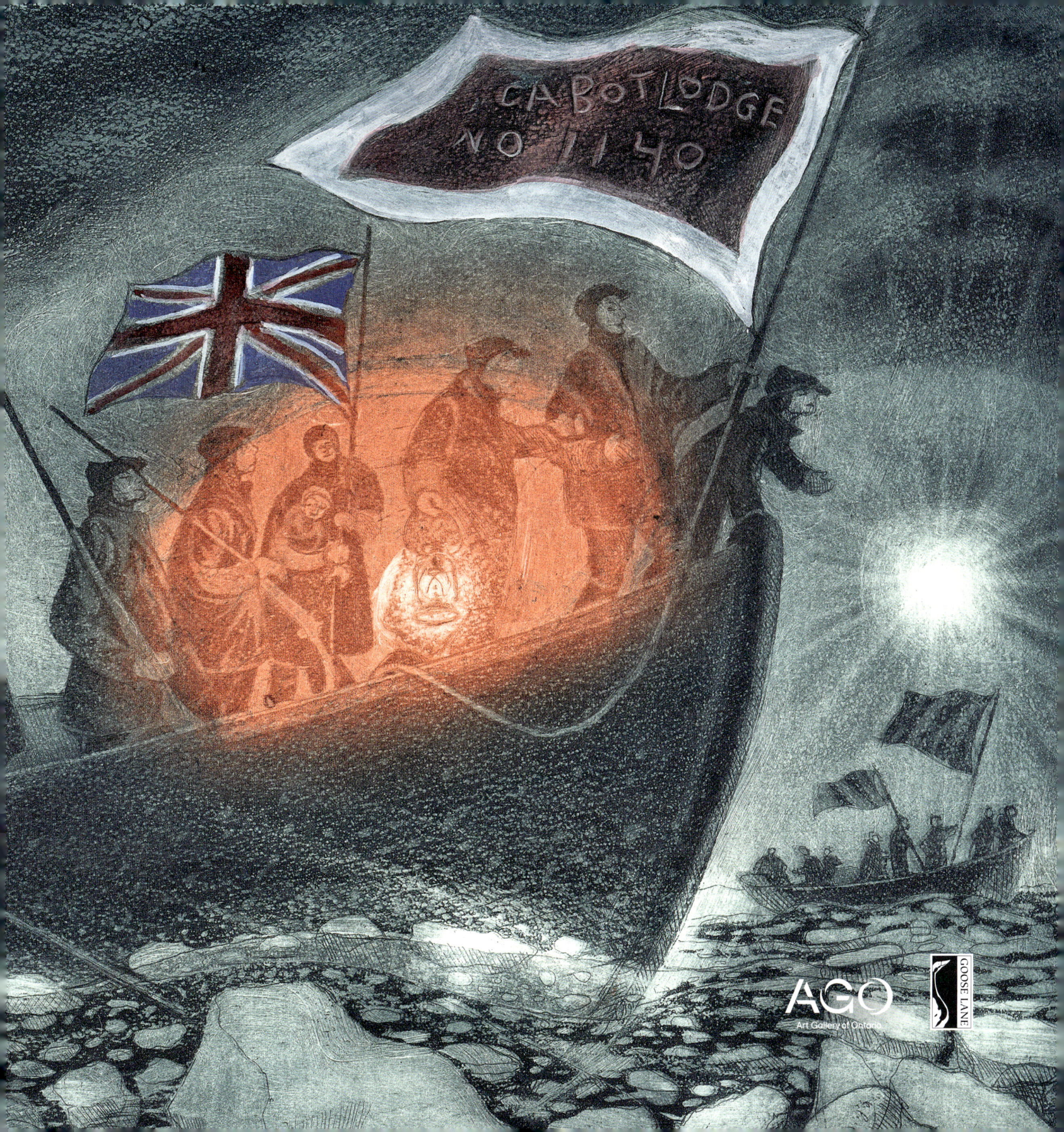

CABOT LODGE
NO 1140

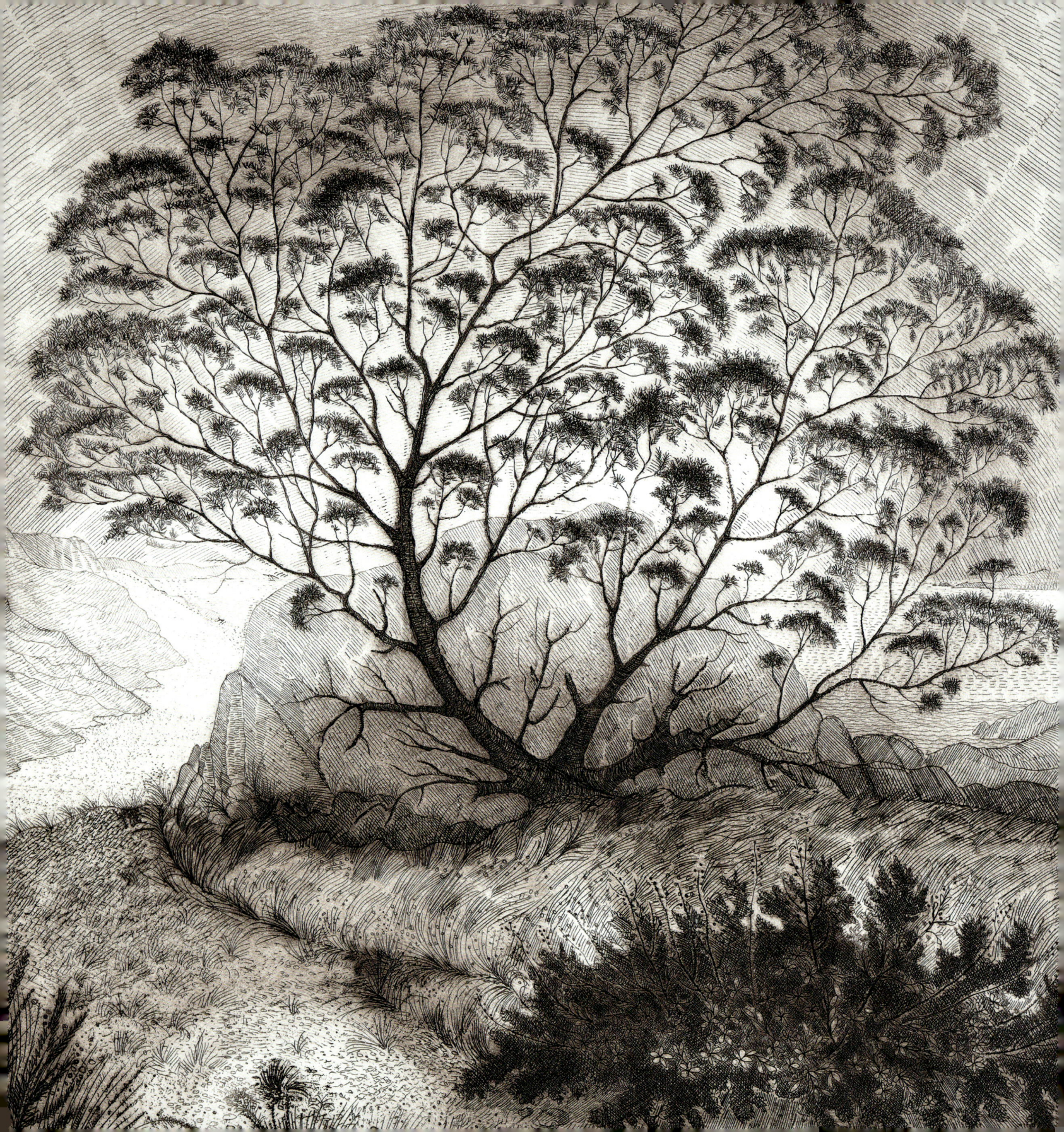

CONTENTS

DIRECTOR'S FOREWORD

In 2011, the Art Gallery of Ontario mounted a significant monographic exhibition by Canadian printmaker David Blackwood that explored the geology, folklore, and history of Newfoundland. These elements were of profound influence on him, and he continued to draw from the particular Atlantic Canadian lifestyle of his youth and that of his ancestors for generations before him. Nearly fifteen years later, *David Blackwood: Myth & Legend*, curated by Alexa Greist, celebrates both the personal and professional life of this prolific artist. The exhibition highlights Blackwood's sacred process of making but is also about what he held most dear: his family and their history in the remote fishing village of Wesleyville, Newfoundland.

The artist's relationship with the AGO began in 1959 when he first arrived in Toronto to study at the neighbouring Ontario College of Art. Following countless formative visits to the Museum and decades of refining his craft, Blackwood and his wife, Anita, had generously donated over 200 works to the AGO by the early 2000s—a massive gift that included prints, drawings, and watercolours. He continued his support of the AGO as a member of the Board of Trustees and was elected Honorary Chair in 2003. Whether in Wesleyville, his later-stage studio in Port Hope, Ontario, or at the AGO, Blackwood manifested a deep sense of home and belonging.

Through the lasting generosity of David and Anita, the AGO has become the collection of record for the artist and the home of his archives. After David's passing in 2022, Anita continued giving his work to the AGO—which now holds 300 works—including several printed proofs and drawings for significant prints spanning the seven decades of his singular career. I extend heartfelt gratitude to Anita Blackwood for her ongoing stewardship of her late husband's legacy. Her support and kindness have guided this exhibition and brought it to fruition.

Sincere thanks to Alexa Greist, Curator & R. Fraser Elliott Chair, Prints and Drawings, for conceiving a beautiful collection of works that have captivated and excited our audiences for decades and will inspire visitors anew in this latest presentation. Additional thanks to Amy Marshall Furness, Rosamond Ivey Special Collections Archivist & Head, Library & Archives, for lending her deep expertise of Blackwood's archive and preserving his fascinating personal records for future generations. I likewise wish to acknowledge several other AGO staff for their collaboration on this exhibition, including Project Managers Katarina Veljovic and Chloé Wittes; Wendy Hebditch, Curatorial Coordinator, European Art and Prints & Drawings; Interpretive Planner Nadia Abraham; Nives Hajdin-Rorabeck, Editor, Publications & Exhibitions; Graphic Designer Aleksandra Grzywaczewska; Exhibition Designer Marco Cheuk; Production Coordinator Evelyn Quinn; and our fundraising team, led by Chief Development Officer Kate Halpenny, for garnering exceptional interest and support for this showcase.

previous (page 12)
Gram Glover's Tree on Bragg's Island
(detail), 1999

right
Self-Portrait [Fragment] (detail), 1981

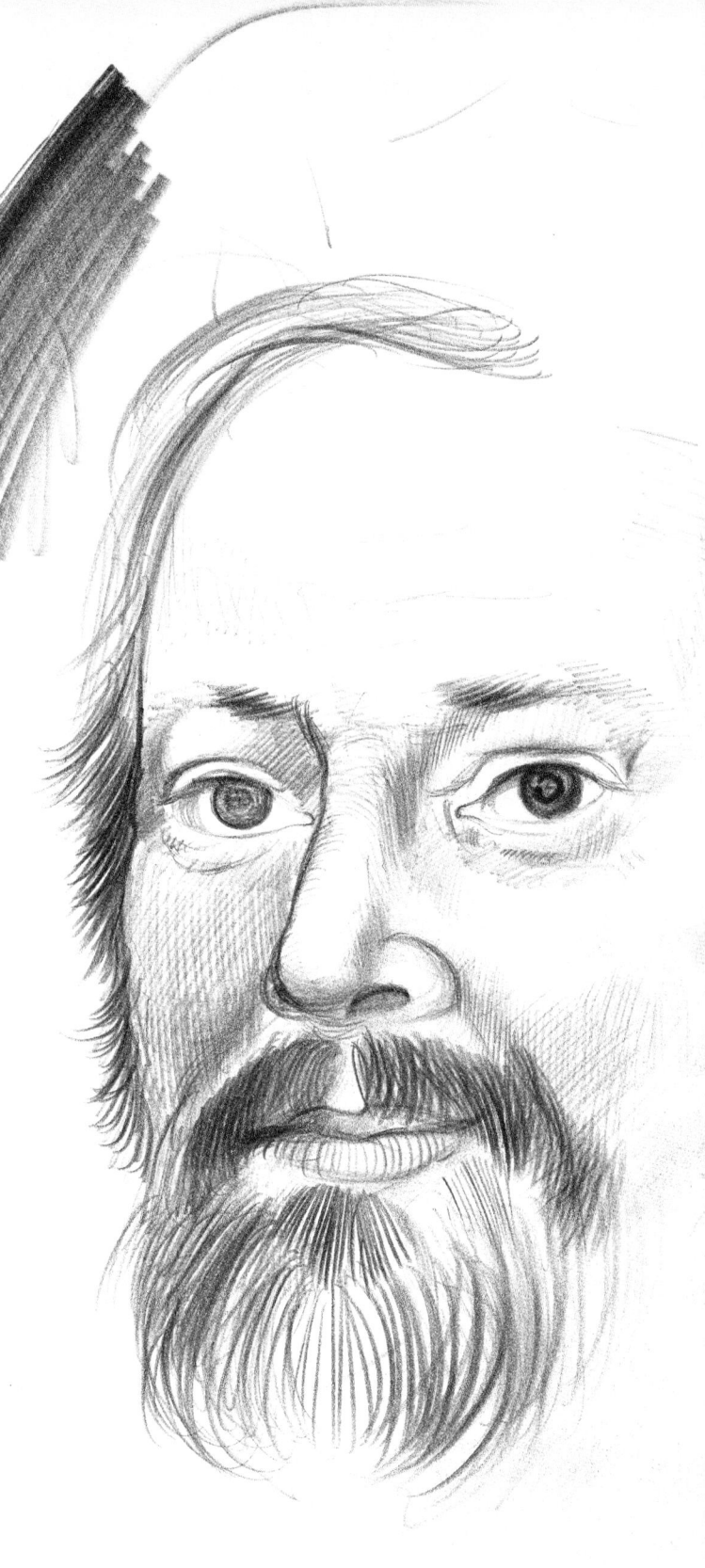

Thank you to Lara Minja of Lime Design for expertly channeling Blackwood's fierce artistry and warmth within these pages, and to Publication Coordinator Kathryn Yuen, Editor Nives Hajdin-Rorabeck, and Jim Shedden, Curator, Special Projects & Director, Publishing, for thoughtfully guiding the creation of this publication.

Thank you to our Supporting Sponsor CIBC and Contributing Sponsor Heffel Foundation. We are also grateful for the lead support of the Volunteers of the AGO, the generous support of Maxine Granovsky Gluskin & Ira Gluskin, and the generous support we received in memory of Martine Vilas and Gerald Conway of Cleveland, Ohio. As well, many thanks to Elizabeth Tory for her additional assistance in support of this project.

David Blackwood was deeply committed to his practice from start to finish. We are delighted to celebrate a master printmaker and his pursuit of pure craftsmanship—someone who left behind a literal and figurative impression on each surface he created and person he encountered. More than ever, we are proud to champion Canadian artists on a global stage and share our unique stories and perspectives with the world.

STEPHAN JOST

Michael and Sonja Koerner Director, and CEO
Art Gallery of Ontario

CURATOR'S ACKNOWLEDGEMENTS

On the evening of July 22, 2022, three weeks after David Blackwood's death, the AGO's Department of Prints & Drawings hosted a celebration of his life and work. Almost 300 people attended the event at the Marvin Gelber Print and Drawing Study Centre, making it clear there was avid support for this beloved artist and an appetite for another showcase of his work. Prior to his passing, David generously donated his works on paper to the Museum and wished for them to be made accessible to the public. It was important to me, as the curator responsible for his collection, that the AGO plan and premier this laudatory project.

David Blackwood was not only an incredibly skilled printmaker, draftsman, and painter but also a beloved teacher. He shared his expertise widely and with generosity, whether in a professional capacity at Trinity School in Port Hope, Ontario—where he taught drawing and painting for 25 years—indirectly as the artist-in-residence at the University of Toronto Mississauga's Erindale College (1969–75), or through the prints that have been studied by generations of Canadian artists. He gave his time to the AGO via service—as the first-ever artist to be named Honorary Chair of the Board of the AGO—and through many engaging talks. After his death, his spirit remained ever-present to visitors who came to pay tribute as well as through donations made in his memory to the Marvin Gelber Print and Drawing Study Centre. These gifts were the impetus to extend our monthly Open Door drop-in hours in the evenings, thereby offering greater access to the AGO's collection of works on paper—a sustained change now directly supported by Anita Blackwood, his wife of 52 years, in David's memory.

I briefly met David once during my tenure at the AGO, but through the time I have spent with Anita and Janita Wiersma, David's most trusted studio assistant, I feel as though I knew him in a unique way. I cannot thank Anita and Janita enough for the information they've shared about David's work and the inspirations behind particular pieces—invaluable knowledge from those who loved and understood him best. Anita's hospitality at the home that she and David shared—beautifully appointed with family heirlooms and the work of artists they knew and admired—is incomparable, while Janita's memory of David's working methods is deep and was given with an openness of spirit in kinship with David's own. I could not have completed this project without their kind assistance and support.

ALEXA GREIST

Curator & R. Fraser Elliott Chair,
Prints and Drawings

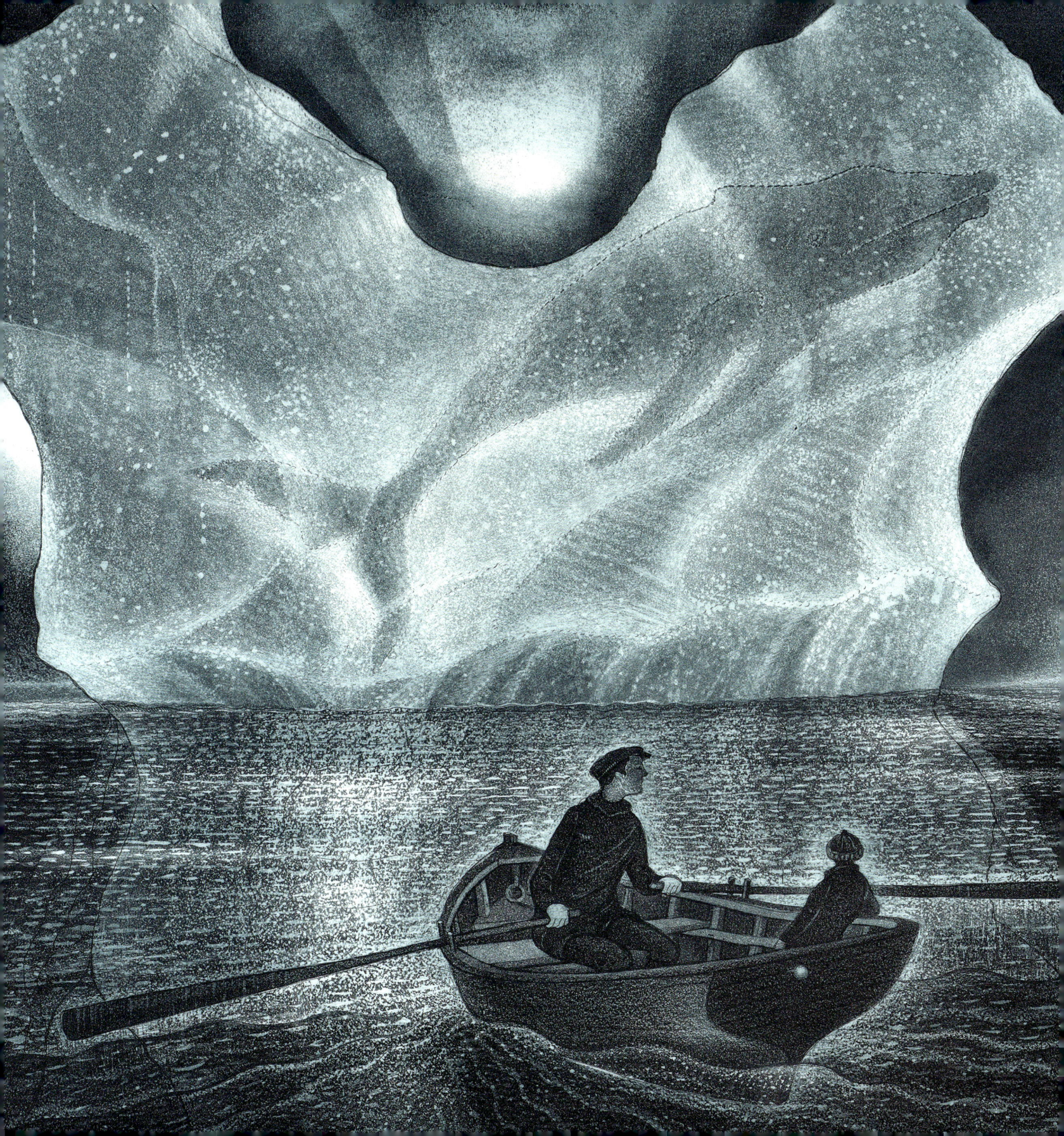

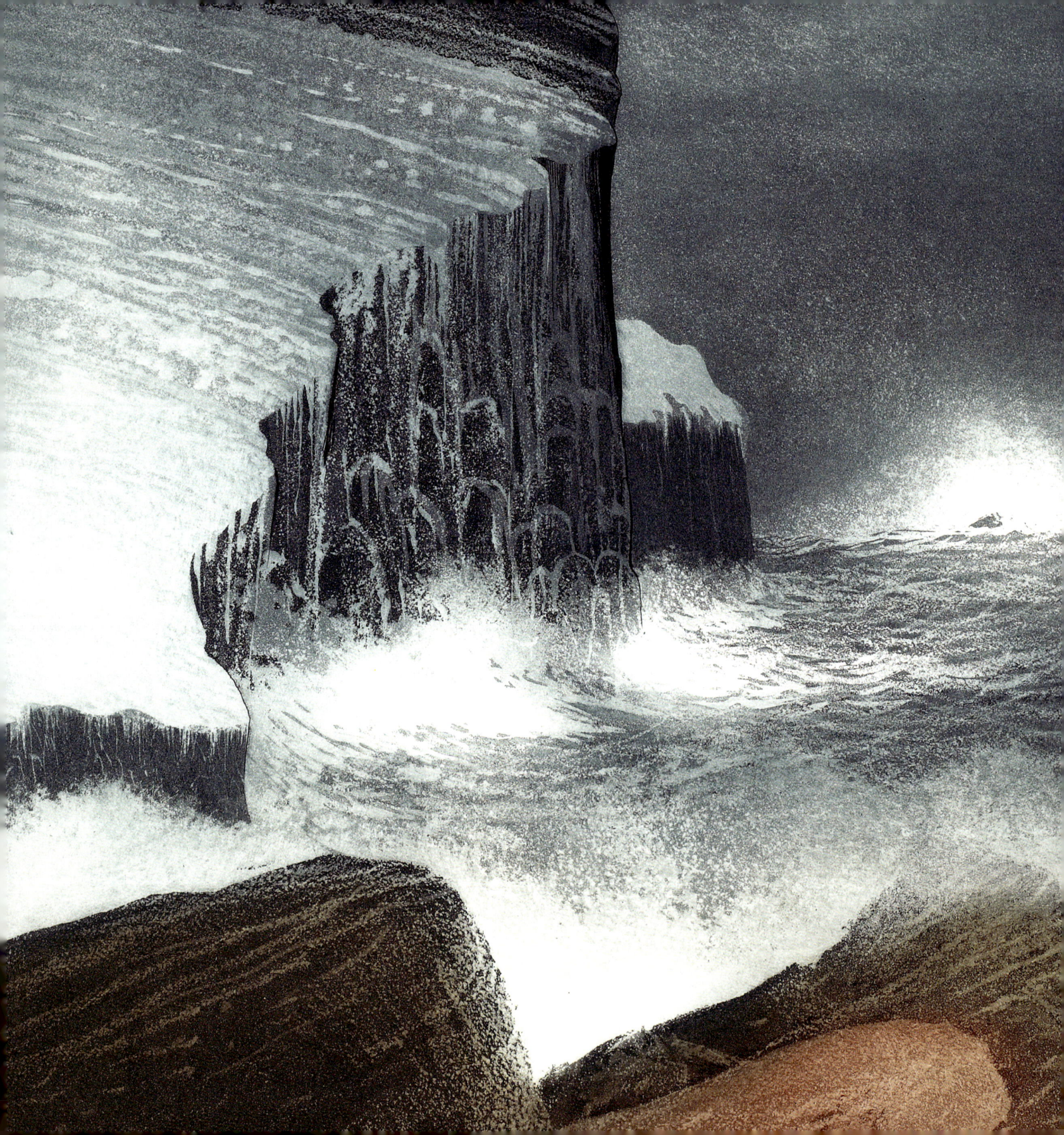

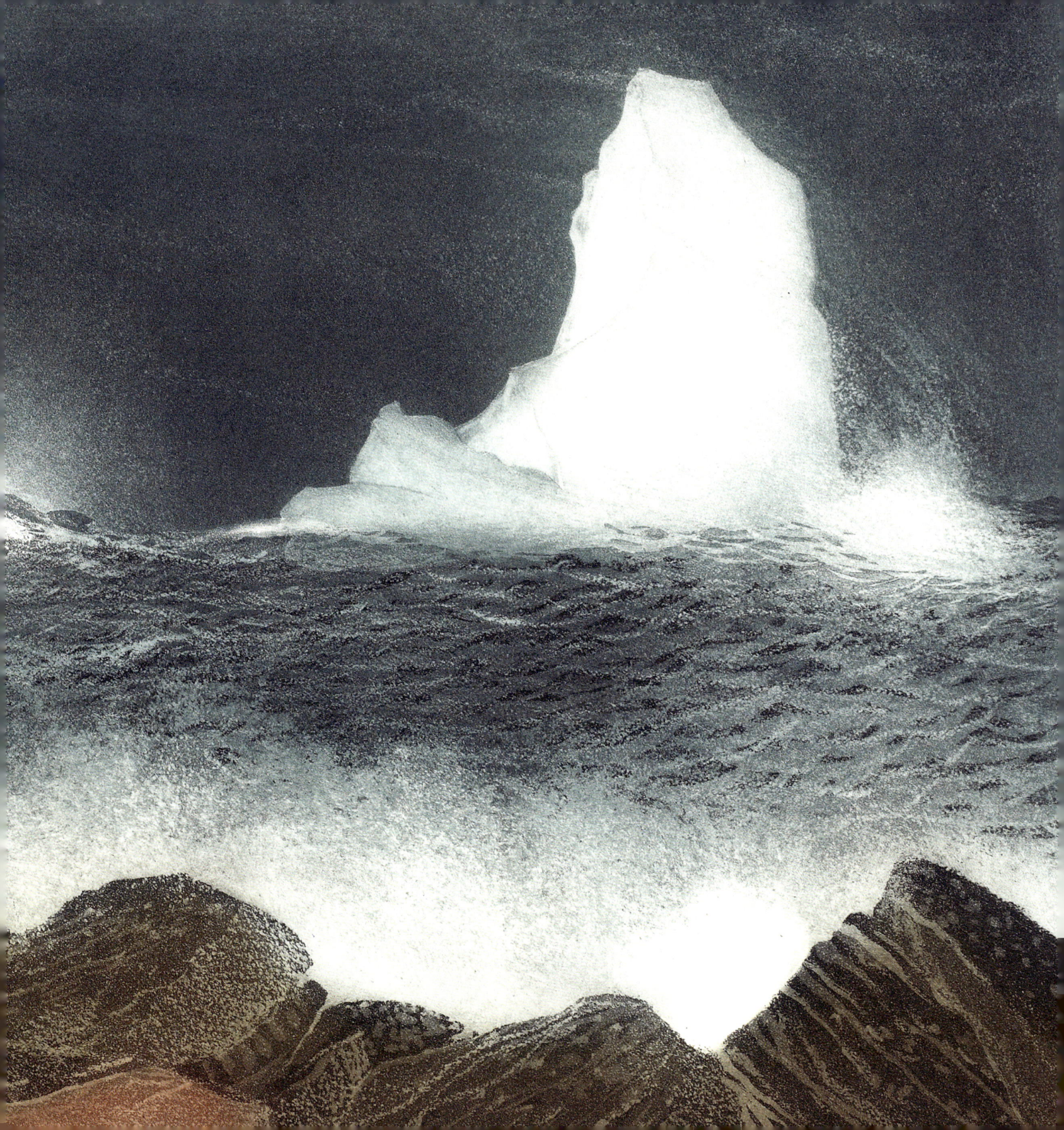

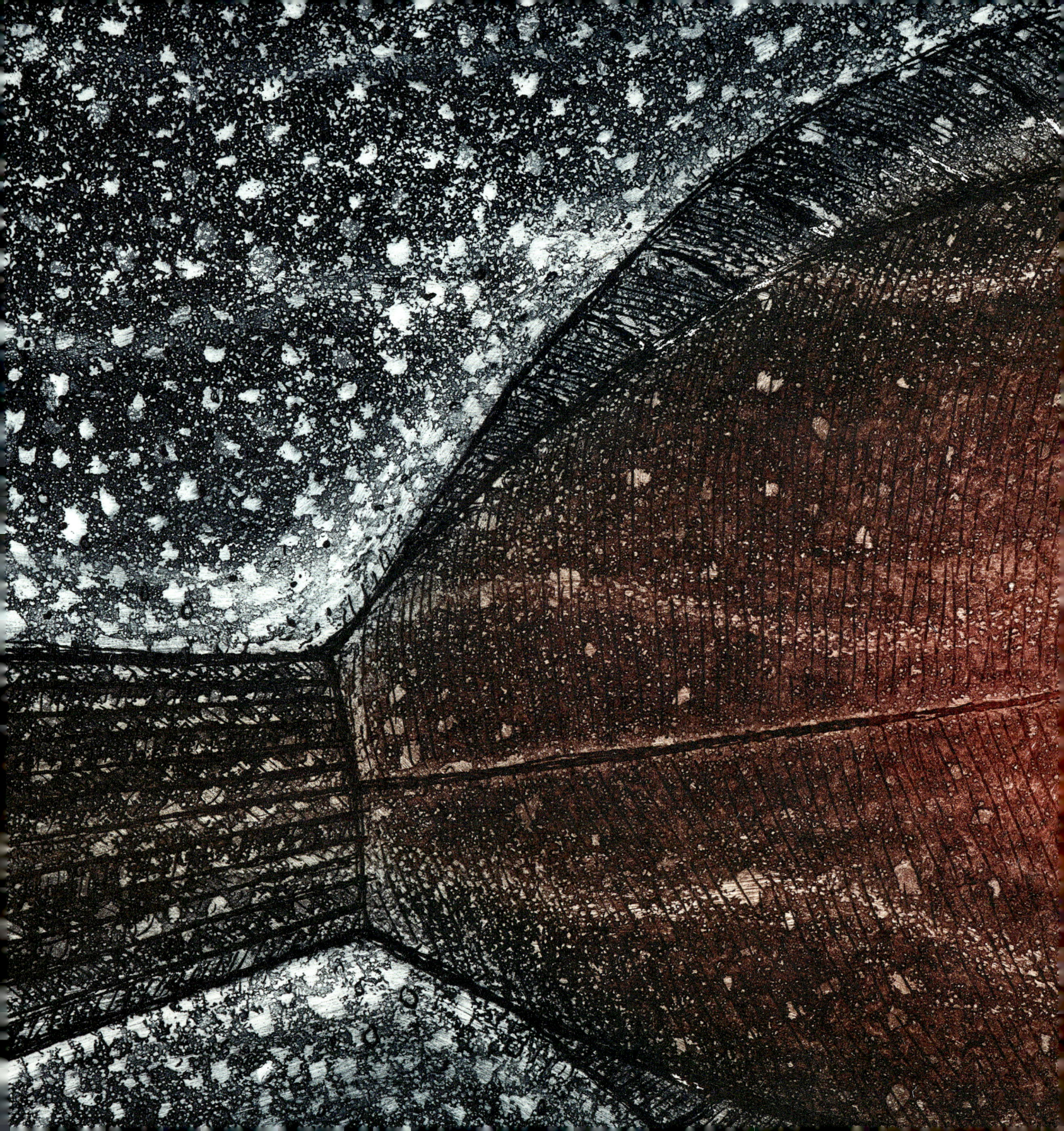

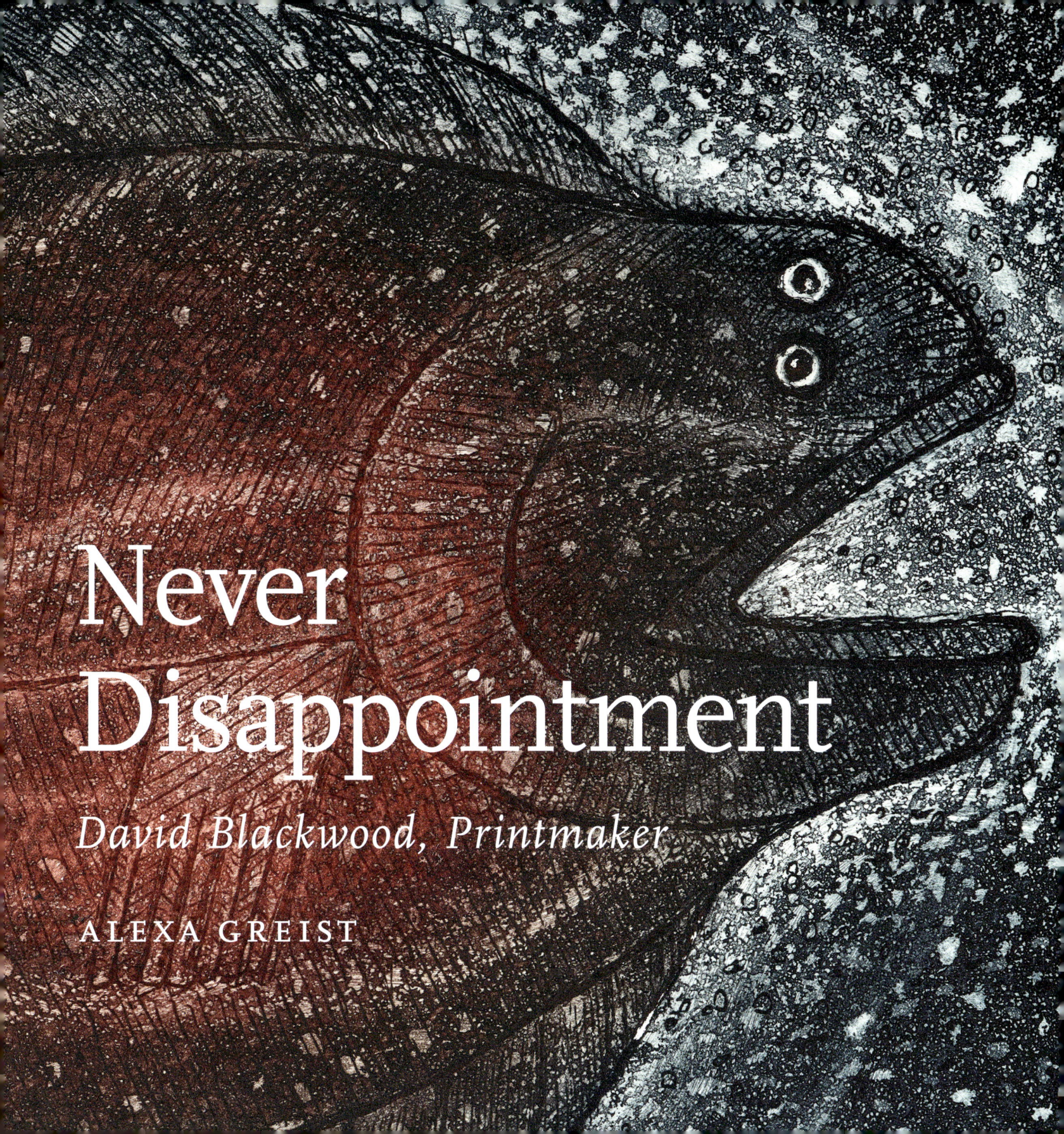

Never Disappointment

David Blackwood, Printmaker

ALEXA GREIST

previous spread
Flatty (detail), 2015

opposite
Note from David Blackwood
to Janita Wiersma, October 2014.

Janith,

, 5 minutes in the
acid will complete this
work.
It can be cleaned off
& printed (one blue, one
brown).

Cleaning Varsol then
mythol Alcohol

At this point we have
no idea of what lurks
beneath the surface!
Regardless, there in never
disappointment.
Very Best
DaWil

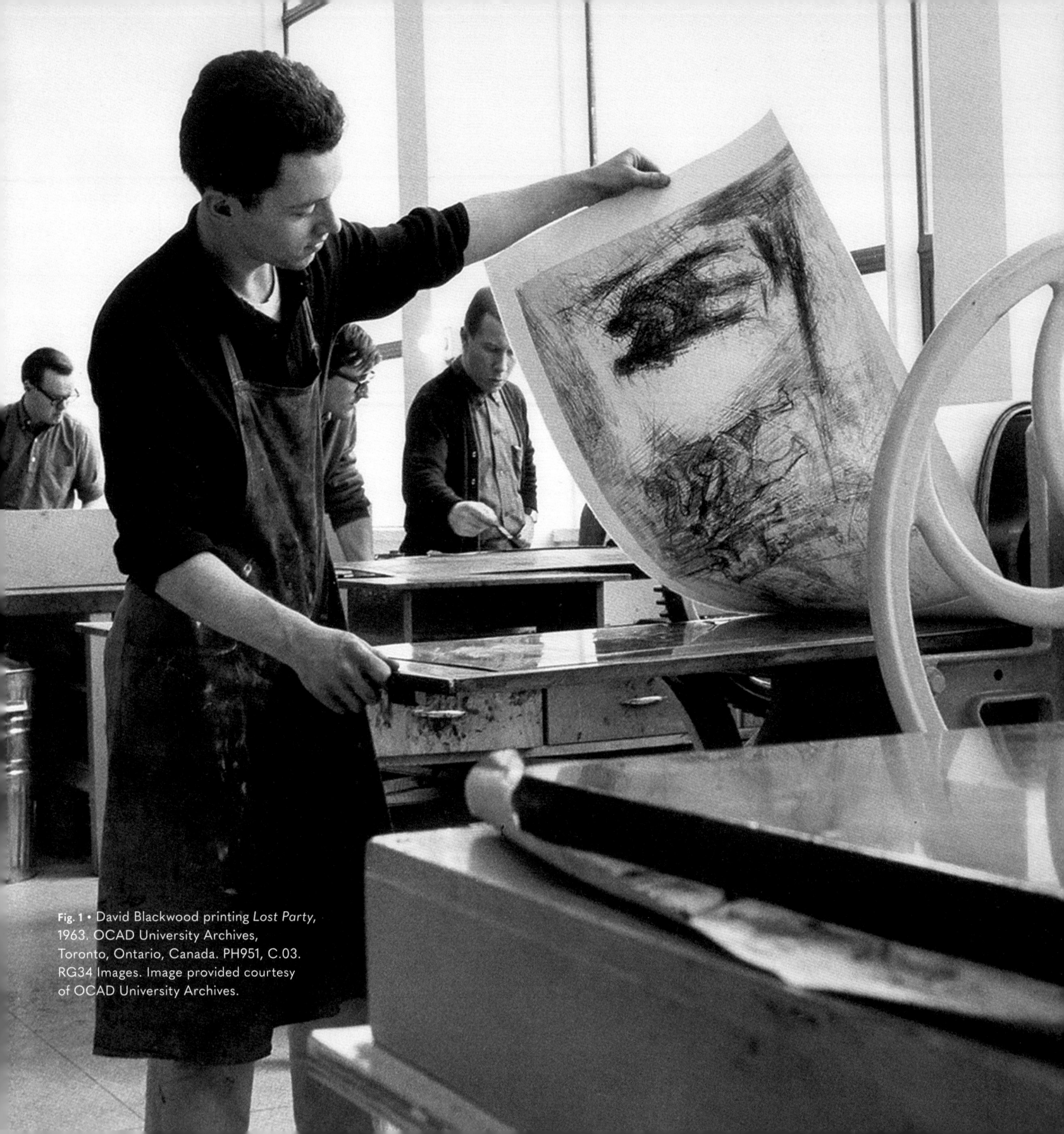

Fig. 1 • David Blackwood printing *Lost Party*, 1963. OCAD University Archives, Toronto, Ontario, Canada. PH951, C.03. RG34 Images. Image provided courtesy of OCAD University Archives.

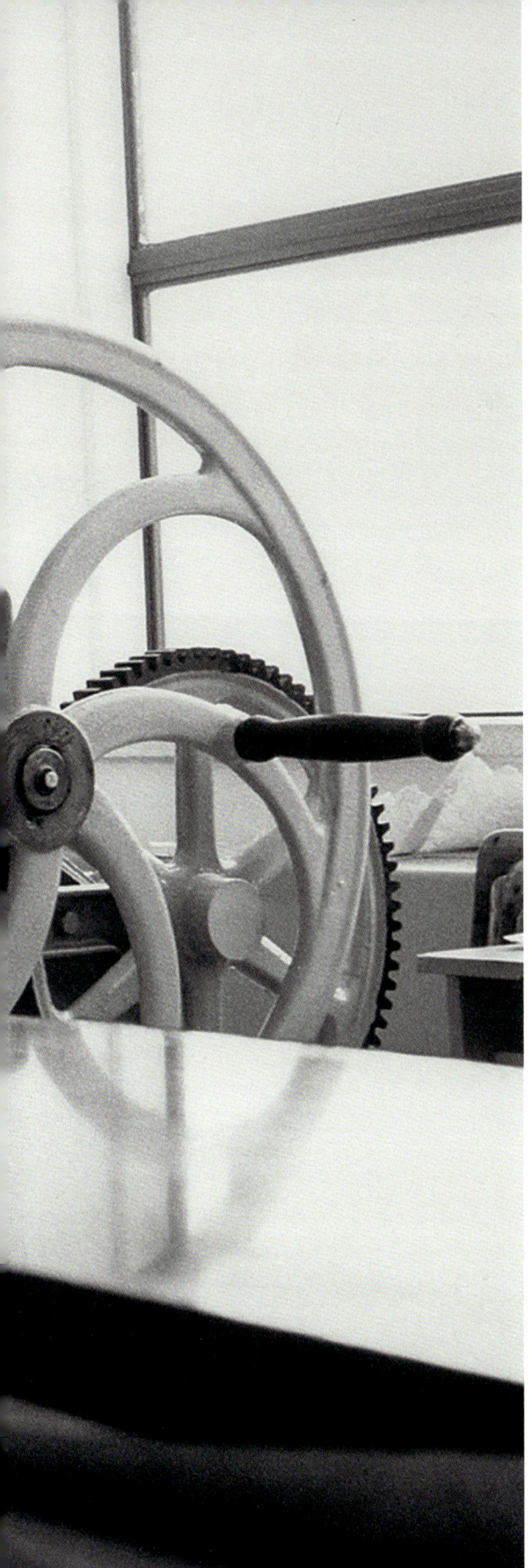

"At this point, we have no idea of what lurks beneath the surface! Regardless, there is never disappointment."

—DAVID BLACKWOOD

David Lloyd Blackwood (1941–2022) was an artist who discovered two key elements early in his artistic trajectory: his ideal medium of *intaglio*[1] printmaking and his defining subjects: the lifestyle of his childhood and the enduring landscape of Newfoundland and Labrador. Blackwood worked primarily in etching with aquatint and embraced the possibilities of the copperplate; not for its experimental and abstract linear qualities—as was the main interest of the Ontario College of Art (OCA) printmaking studio, where he began his formal studies at the age of 18 in 1959—but rather for its properties that allowed simple line and tone to create immersive effects. This experimentation opened an entire world in his hands (fig. 1).[2]

Using a restrained palette of inks on a diverse field of *intaglio* textures, Blackwood used colour sparingly and to great effect; warm, and even violent, reds and oranges punctuate dark seas and skies in many of his most famous prints. There are exceptions, such as interior scenes where the richness of accumulated textiles and domestic decorations reflect the warm nature of home. He captured

1 A technique in which the image is incised into the plate and the resulting recesses are filled with ink. *Intaglio* differs from the process of relief printing, where the design prints from raised areas.

2 Katharine Lochnan, "Black Ice: David Blackwood's Prints of Newfoundland," in *Black Ice: David Blackwood, Prints of Newfoundland* (Douglas & McIntyre, 2011), 10.

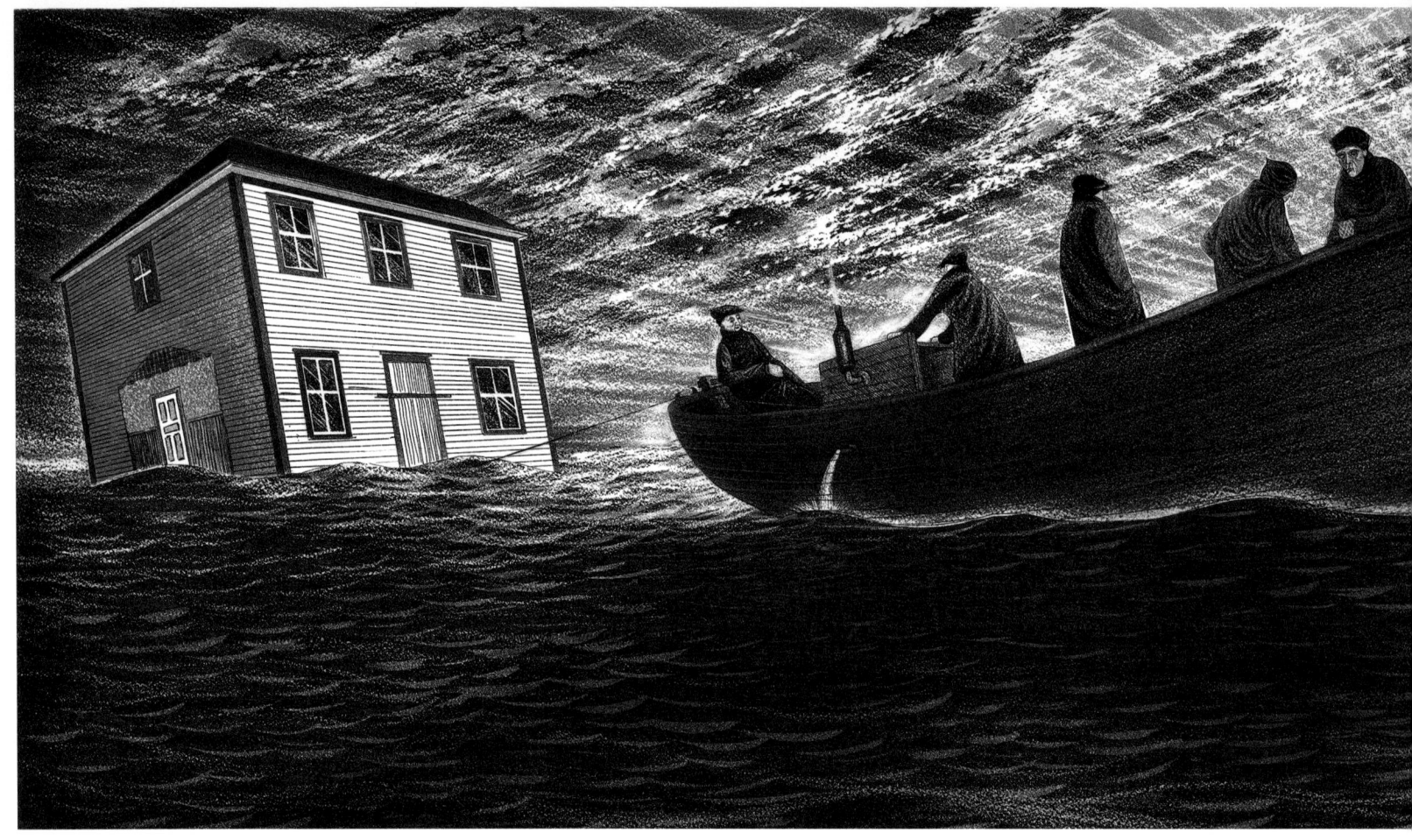

the outport spaces that disappeared with the resettlements, or centralization, of their residents through various government programs under Newfoundland Premier Joseph Roberts Smallwood from 1949 to 1972. Many of the artist's prints seek to preserve spaces that were either torn down or moved to other locations (fig. 2), in addition to the vanishing ways of life that had brought people to settle in the harsh climate of the outport settlements in the first place.

During his printmaking career, Blackwood worked through his large, narrative prints in much the same way. He began with smaller sketches that led to an overall pencil drawing at the same scale as the plate.[3] He might have played with sections of the transfer drawing, by cutting the foreground in *Wesleyville: Burning*

3 David Blackwood in William Gough, *David Blackwood: Master Printmaker* (Douglas & McIntyre, 2001), 166. The written account of his technique in this catalogue is concise and clear. The National Film Board of Canada made a short documentary in 1976 showing Blackwood working through a plate from start to finish. This film is an invaluable record of both the *intaglio* process in general and of a particular artist's masterful use of the technique. See *Blackwood*, dirs. Tony Ianzelo and Andy Thomson, 1976, National Film Board of Canada, nfb.ca/film/blackwood/.

4 Email from Janita Wiersma, March 5, 2025.

5 Gough, 166.

6 Email from Janita Wiersma, April 23, 2025.

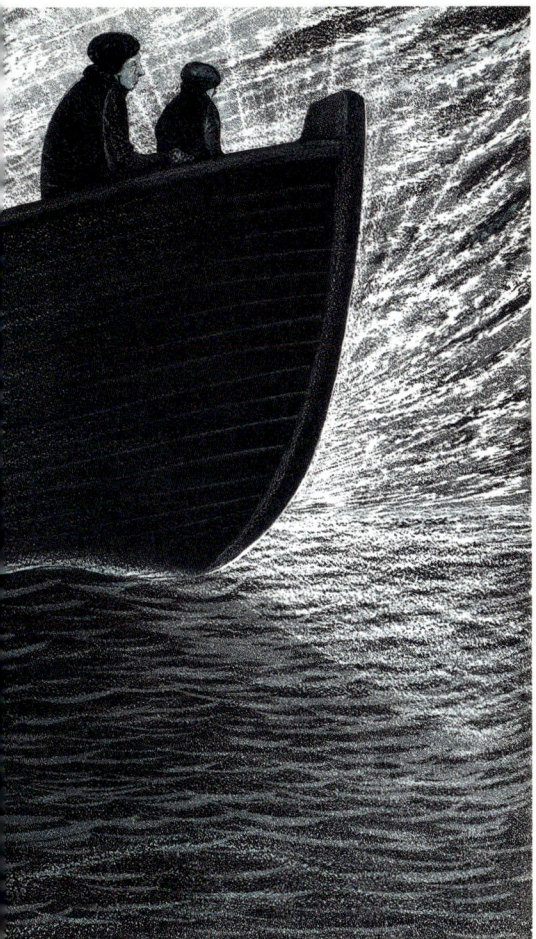

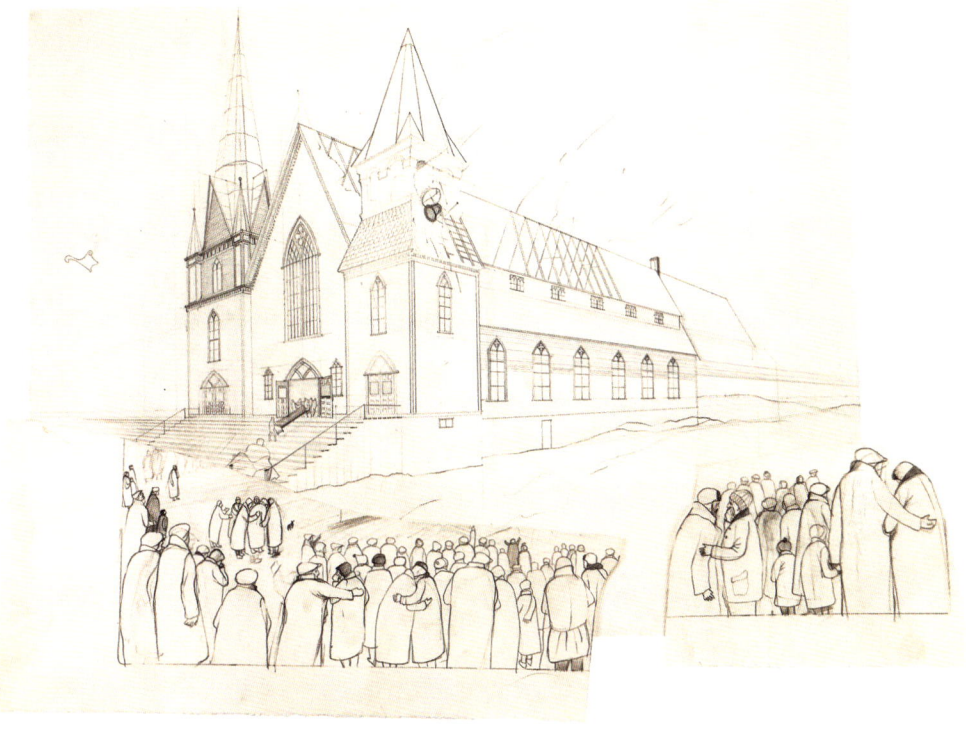

left

Fig. 2 • *Uncle Eli Glover Moving*, 1982. Etching and aquatint on paper, H/C, 35.4 × 85.8 cm. Art Gallery of Ontario, Gift of David and Anita Blackwood, Port Hope, Ontario, 1999 (99/963).

right

Fig. 3 • Three preparatory drawings for *Wesleyville: Burning of the Methodist Church*, 1976. Drawing 1 [centre]: graphite on paper, 61 × 83.8 cm; drawing 2 [left]: graphite on tracing paper, 25.4 × 55.9 cm (irregular); drawing 3 [right]: graphite on tracing paper, 20.3 × 27.9 cm (irregular). Edward P. Taylor Library & Archives, Art Gallery of Ontario.

of the Methodist Church (fig. 3), for example, to move it around on the plate and even redraw entire sections.[4] To transfer full-scale drawings, Blackwood used a two-step process to press down through the waxy, prepared ground—a substance applied to the surface of the plate that protects it from acid—to reveal the copper surface below.[5] First, he used transfer paper layered between the plate and the drawing, going over the lines of the drawing with a pencil to transfer the image onto the hard wax ground. He then went over the transferred lines again with an etching needle to remove a small amount of the ground, exposing the copper surface below.[6] In etching, acid is used to "bite" away the lines that are exposed through this scratching, and it is these removed spaces, or "valleys," that hold ink for printing under high pressure. Blackwood's process—in which he would apply an acid-resistant ground and then draw through it before the acid etched the plate—underwent many iterations; each one resulted in unpredictable outcomes, such as lines etched more deeply than intended, or "foul biting" wherein acid might penetrate part of the carefully prepared ground. To create tonal areas, Blackwood used aquatint in its traditional form, where powdered resin is applied to the plate and then warmed to adhere the various-sized, scattered particles of resist to the plate before another dip into the acid. After each bath in the acid, he would remove the ground and pull a print from the plate to check its progress. The resulting prints are called proofs or states of a print, and these working proofs give us a glimpse into how Blackwood built his prints.[7]

The experimentation and observation did not end once Blackwood reached the final state of the print. Rather, he often printed impressions in varying shades of grey and blue, or even red, sometimes while seeking the final proof and other times even after he had started editioning a print. This experimentation was part of the process and for Blackwood, that process didn't have to end with a "final" proof.[8] He rarely finished editioning his prints as he insisted on printing them himself, and often he was ready to begin working on another project before completing a full edition.[9] He occasionally employed studio assistants part-time, but Blackwood ultimately did all the platework and presswork himself. However, there was one exception.

In the last decade of his life, Blackwood allowed a trusted printmaker, Janita Wiersma, to assist him directly in his studio while he recovered from a life-threatening illness in 2015.[10] Upon being moved to Toronto's Bridgeport rehabilitation facility after a year of hospitalization at Mount Sinai, the artist asked for drawing materials and, soon after, a copperplate and his *intaglio* tools. The small print *Flatty* (fig. 9) was the result of his first foray back into printmaking.[11] A "flatty" is one of four types of flatfish found in Newfoundland waters, but it is also likely a reference to Blackwood's much-diminished frame and loss of muscle. Here, the fish acts as a stand-in for an individual so weak that he had to

7 Blackwood stated that it often took him months to finalize a working proof and copperplate to then print an edition. For example, he noted that he printed his first working proof for *Portrait of Heber Field as a Great Mummer* on April 26, 2000, and he pulled the twelfth, and final, working proof on October 18. Blackwood in Gough, 166.

8 Email from Janita Wiersma, March 5, 2025.

9 Email from Anita Blackwood, March 5, 2025.

10 Conversation with Anita Blackwood and Janita Wiersma in Port Hope, Ontario, July 20, 2024. Wiersma began working as a studio assistant to Blackwood in 2011.

11 Ibid., August 13, 2024.

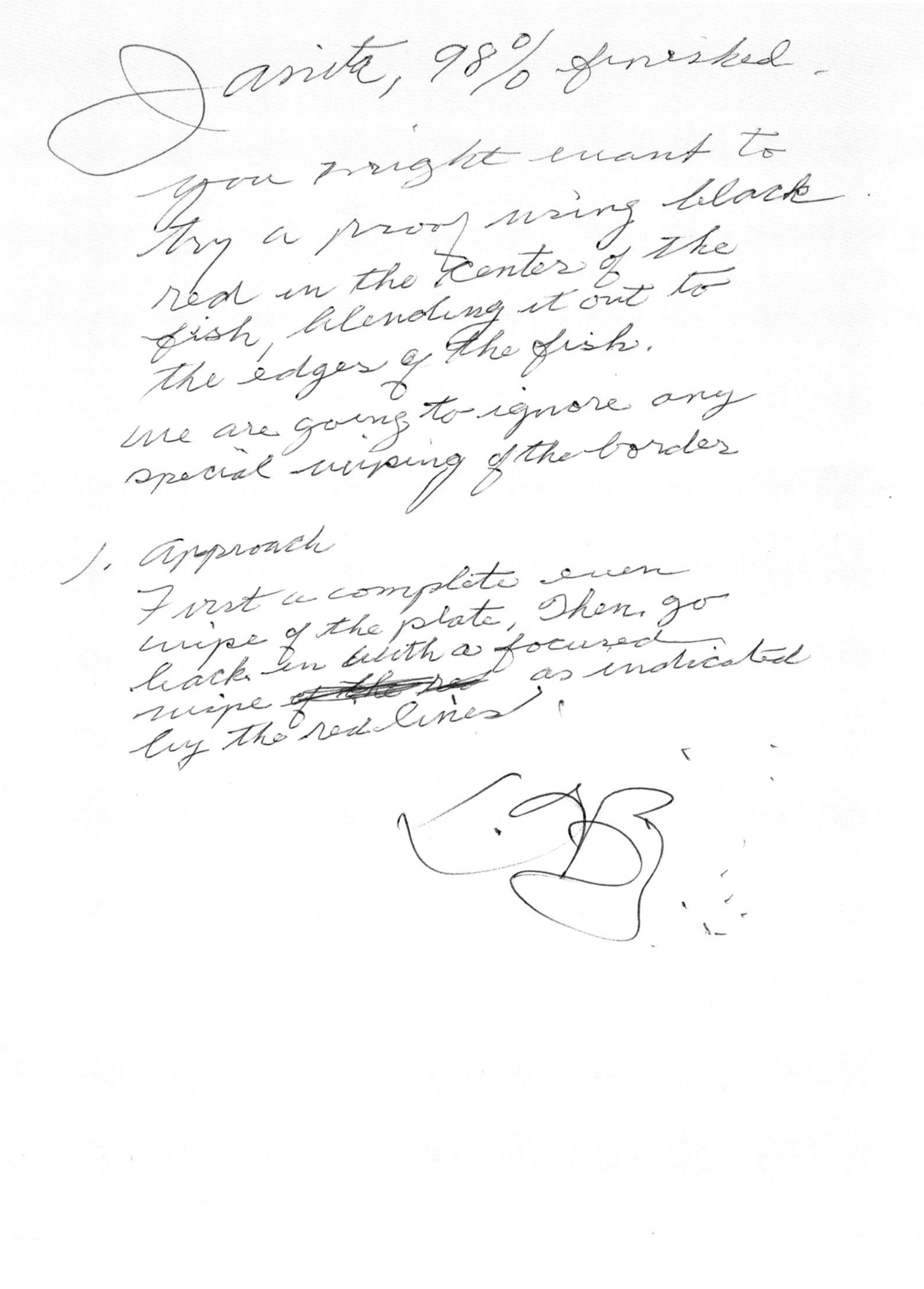

Janita, 98% finished.

You might want to try a proof using black red in the center of the fish, blending it out to the edges of the fish.

We are going to ignore any special wiping of the border

1. Approach
First a complete even wipe of the plate, Then go black in with a focused wipe ~~the red~~ as indicated by the red lines

Fig. 4 • Note from Blackwood to Janita Wiersma with printing instructions for *Flatty*, 2014.

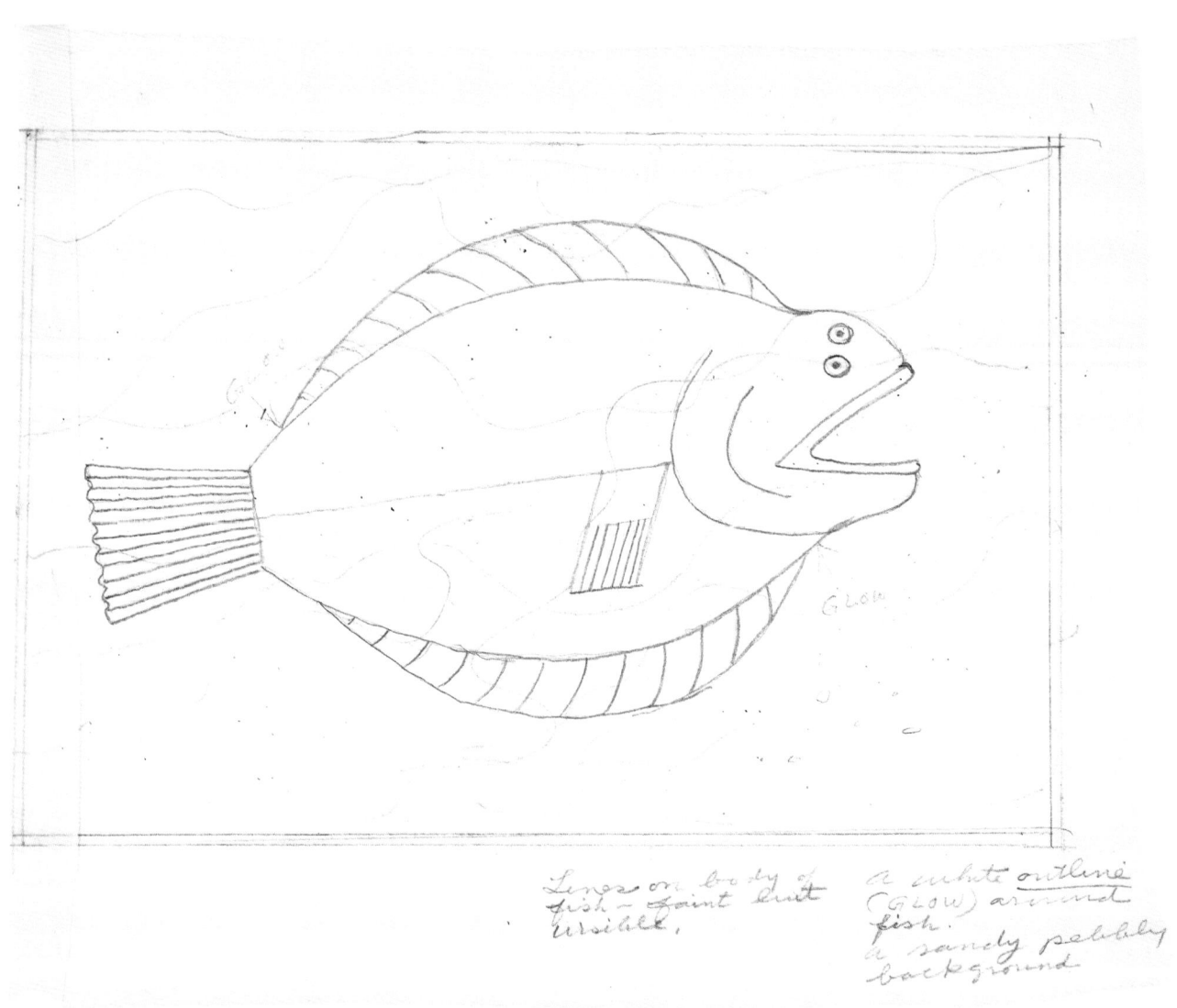

Lines on body of
fish — faint but
visible.

a white outline
(GLOW) around
fish.
a sandy pebbly
background

Fig. 5 • *Flatty (tracing)*, 2014.
Graphite on tracing paper, 27.9 × 35.6 cm.
Edward P. Taylor Library & Archives,
Art Gallery of Ontario.

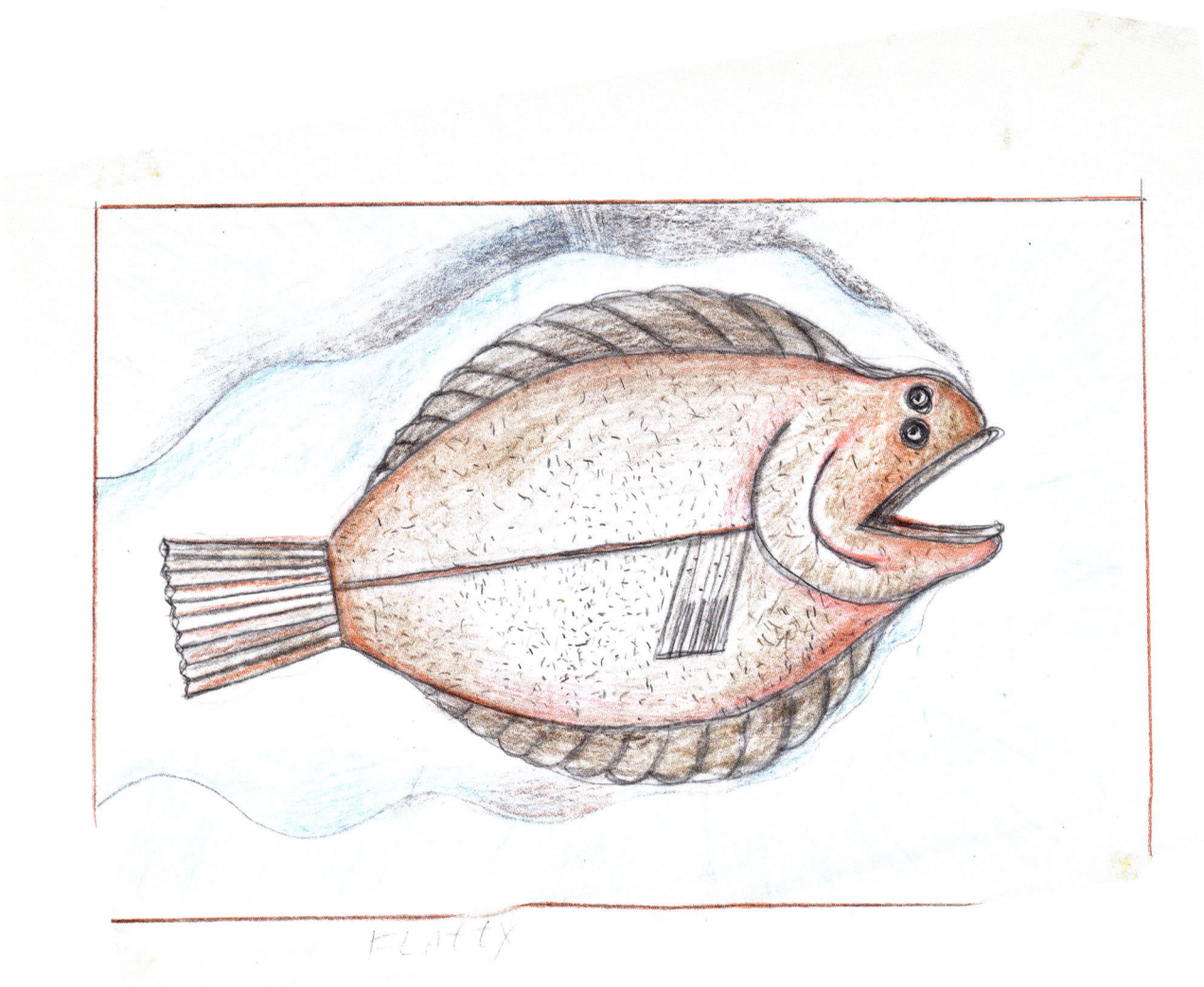

Fig. 6 • *Flatty (working drawing)*, 2014.
Coloured pencil on tracing paper, 24.4 × 35.6 cm.
Edward P. Taylor Library & Archives,
Art Gallery of Ontario.

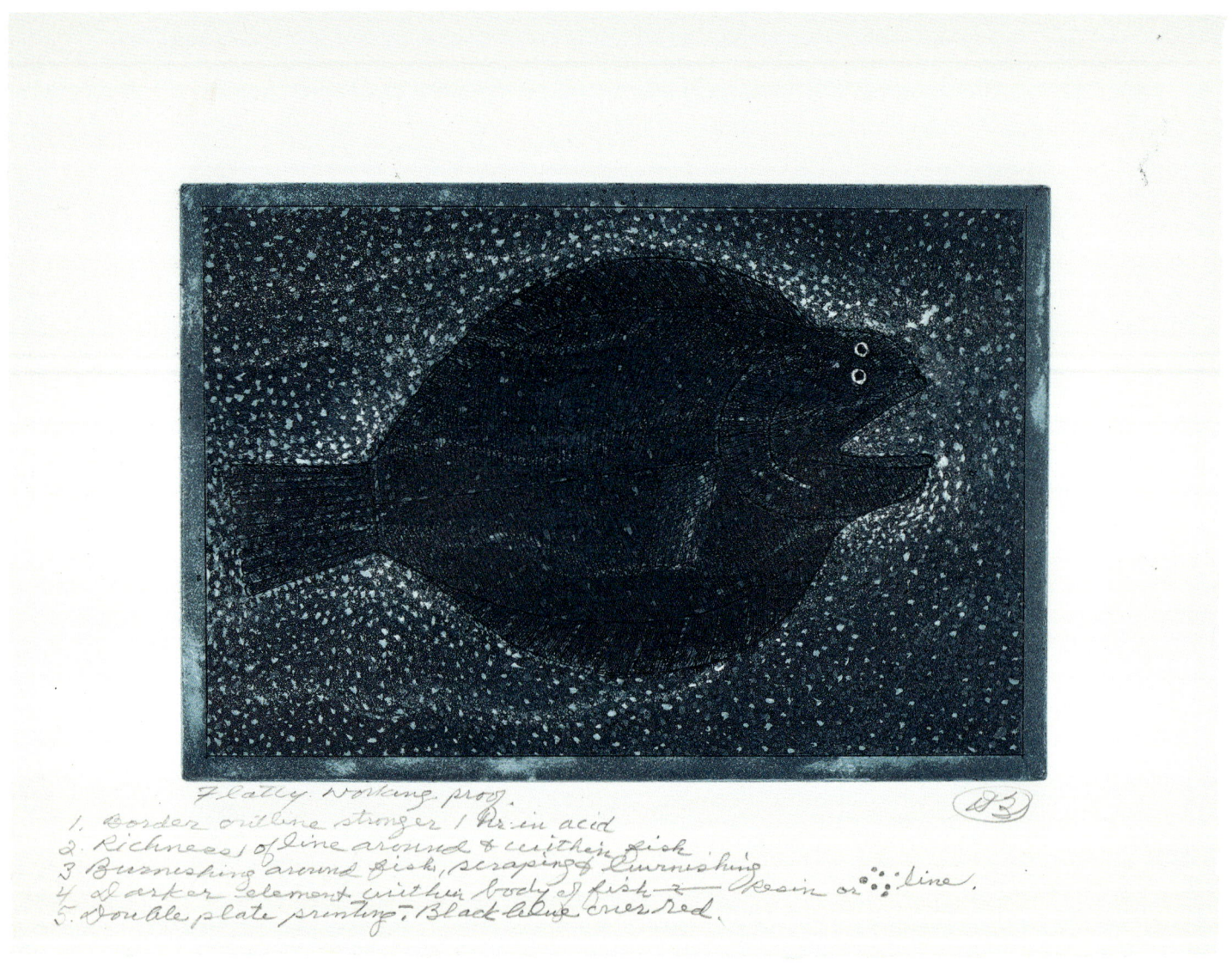

Flatty Working proof.
1. *Border outline stronger / Re-in acid*
2. *Richness, of line around & within fish*
3. *Burnishing around fish, scraping & burnishing*
4. *darker element within body of fish — Resin or ∴line.*
5. *Double plate printing. Black & blue over red.*

Fig. 7 • *Flatty (working proof with artist's notes),*
2014. Etching, aquatint, and graphite on paper,
20.3 × 30.5 cm. Edward P. Taylor Library &
Archives, Art Gallery of Ontario.

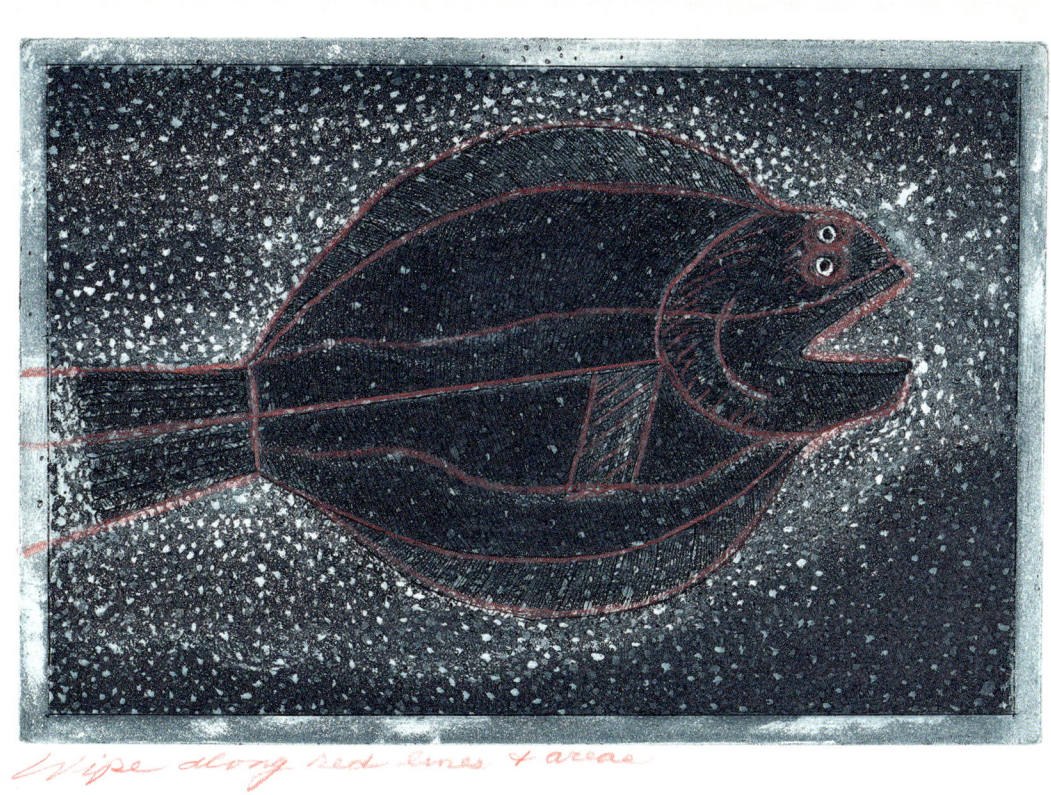

Fig. 8 • *Flatty (working proof with wiping lines and notes)*, 2014. Etching, aquatint, and coloured pencil on paper, 20.3 × 30.5 cm. Edward P. Taylor Library & Archives, Art Gallery of Ontario.

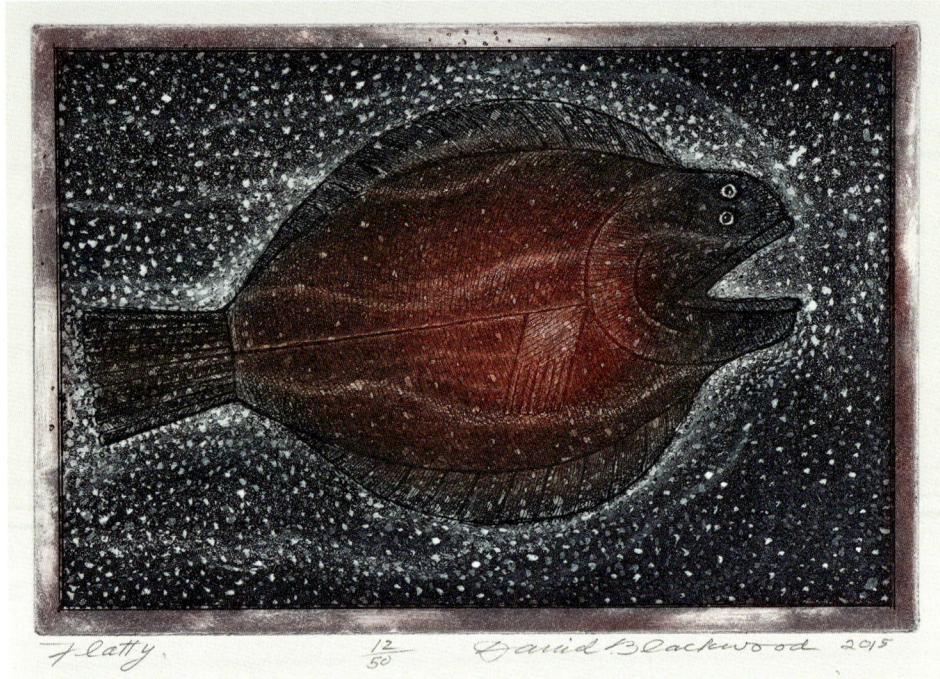

Flatty. 12/50 *David Blackwood* 2015

Fig. 9 • *Flatty*, 2015. Etching and aquatint on paper, edition 12/50, 20.2 × 30.5 cm. Art Gallery of Ontario, Promised Gift of David and Anita Blackwood, Port Hope, Ontario.

be propped up by pillows in his bed to sit and work. Wiersma worked alongside Blackwood to realize this print, with Anita bringing the plate back and forth between Blackwood's studio in Port Hope and his room at Bridgeport in Toronto. Their rich conversations while creating the print together are recorded on various proof states (figs. 4–8).

Blackwood never gave up on a print. A plate could have been bitten unexpectedly deep, but instead of walking away, he would return and rework until it met his vision. Once, during a move from one studio to another, he misplaced an unfinished plate from 1970. The work, *Search Party: Lost* (fig. 10), was subsequently located in late 2019 and finished in March 2021.[12] Blackwood began the work in the years following his first printmaking successes and it was part of what would become known as "The Lost Party" series (although the artist did not define it as a set series). In this plate, a group of men cling to an iceberg as they desperately attempt to gain the attention of a ship on the horizon, following Newfoundland's worst sealing disaster.[13] When the work was rediscovered, it existed only as a line etching, and the ship was not yet present on the horizon. It is still unclear why Blackwood subsequently added this tantalizing detail.[14]

12 Conversation with Anita Blackwood and Janita Wiersma in Port Hope, Ontario, July 20, 2024.

13 251 men from two ships died in the tragedy. See Lochnan, *Black Ice*, 79–80 and 85–95.

14 Wiersma stated that although she and Blackwood did not discuss the ship, she believes it was likely a hopeful sign. Even though the event had occurred more than a century prior, the artist did not want to leave the men lost and without hope. Email from Wiersma, March 5, 2025.

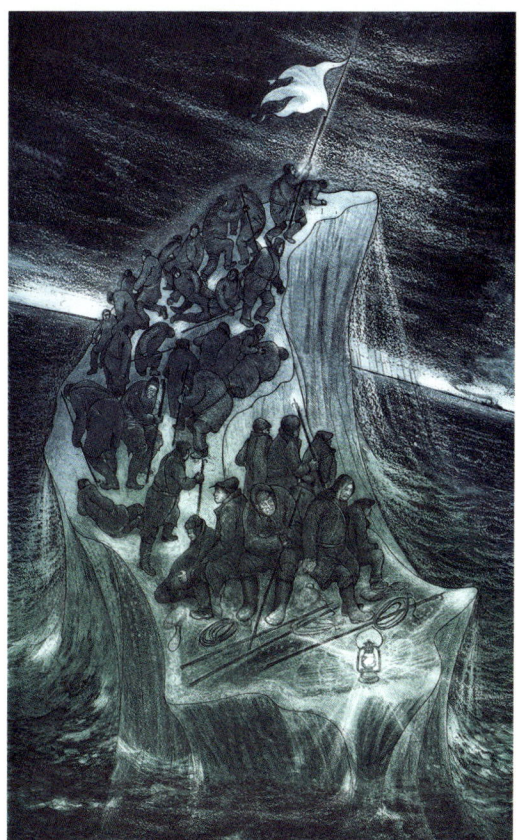

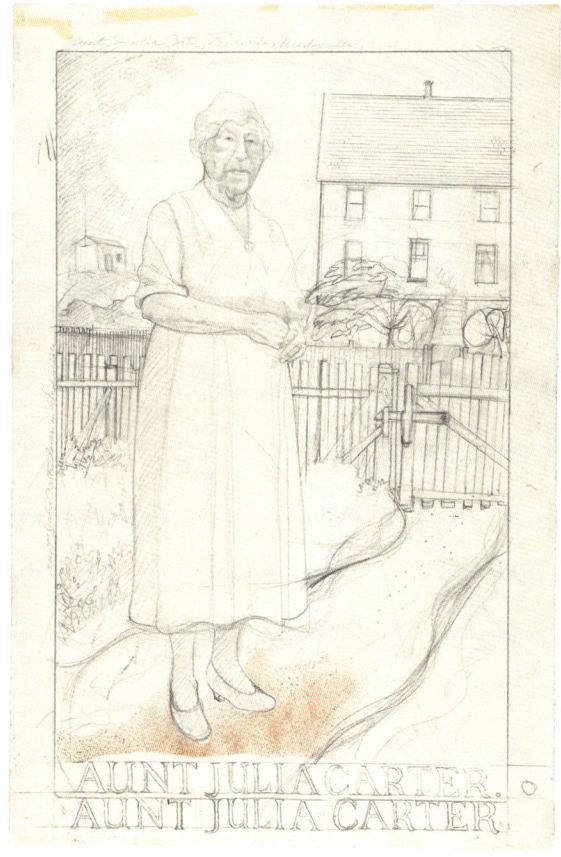

left

Fig. 10 • *Search Party: Lost*, 1970–2021. Etching and aquatint on paper, edition 33/50, 80.8 × 50.7 cm. Art Gallery of Ontario, Promised Gift of David and Anita Blackwood, Port Hope, Ontario.

right

Fig. 11 • *Aunt Julia Carter, Midwife, Wesleyville*, 2020. Graphite and watercolour on paper, 91.9 × 61.2 cm. Art Gallery of Ontario, Promised Gift of David and Anita Blackwood, Port Hope, Ontario.

Rooted in the Newfoundland of his childhood, the final print that the prolific artist began prior to his death was an image of Aunt Julia Carter (fig. 11), a midwife in Wesleyville, who delivered Blackwood and many others in the town where he grew up. Extant only as the full-scale outline drawing that he made in preparation for transfer to the copperplate, the work depicts the solid figure of Carter—an aunt not by blood but nevertheless of great personal significance— standing on a pathway leading to a gate in front of her house. For his last planned work to celebrate the woman who guided him into the world is a poignant final expression to leave behind for all who loved the man and his work. ⛵

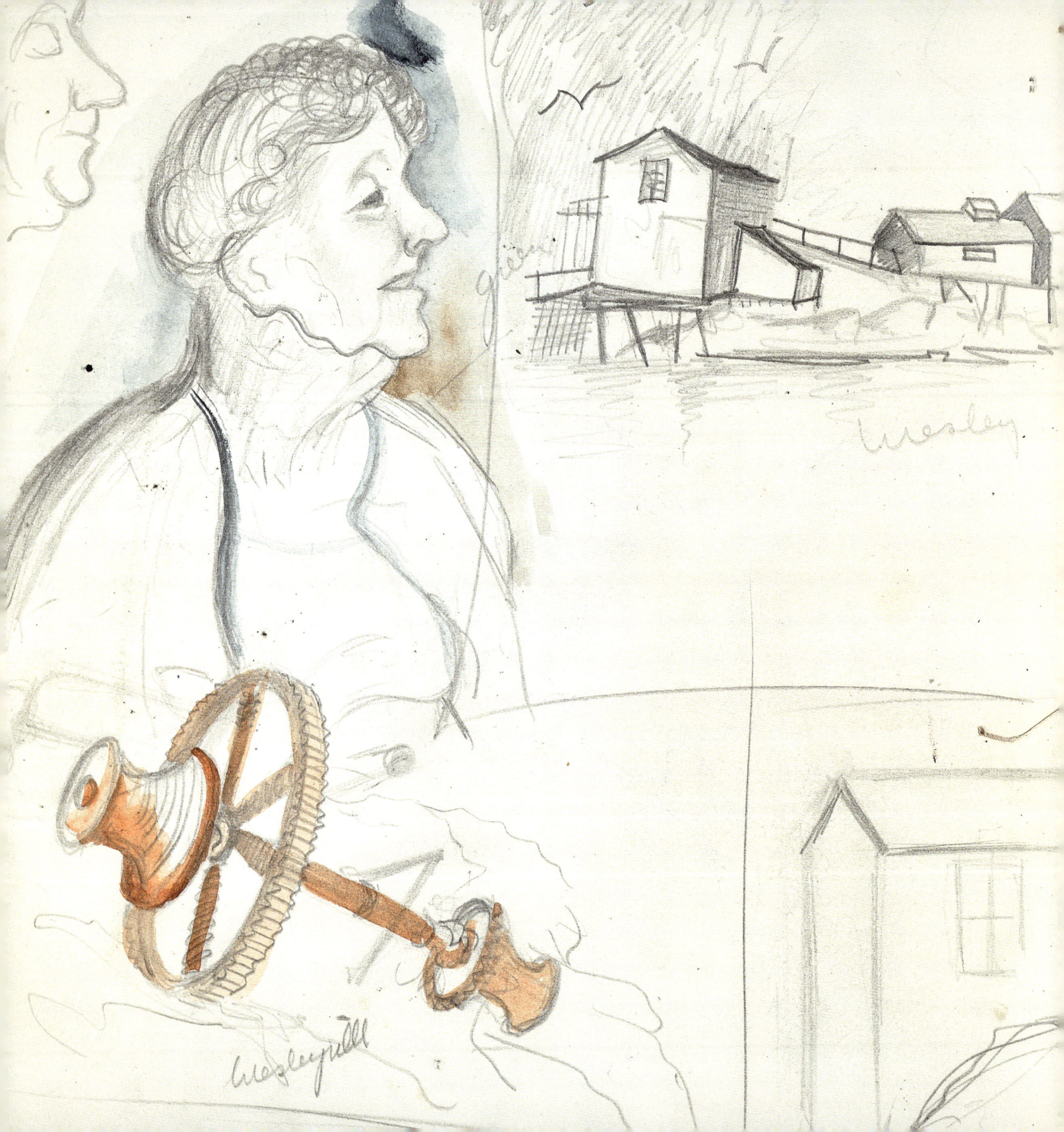

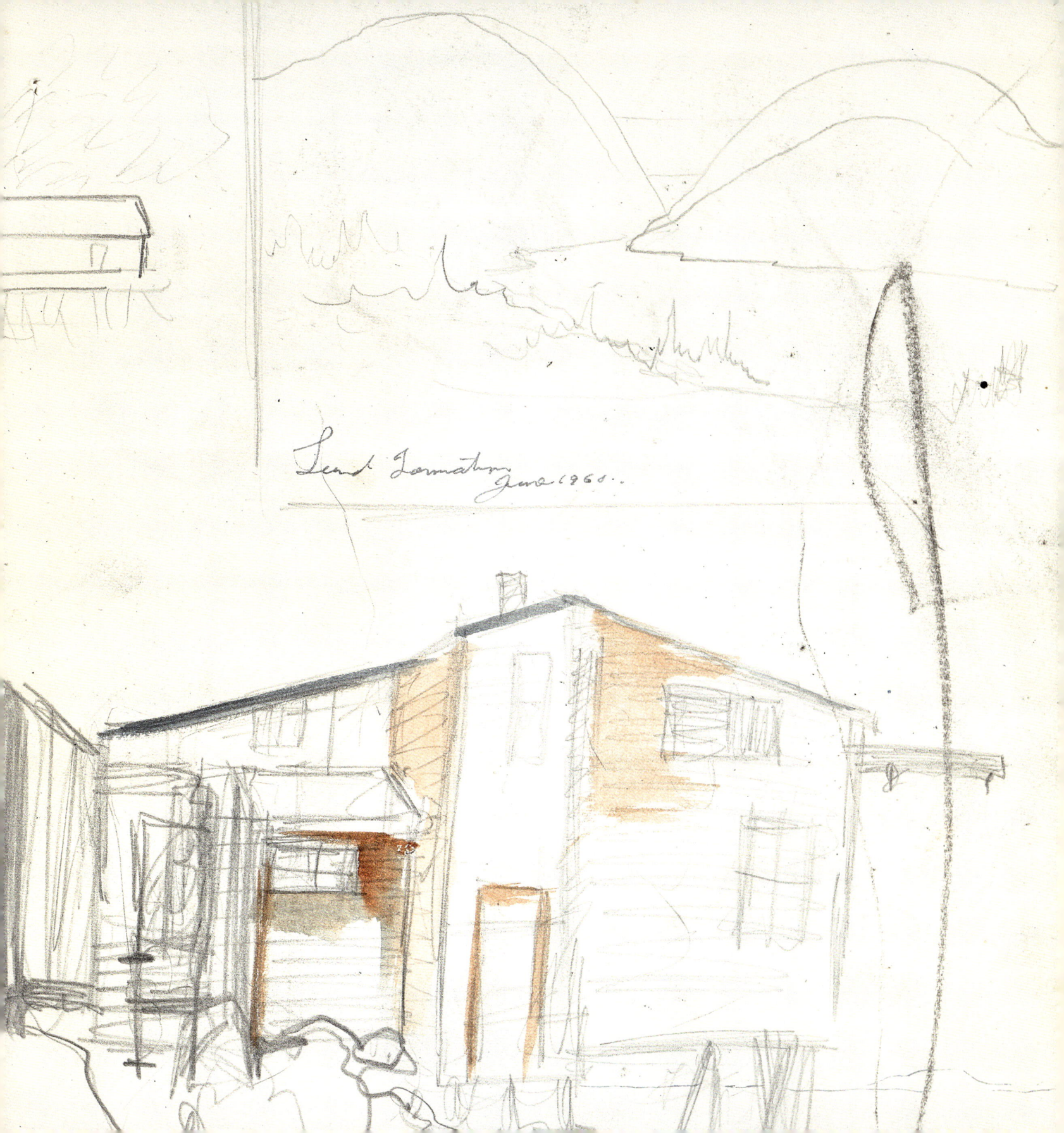

Sand Formation.
June 1960.

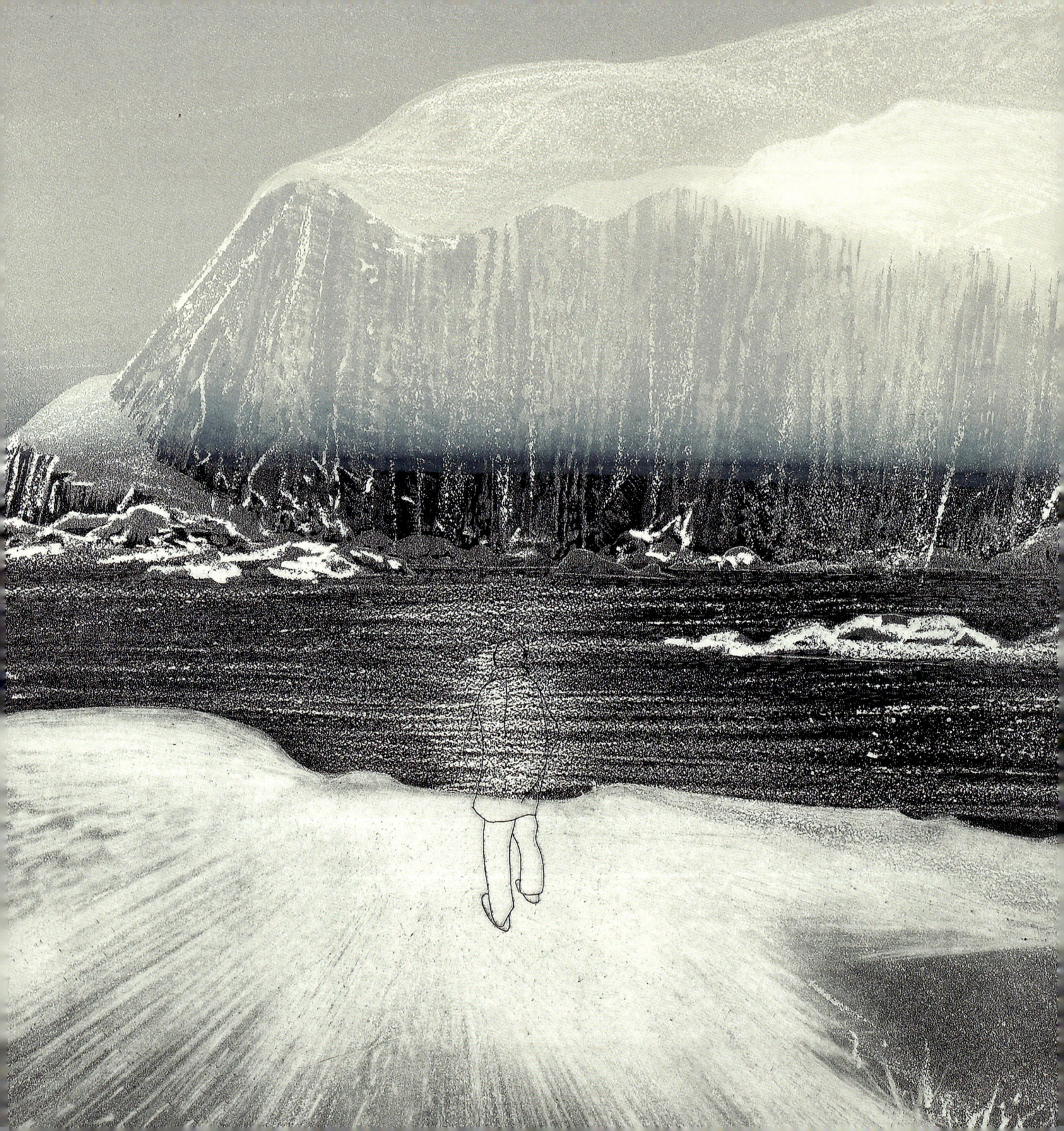

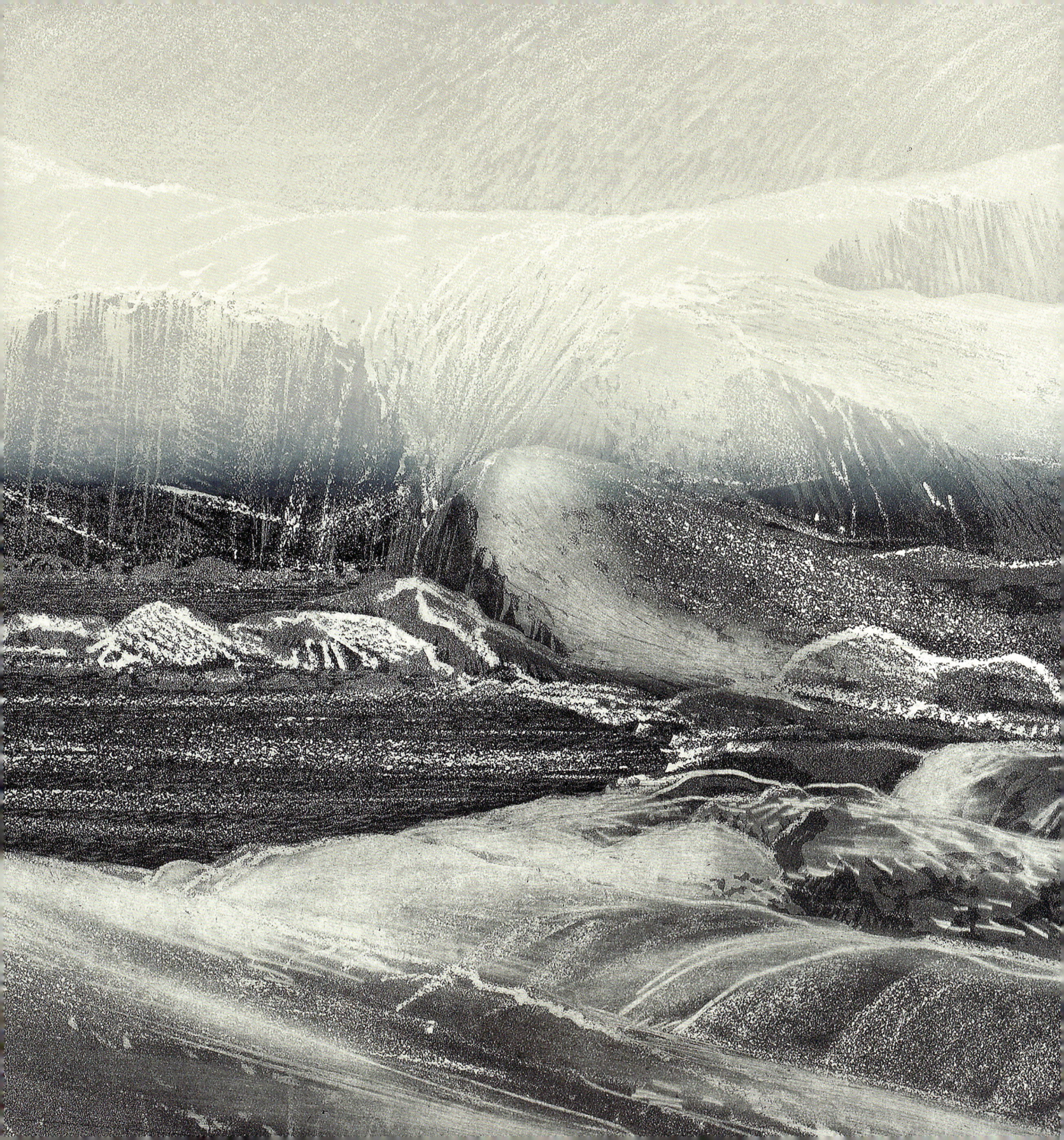

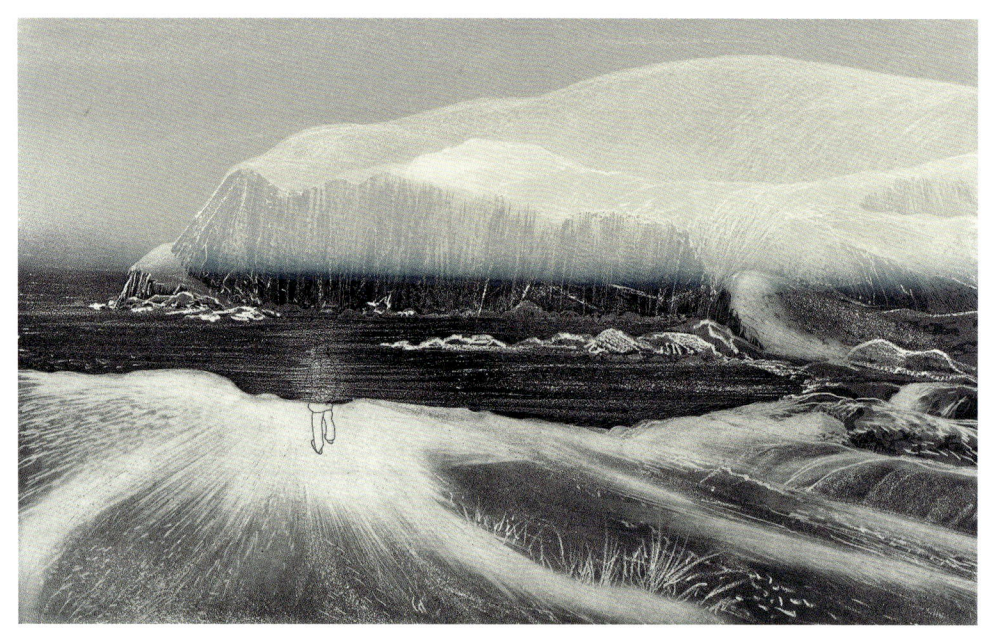

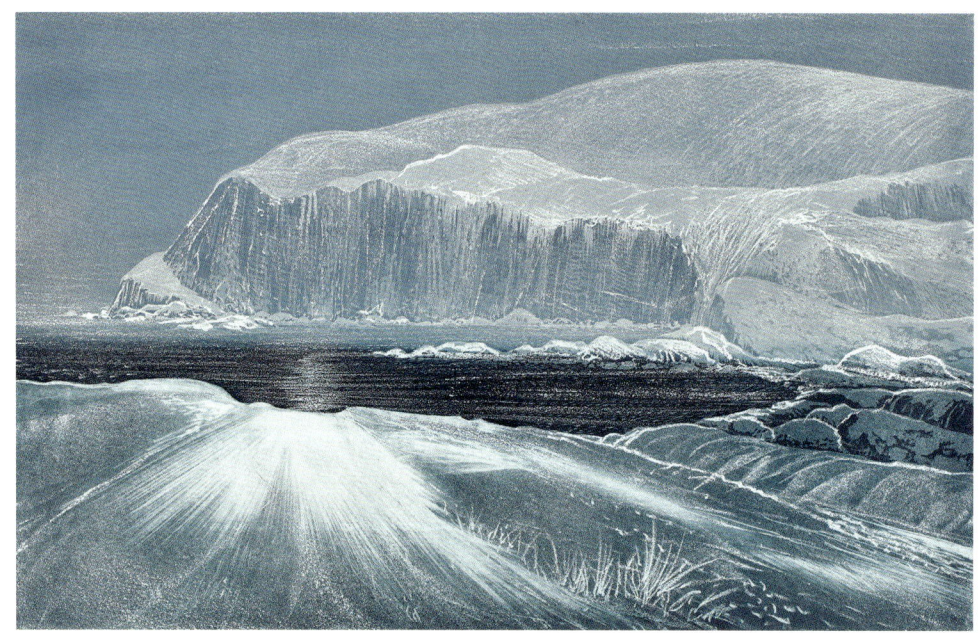

JANUARY VISIT HOME 1975

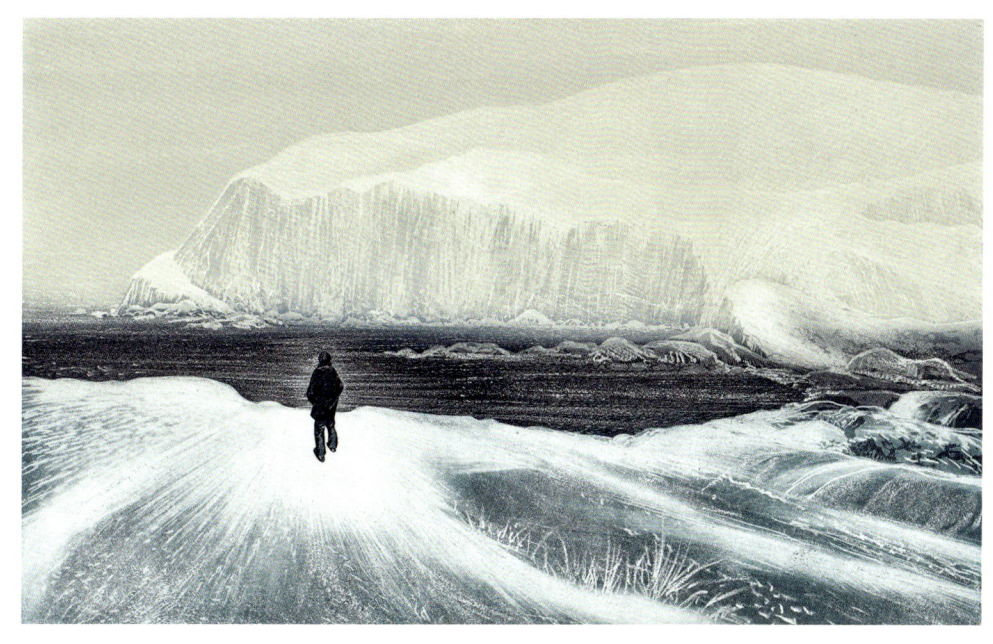

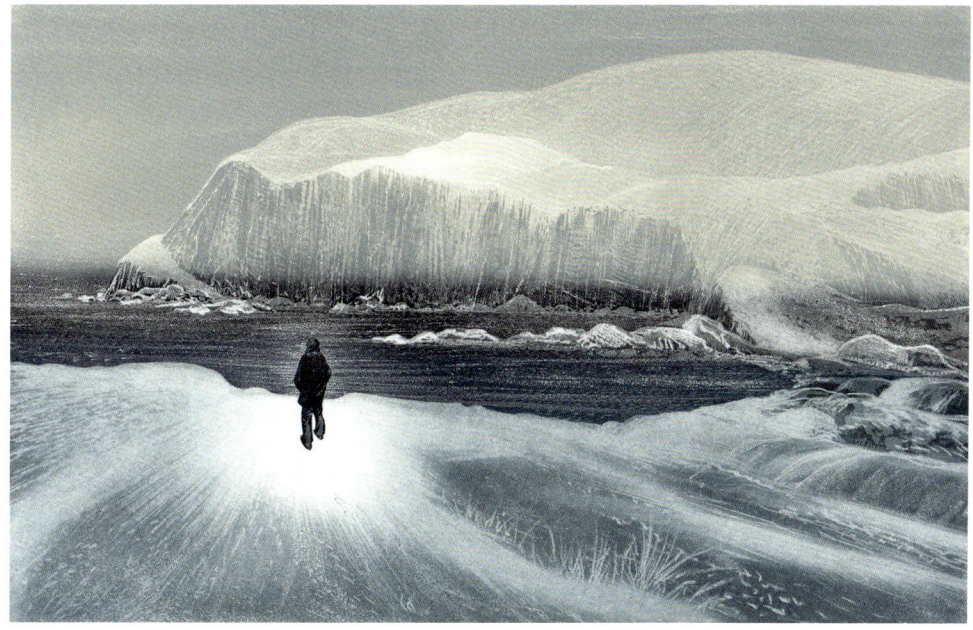

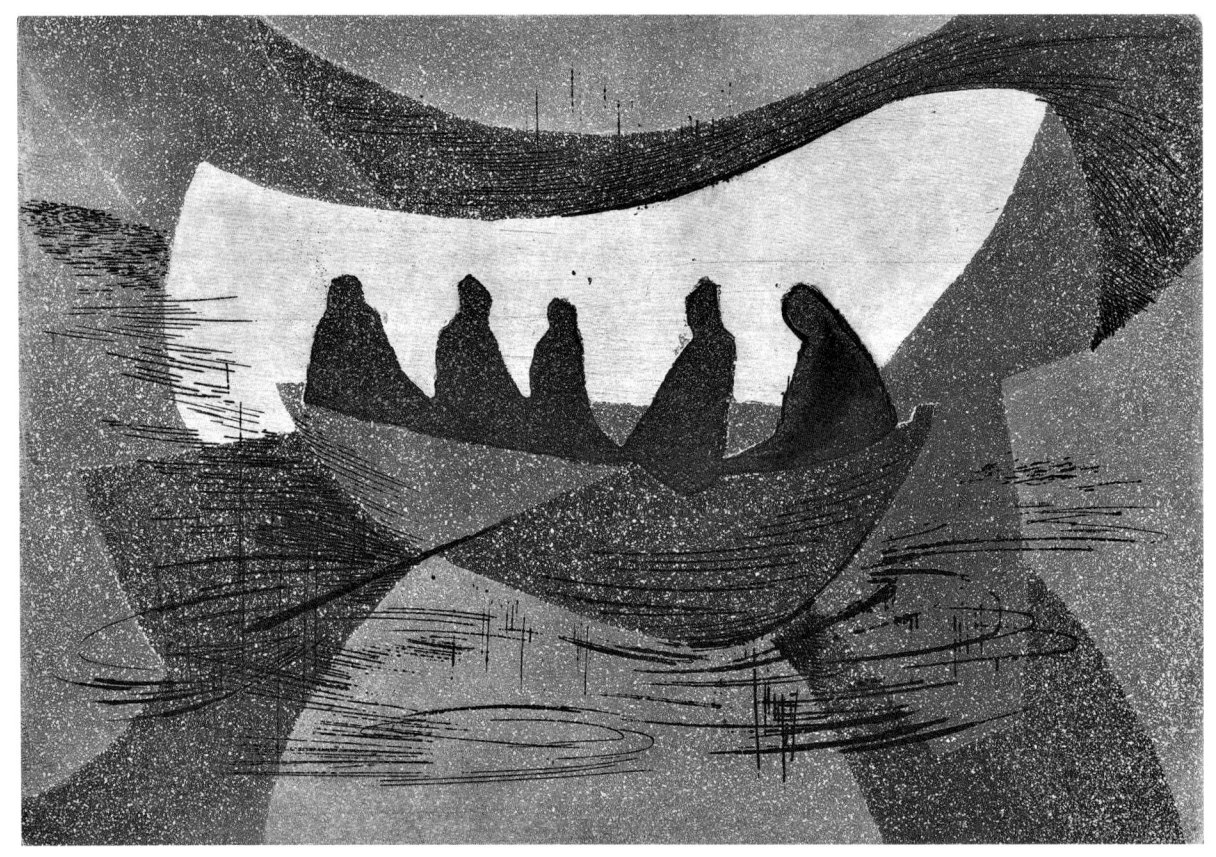

SURVIVORS 1961

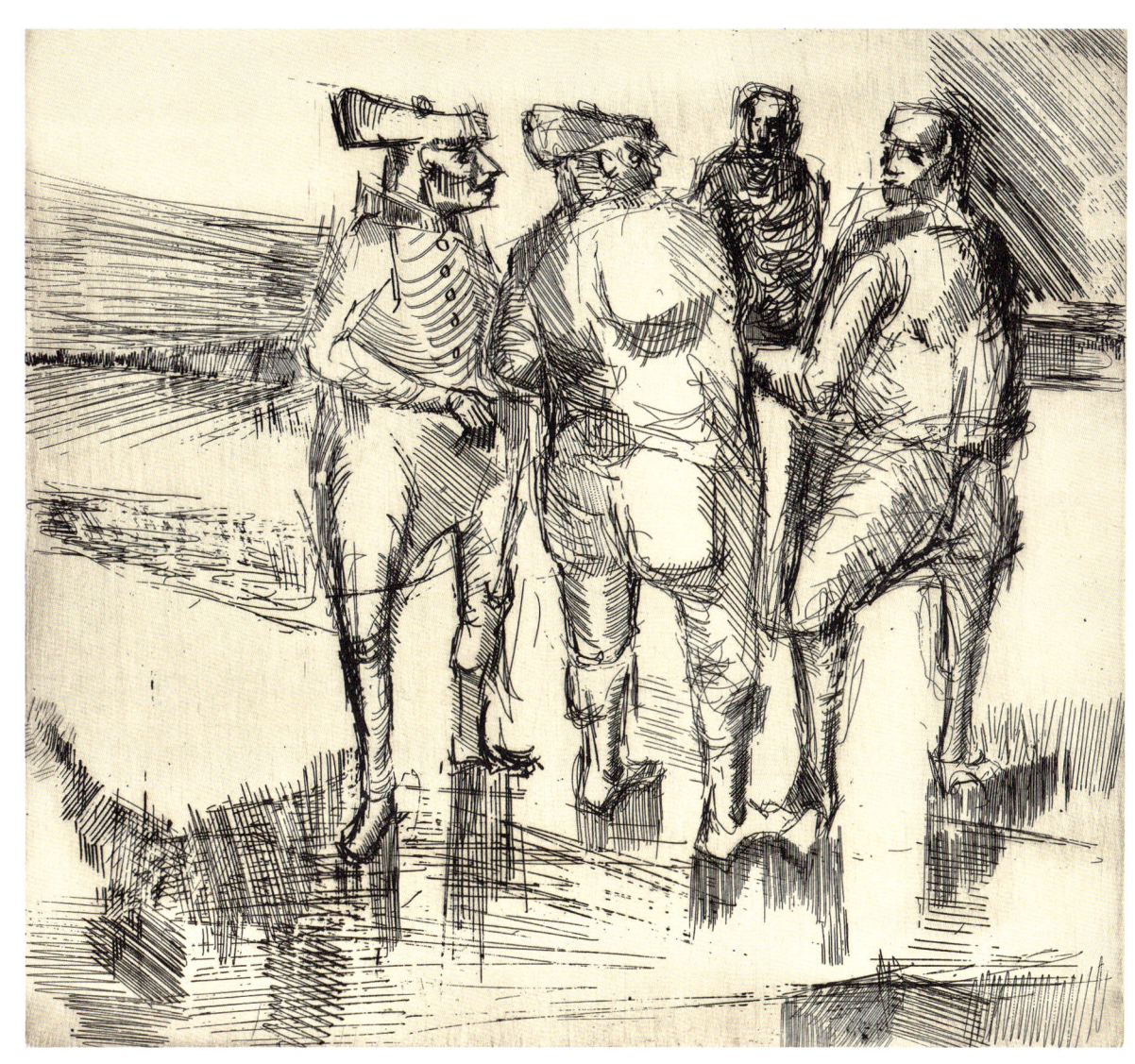

GATHERING 1962 **43**

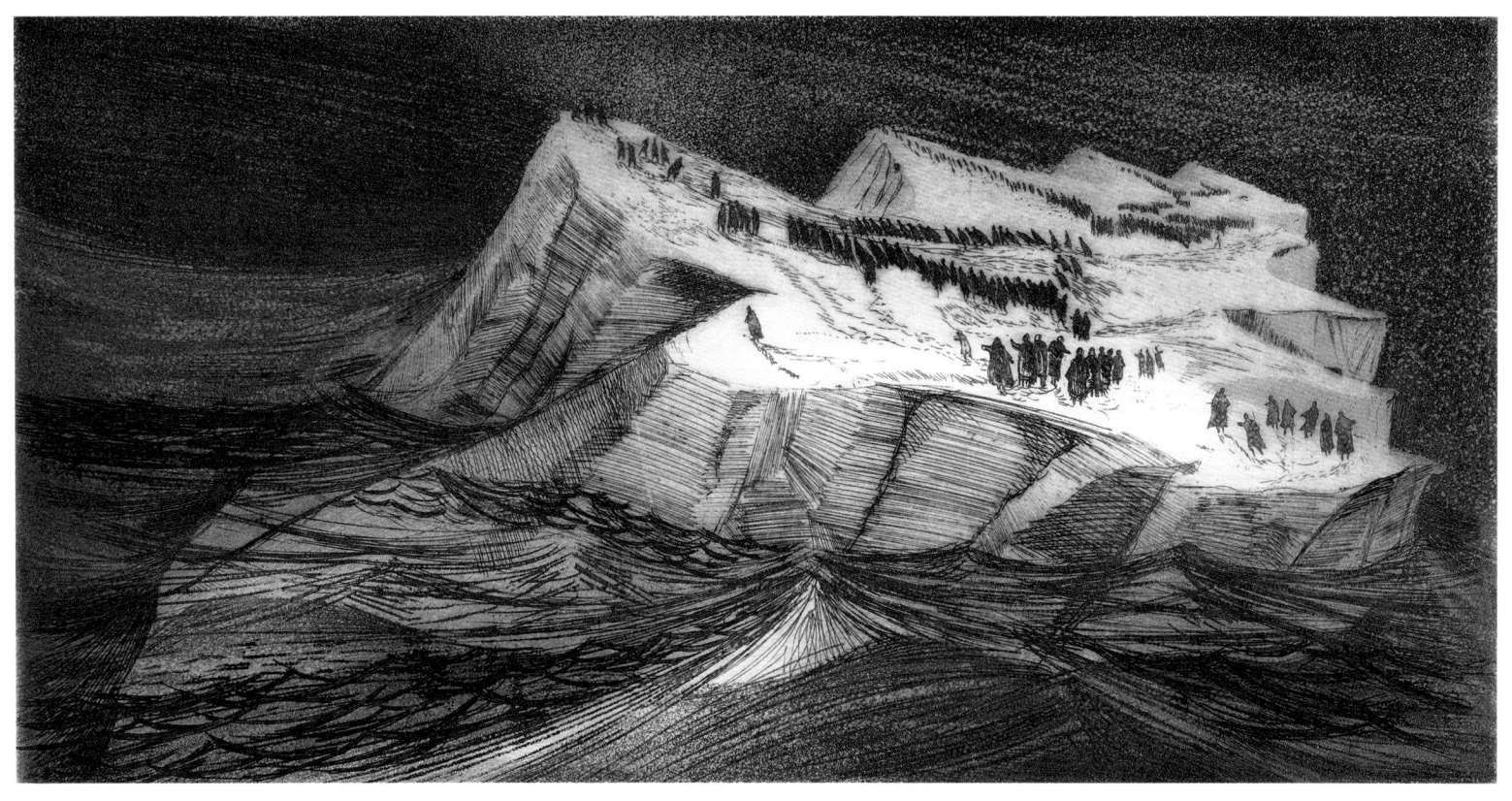

GREAT LOST PARTY ADRIFT   1965

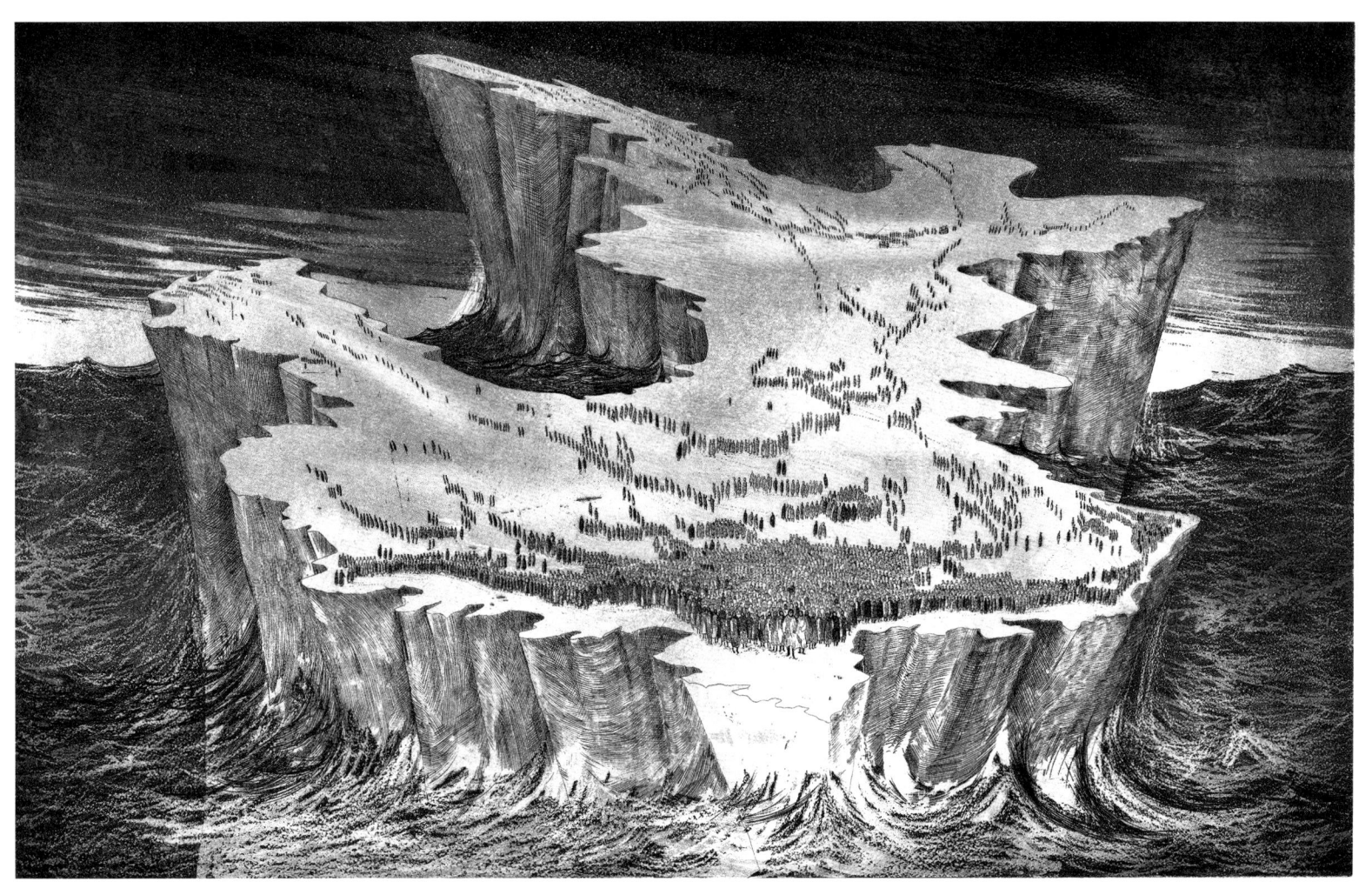

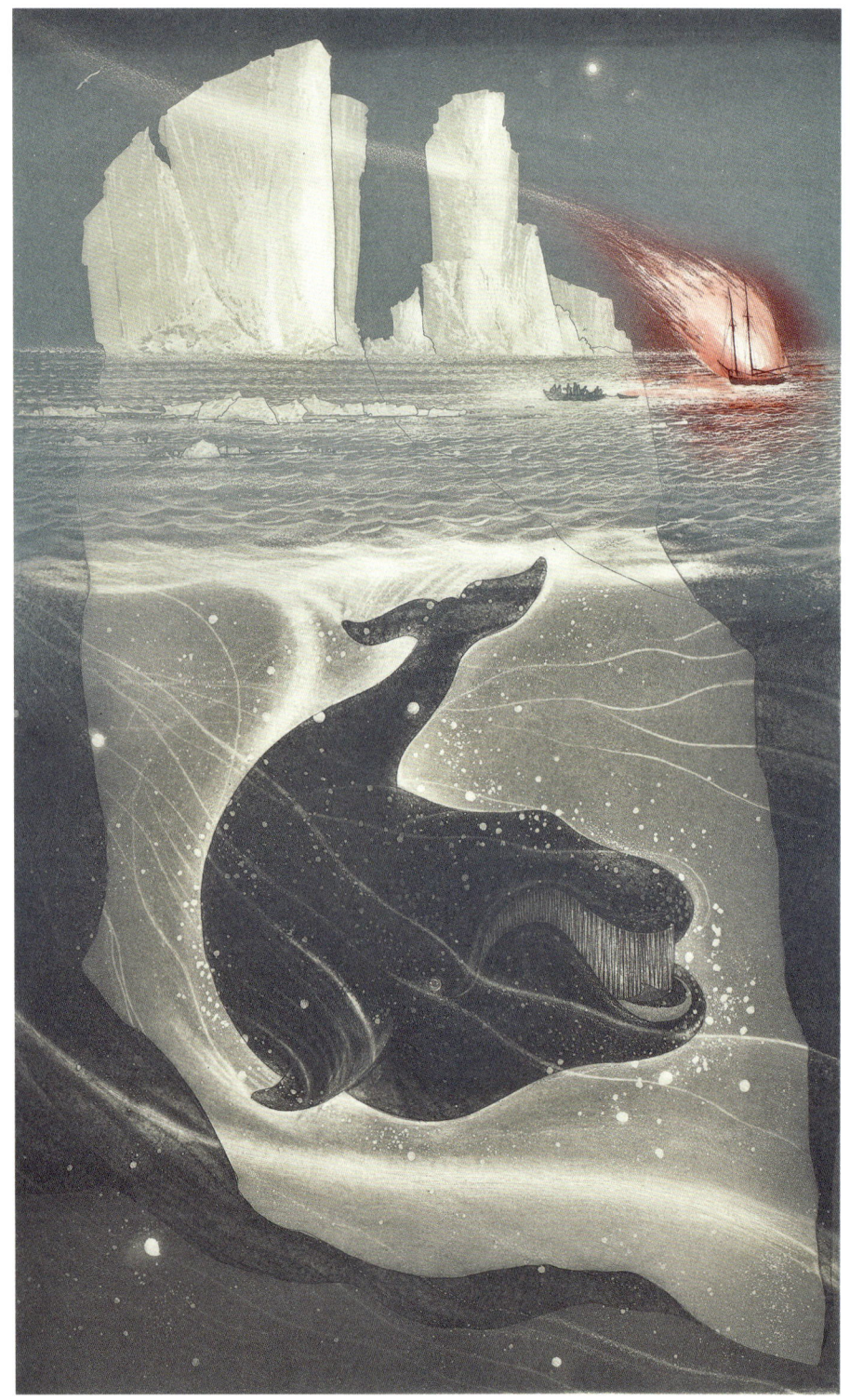

FIRE DOWN ON THE LABRADOR   1980

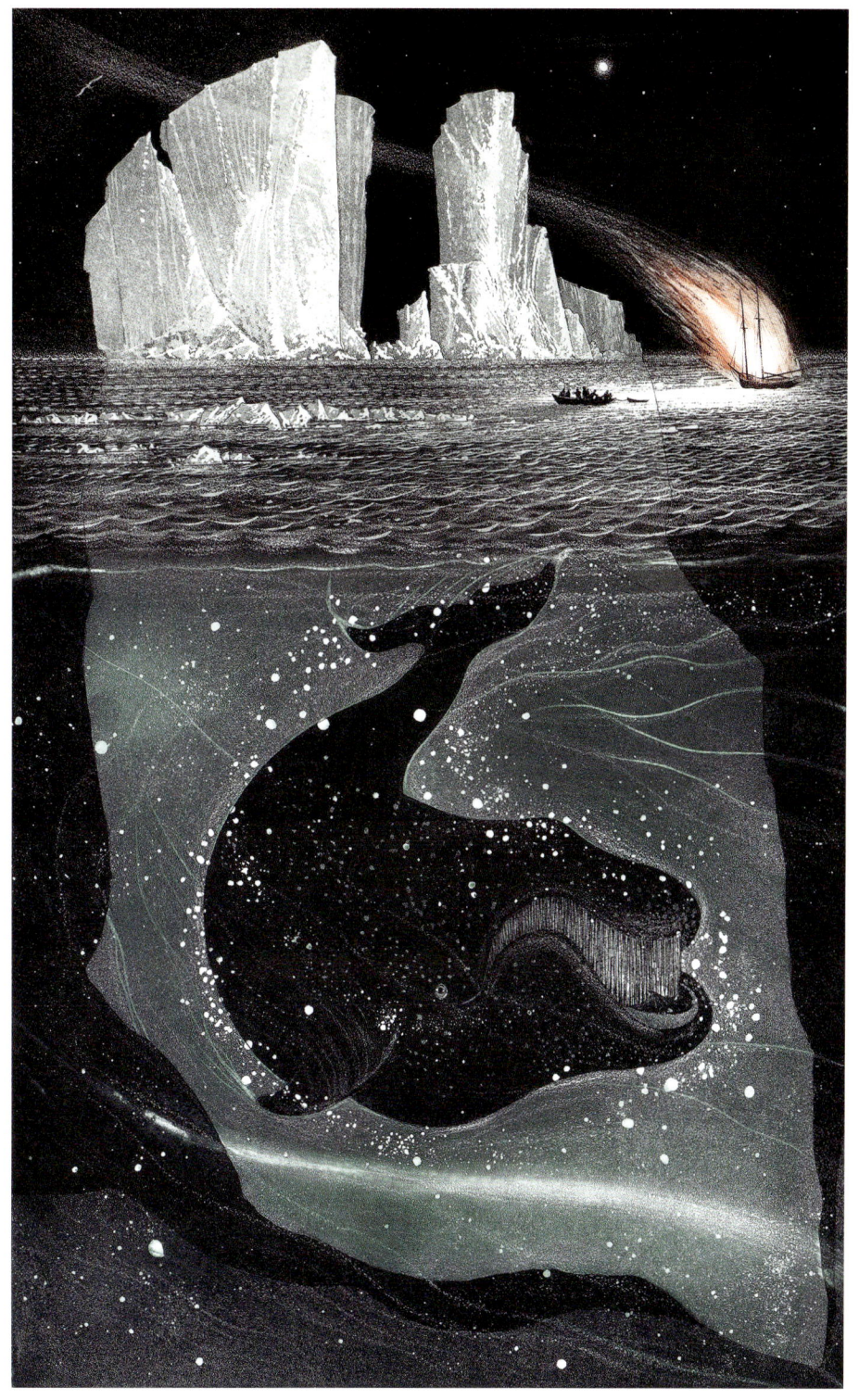

FIRE DOWN ON THE LABRADOR 1980

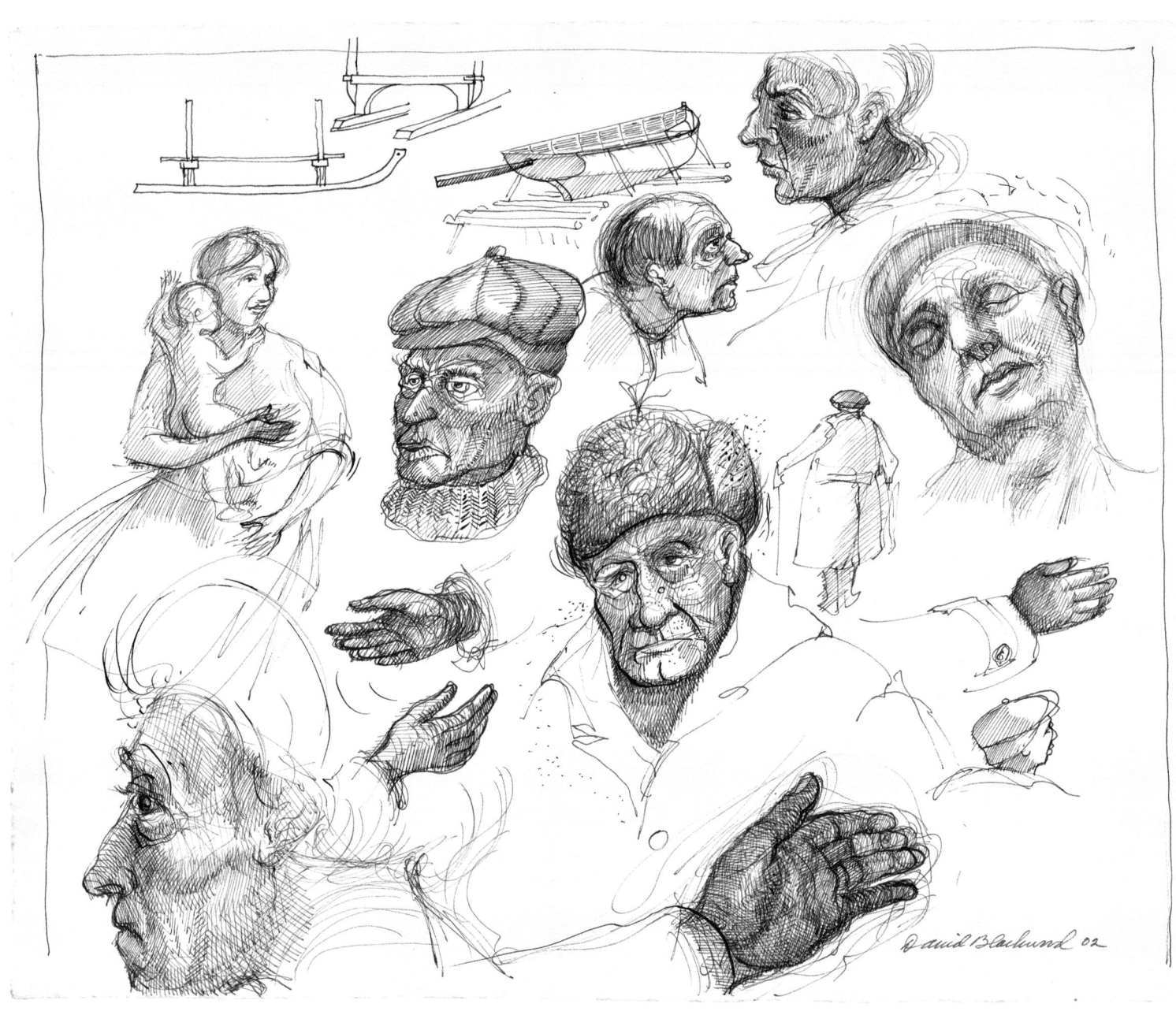

STUDIES HANDS, HEADS 2002

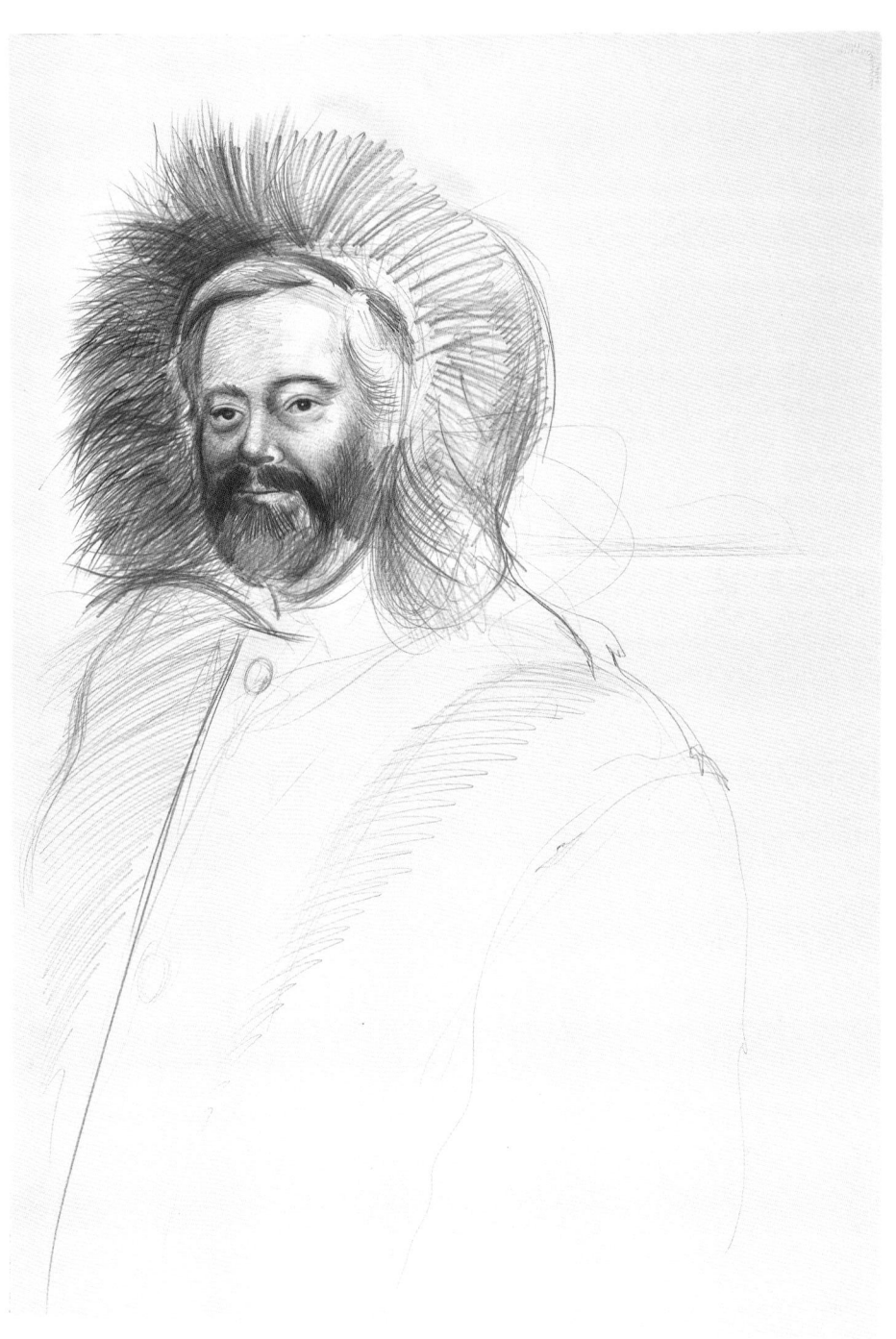

SELF-PORTRAIT [DAVID L. BLACKWOOD]   1981

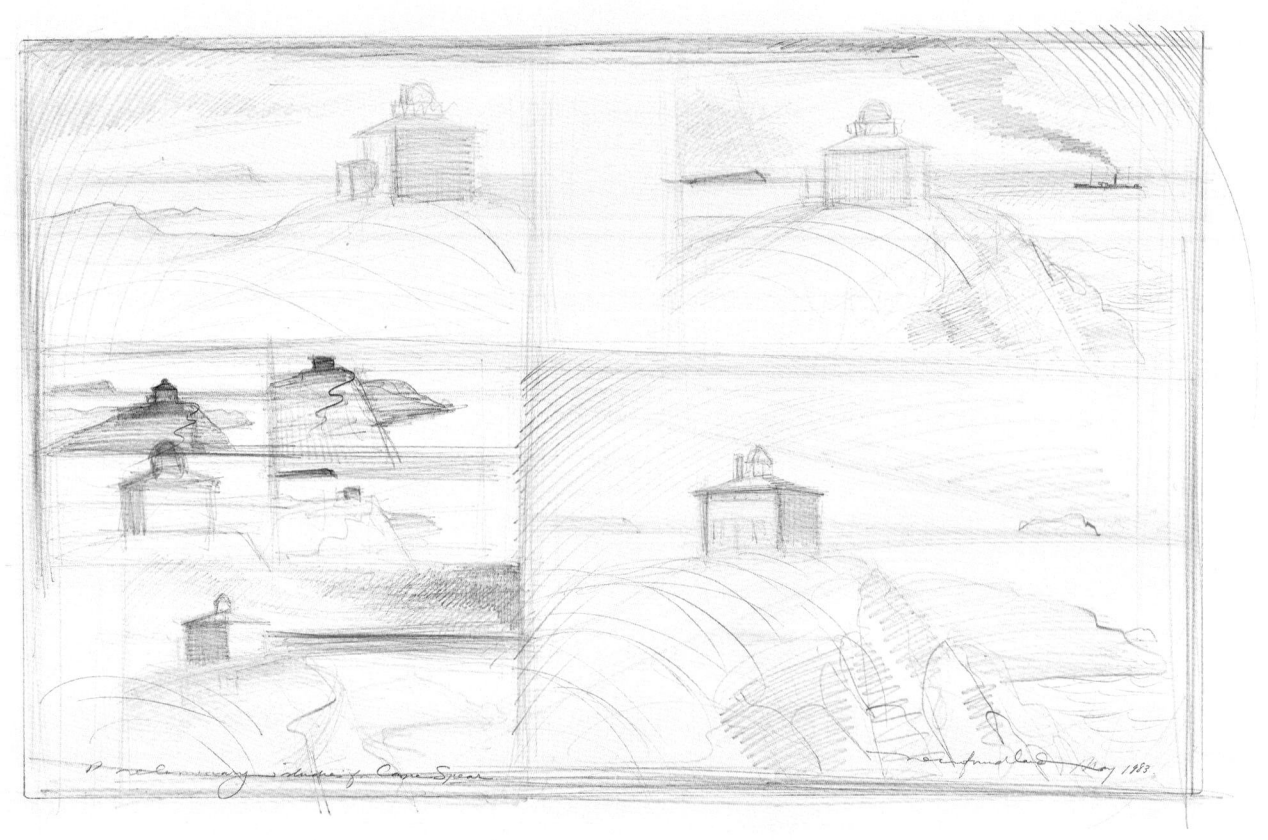

CAPE SPEAR, NEWFOUNDLAND 1983

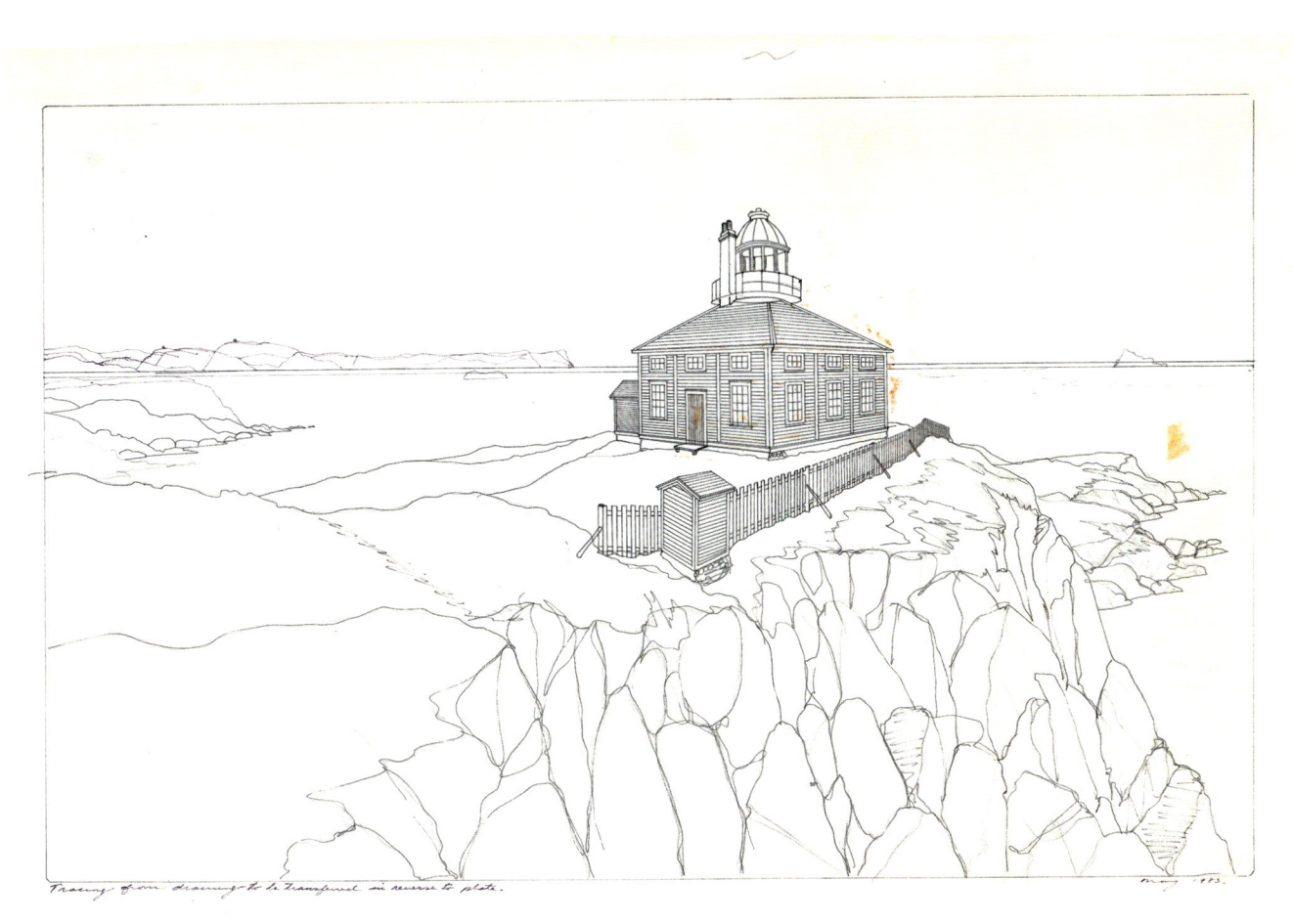

Tracing from drawing to be transferred in reverse to plate.

CAPE SPEAR, NEWFOUNDLAND 1983

CAPE SPEAR, NEWFOUNDLAND 1983

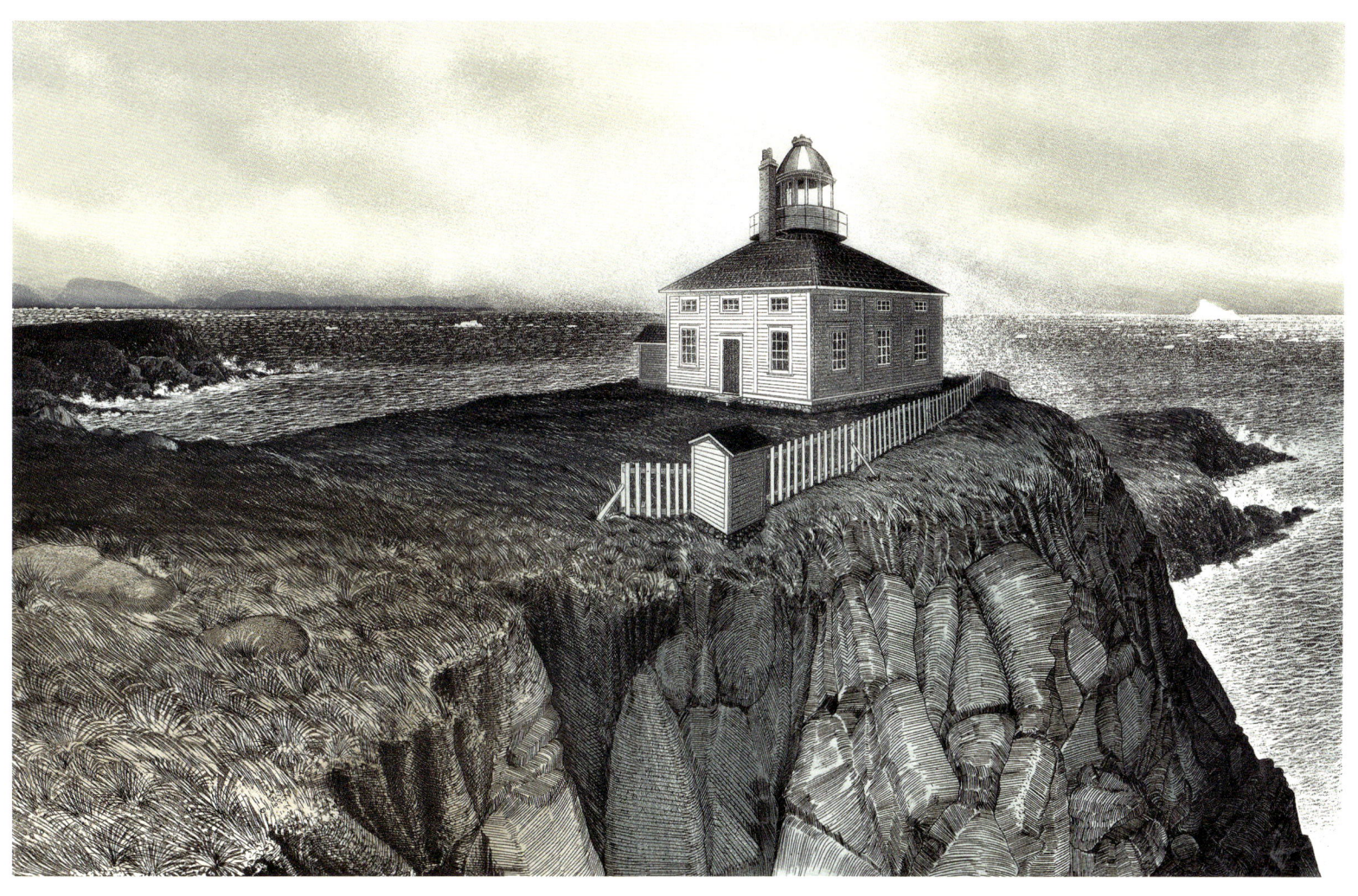

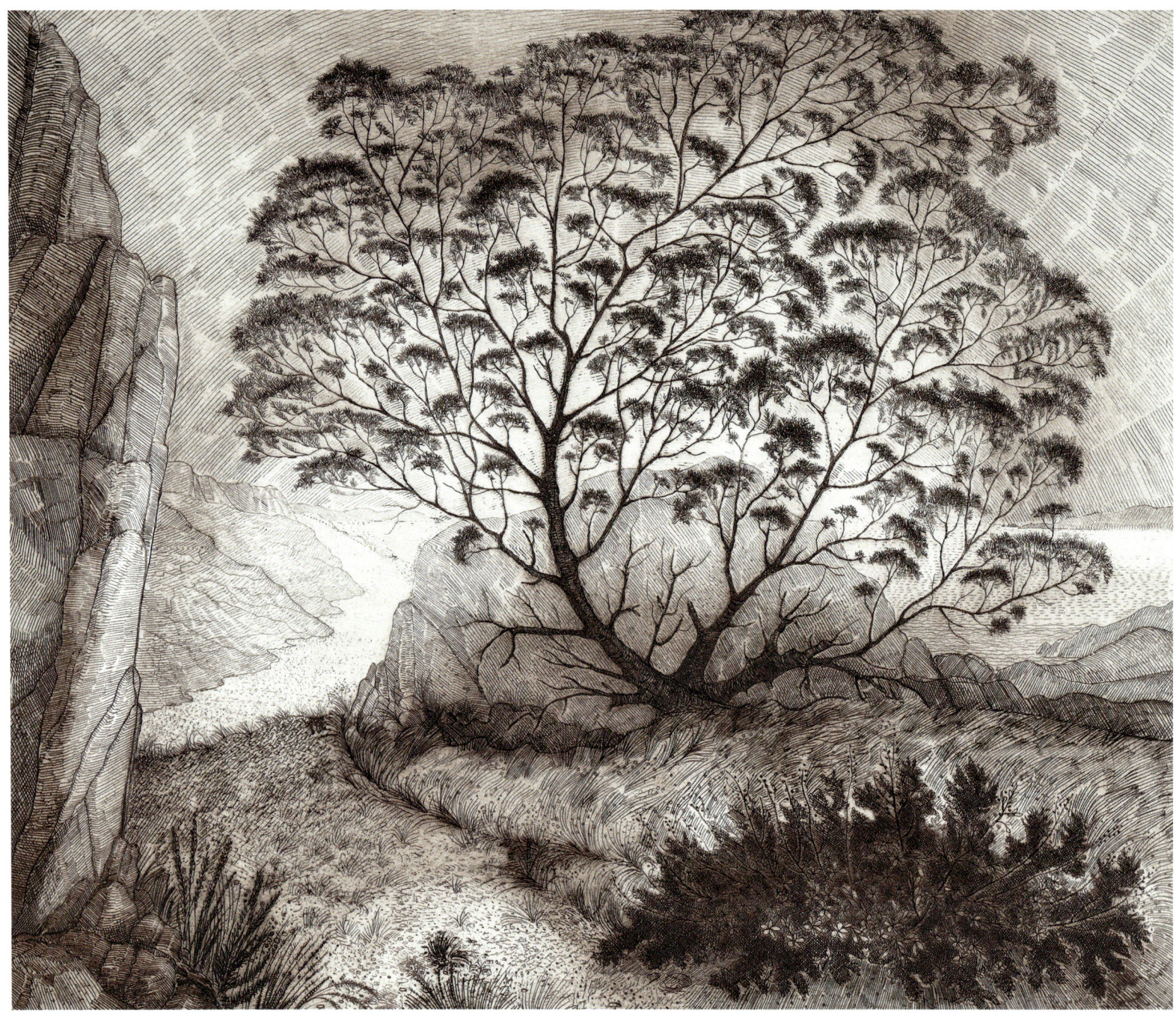

GRAM GLOVER'S TREE ON BRAGG'S ISLAND 1999

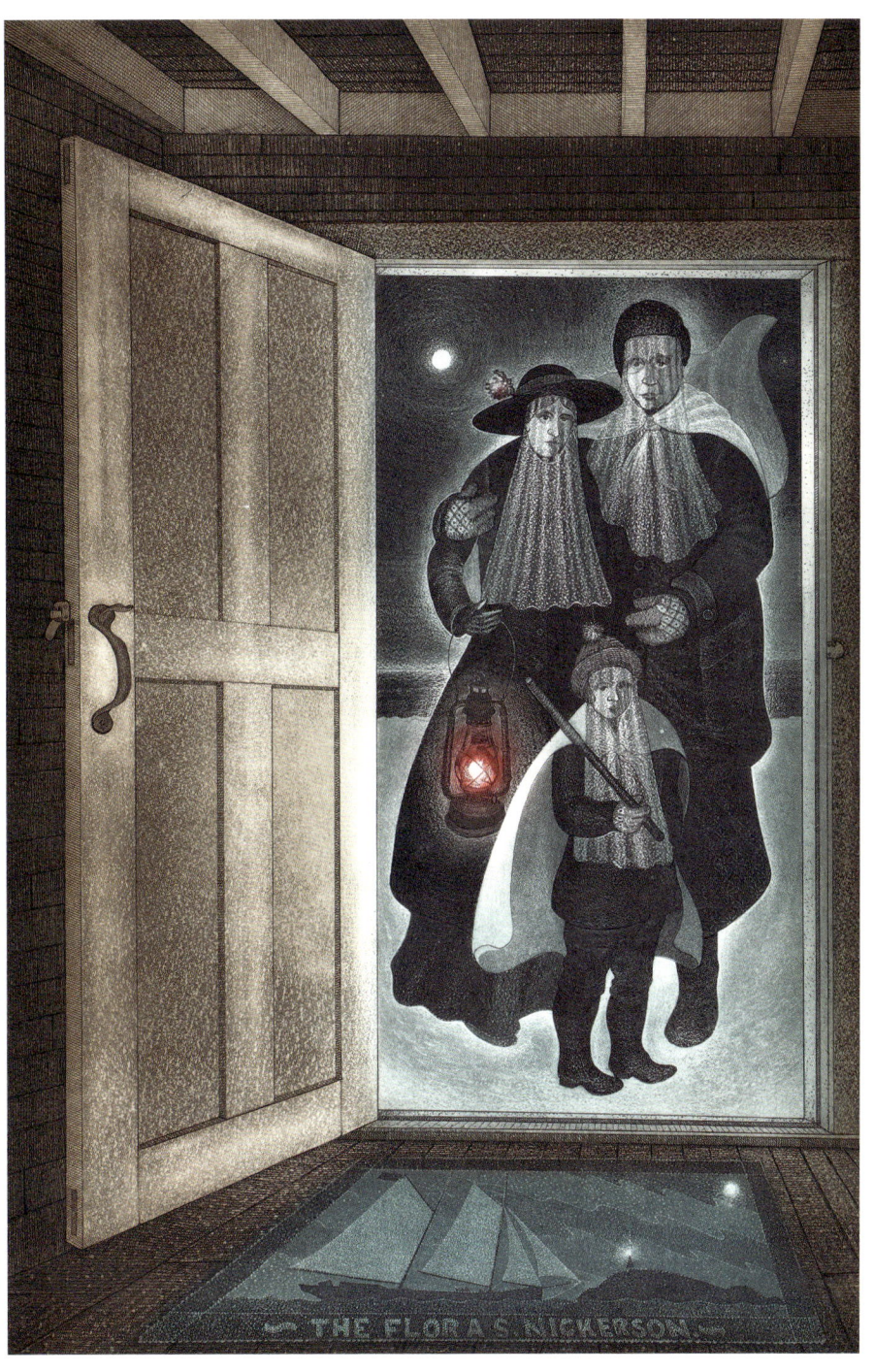

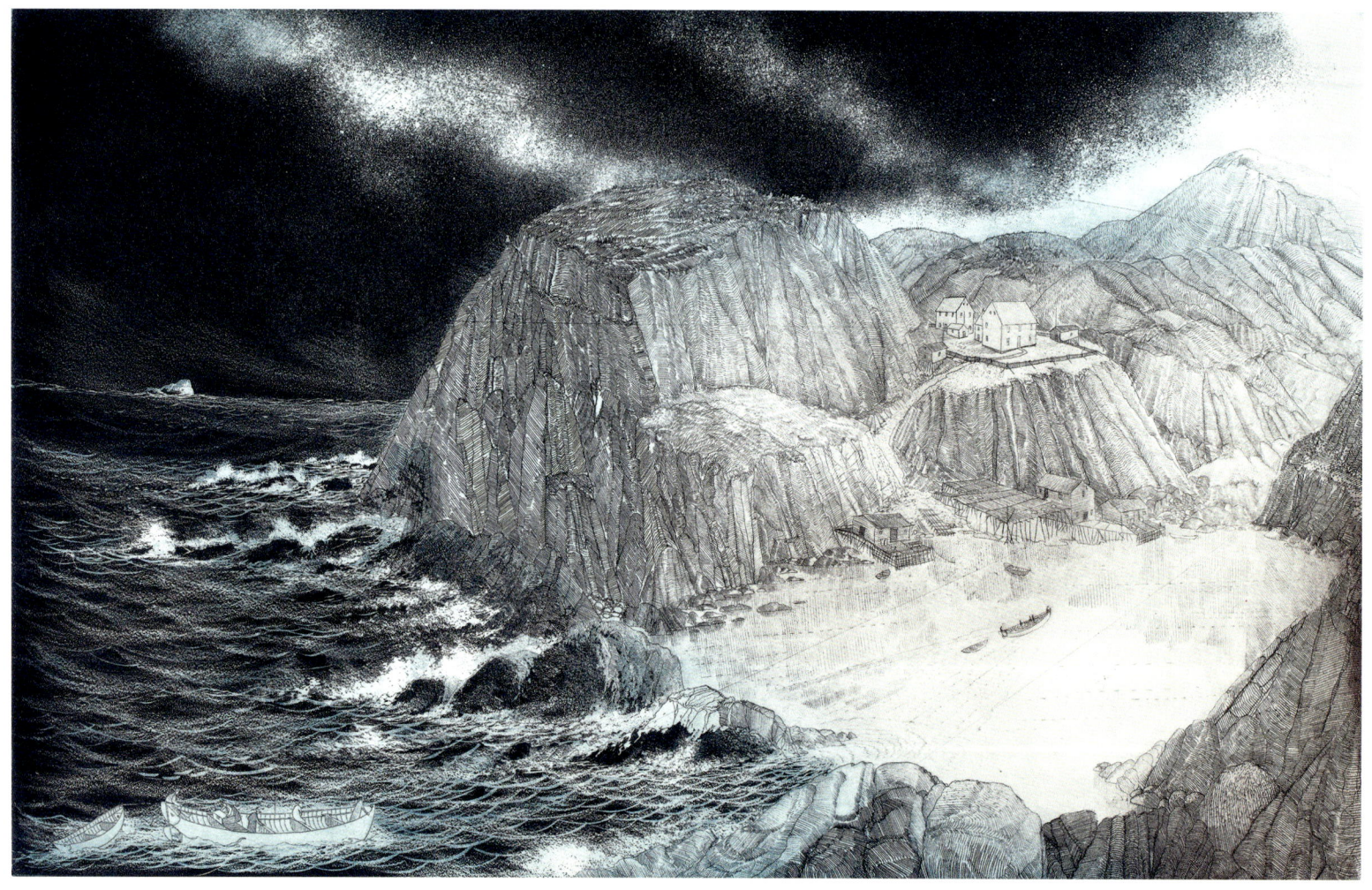

HAVEN 1994

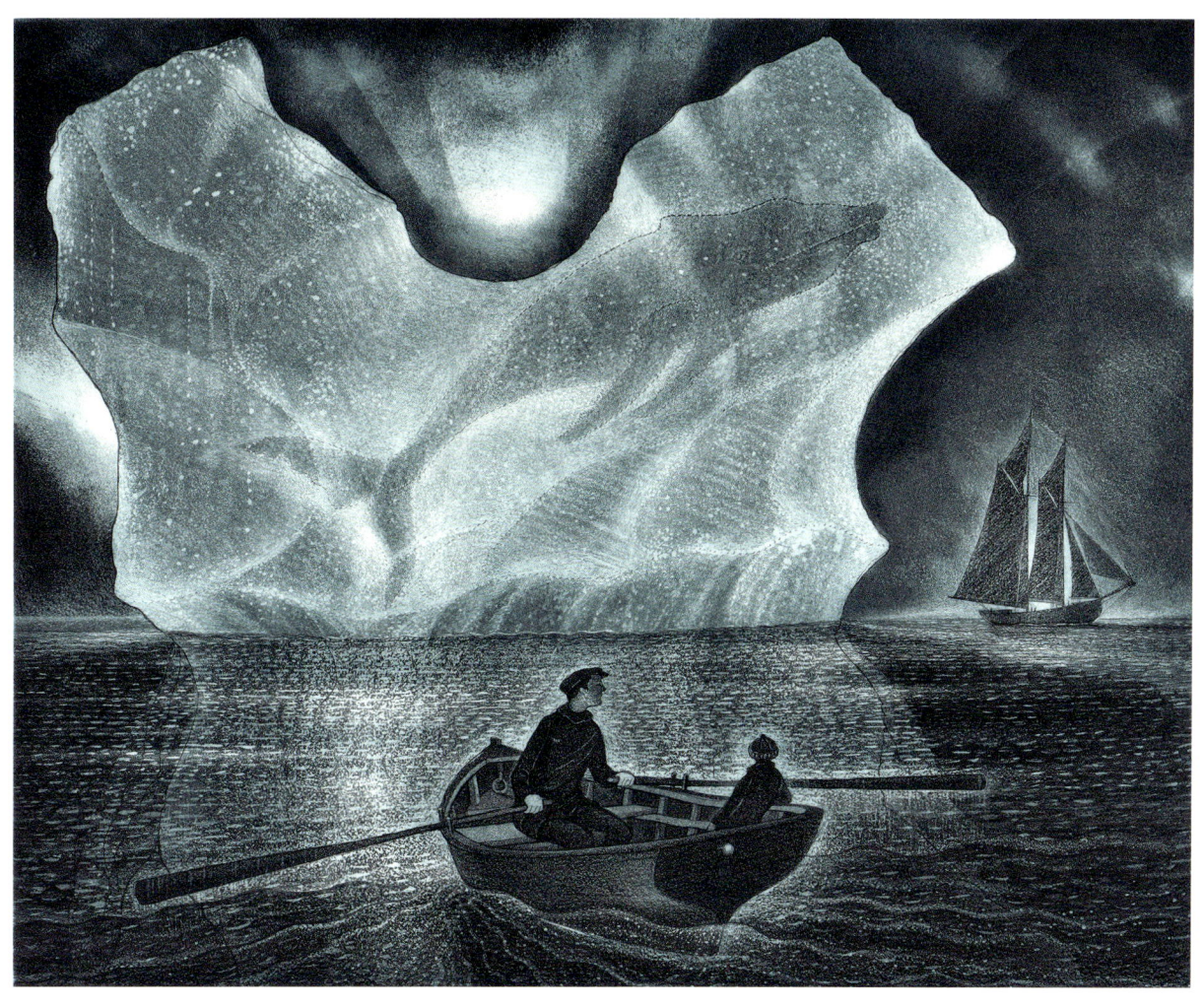

THE FLORA S. NICKERSON DOWN ON THE LABRADOR   1978

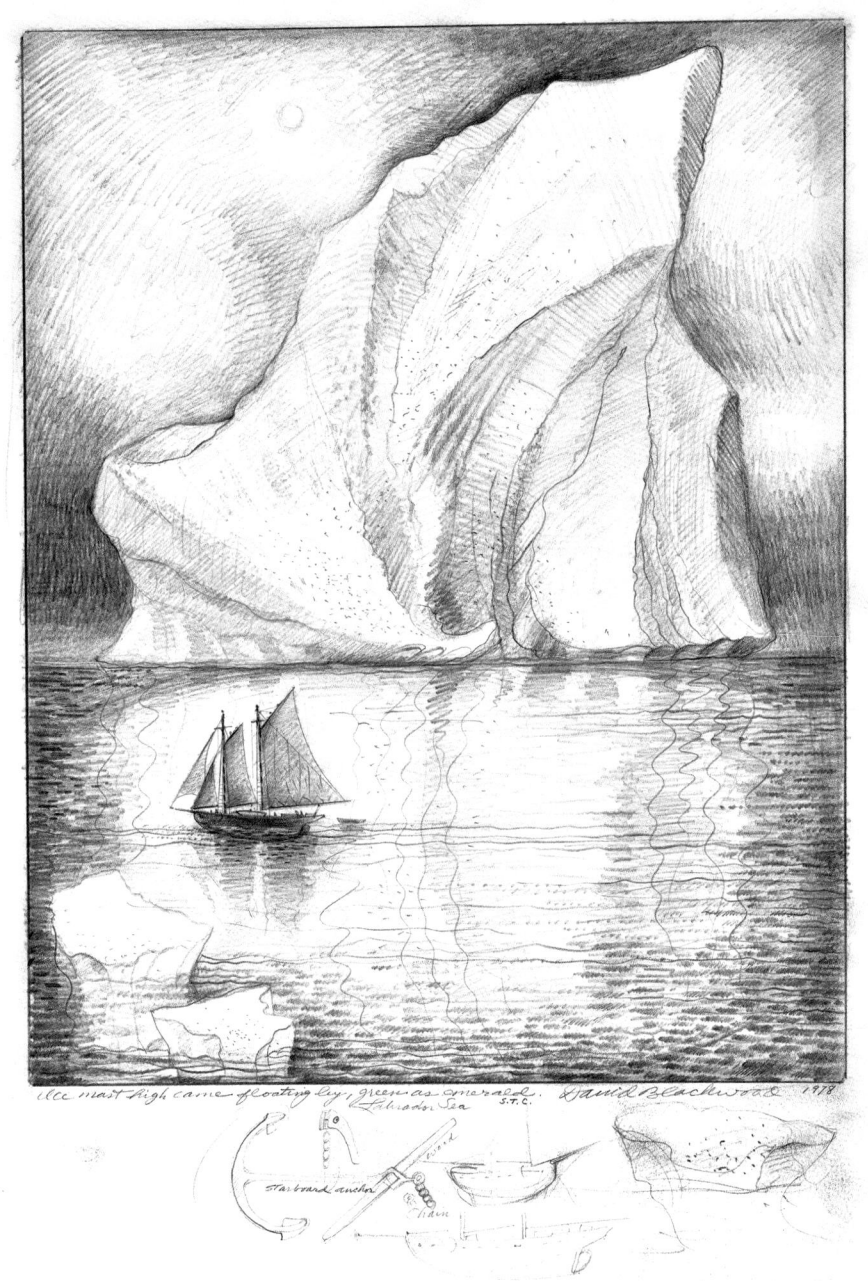

Ice mast high came floating by, green as emerald. David Blackwood 1978
Labrador Sea S.T.C.

Starboard anchor

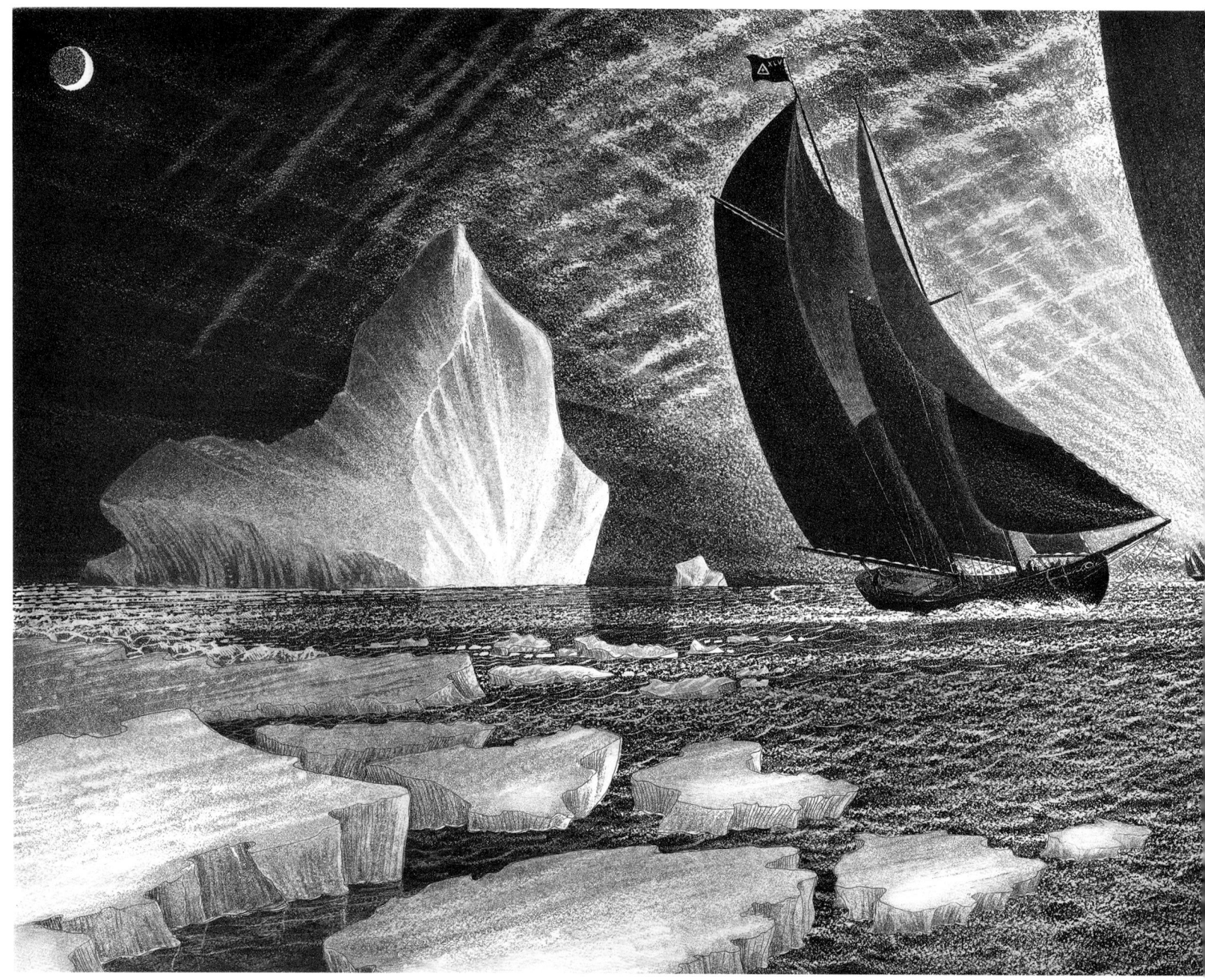

OUTWARD BOUND FOR THE LABRADOR   1985

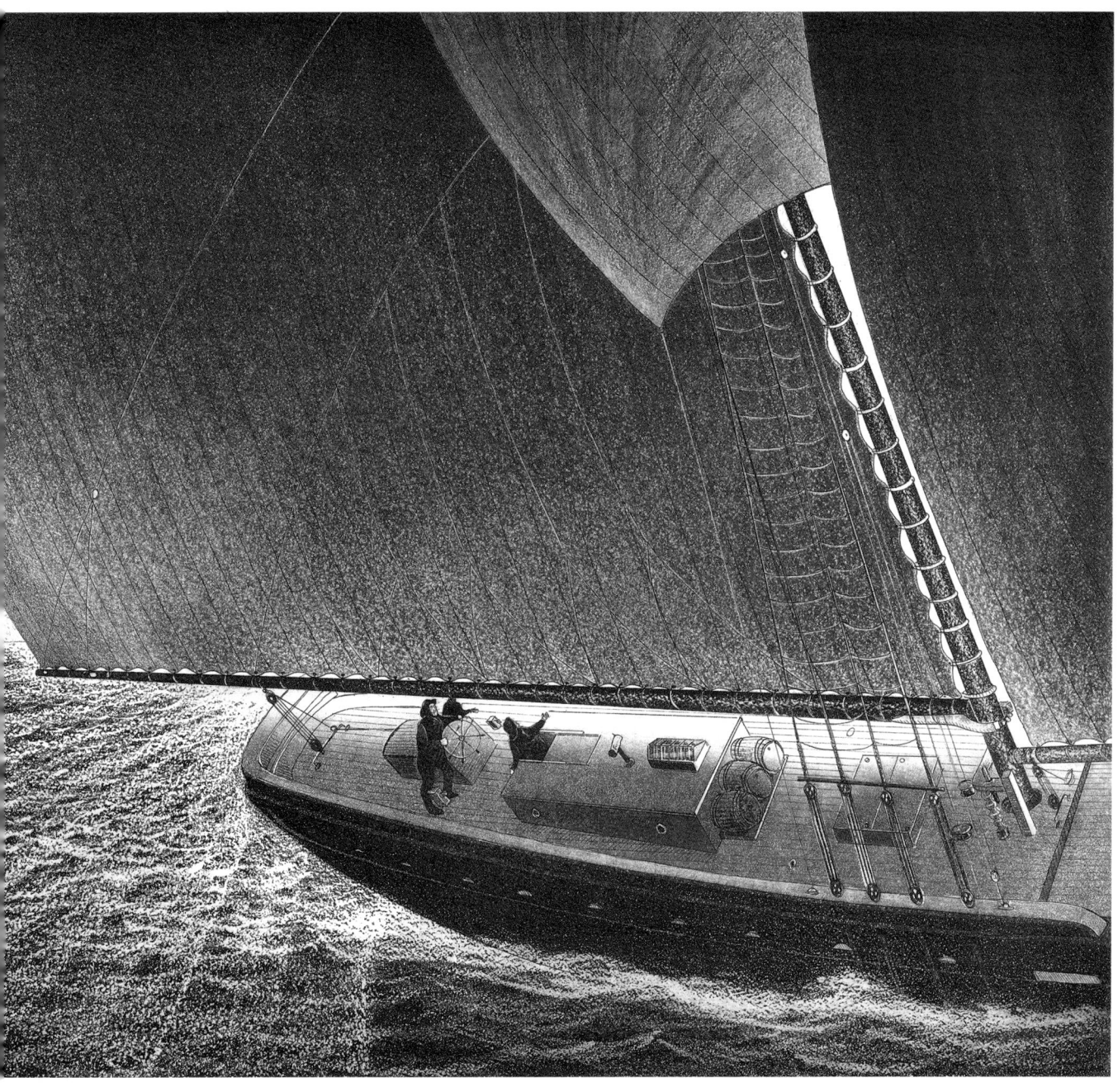

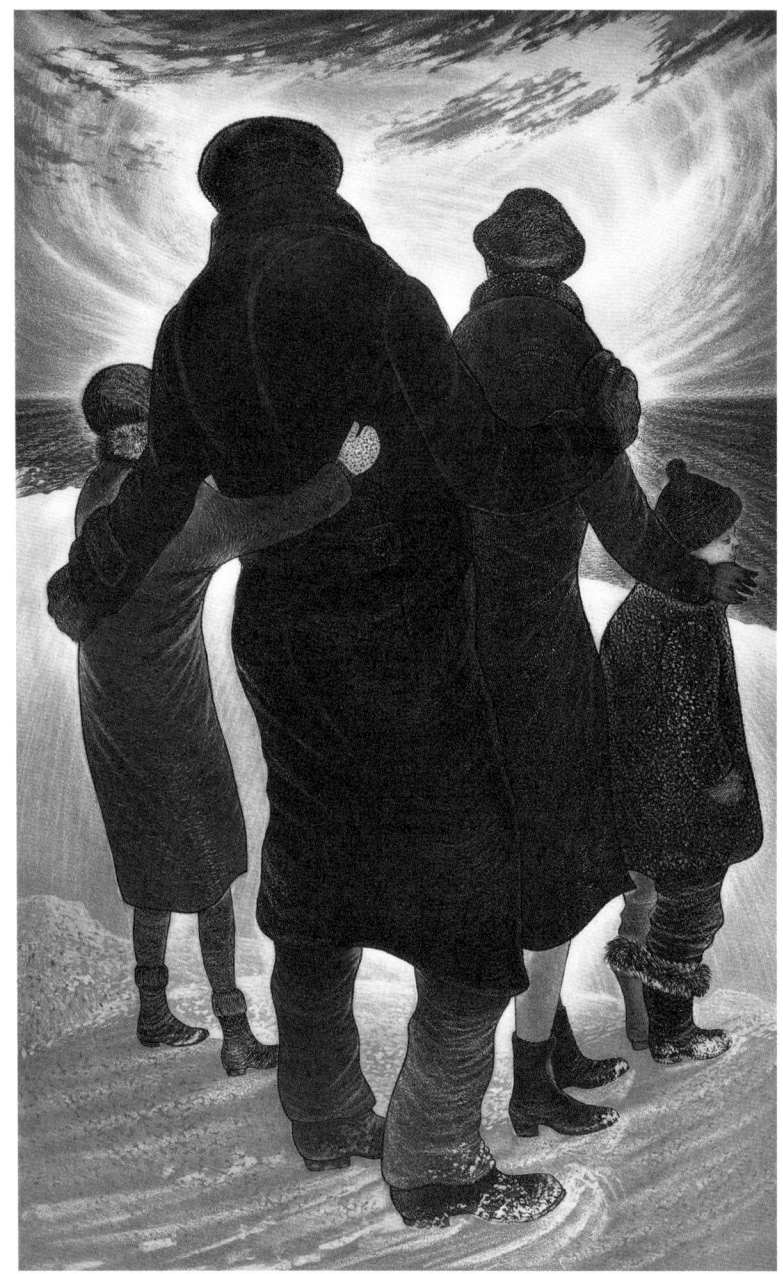

THE FAMILY   1982

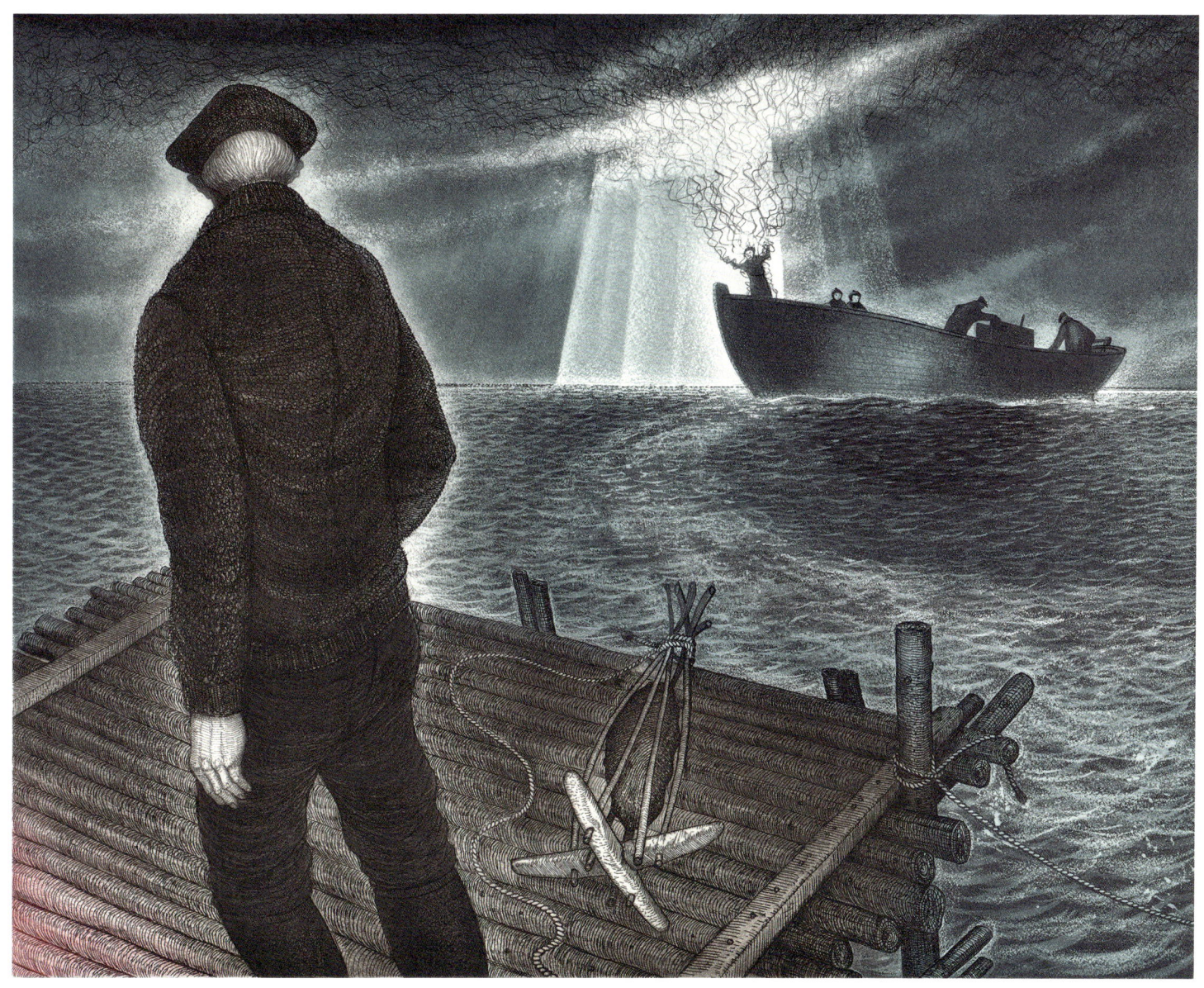

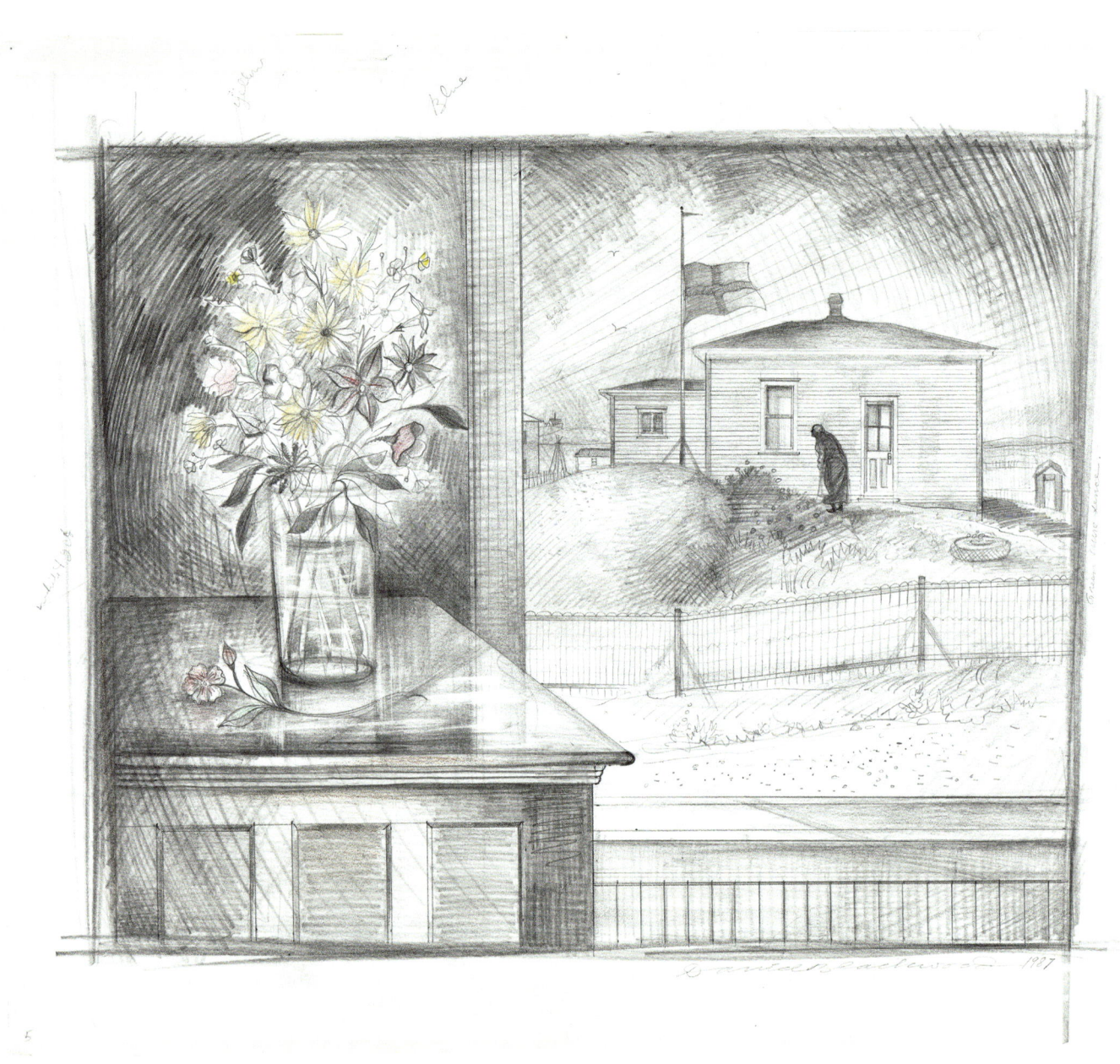

AUNT GERTI HANN HOME IN WESLEYVILLE 1987

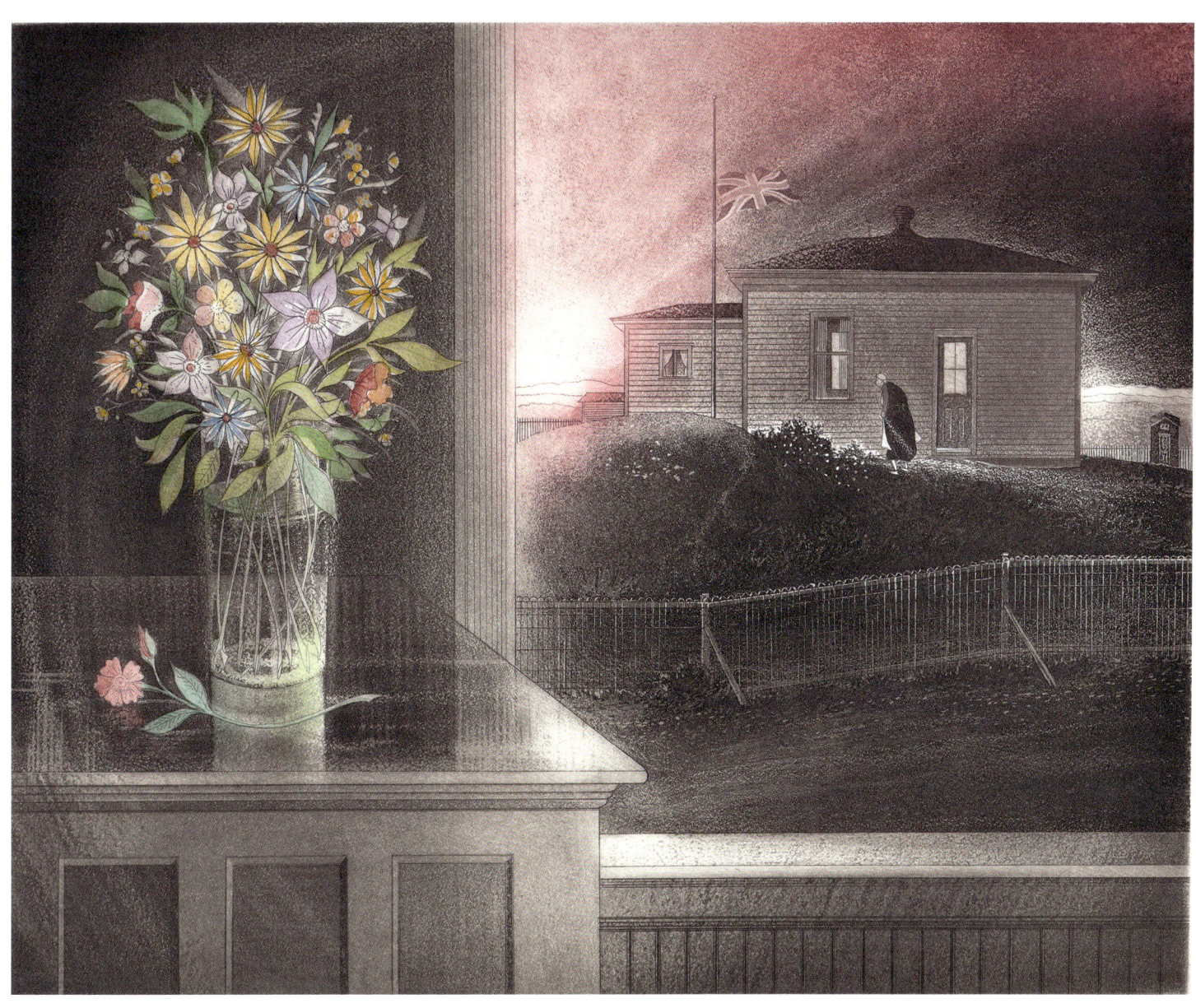

AUNT GERTI HANN HOME IN WESLEYVILLE 1987   **65**

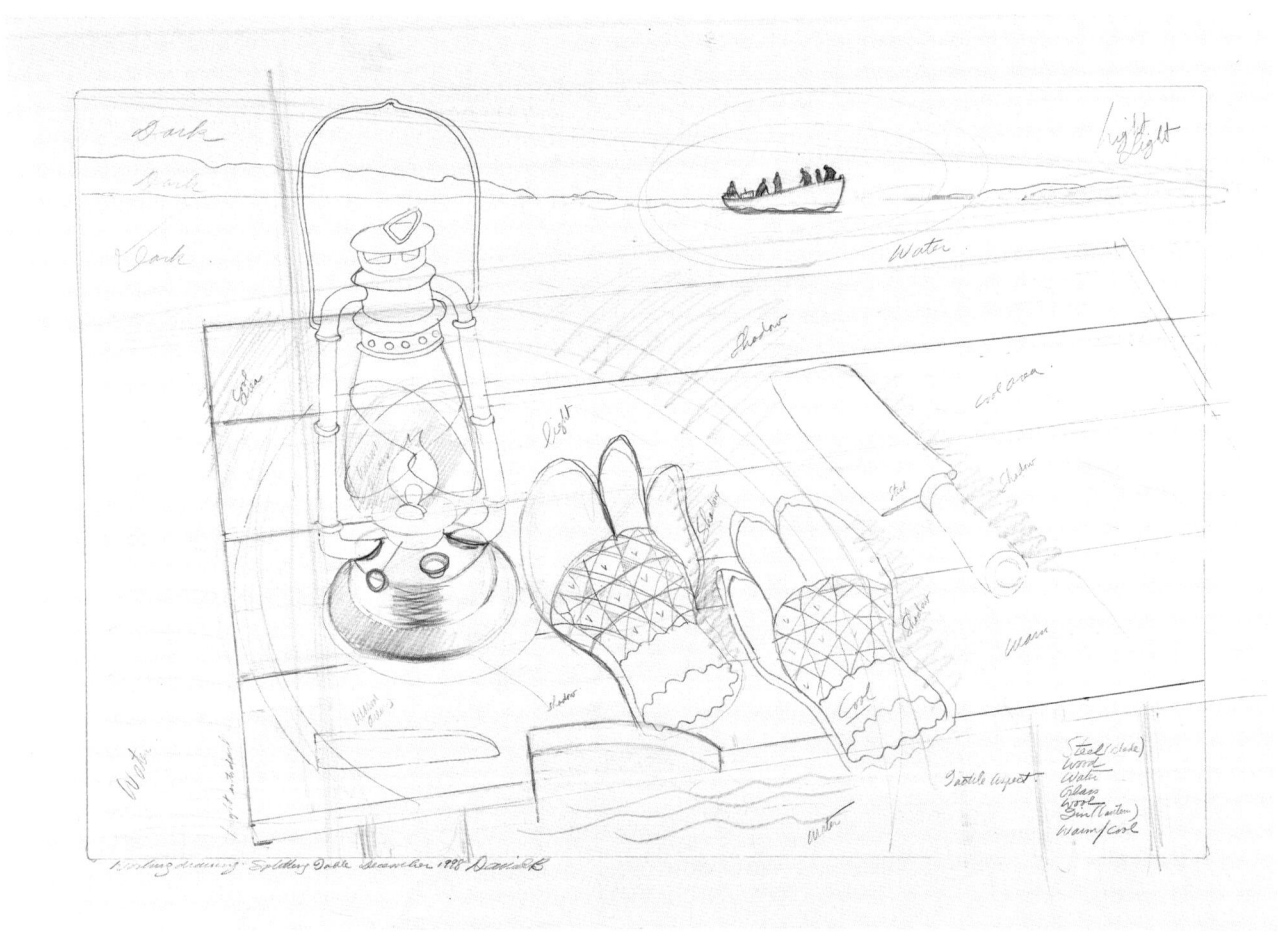

FOR EDGAR GLOVER: THE SPLITTING TABLE (WORKING DRAWING) 1998

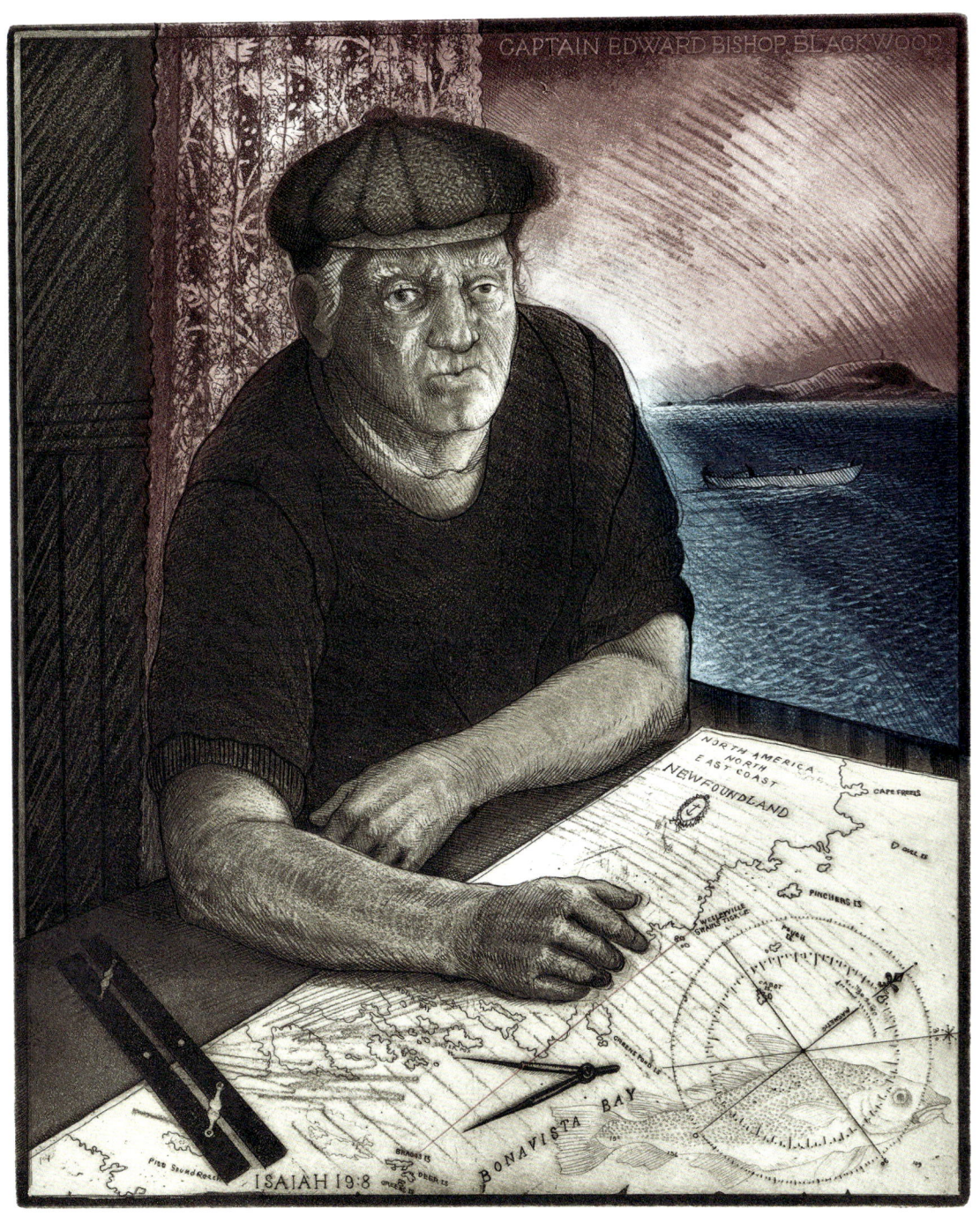

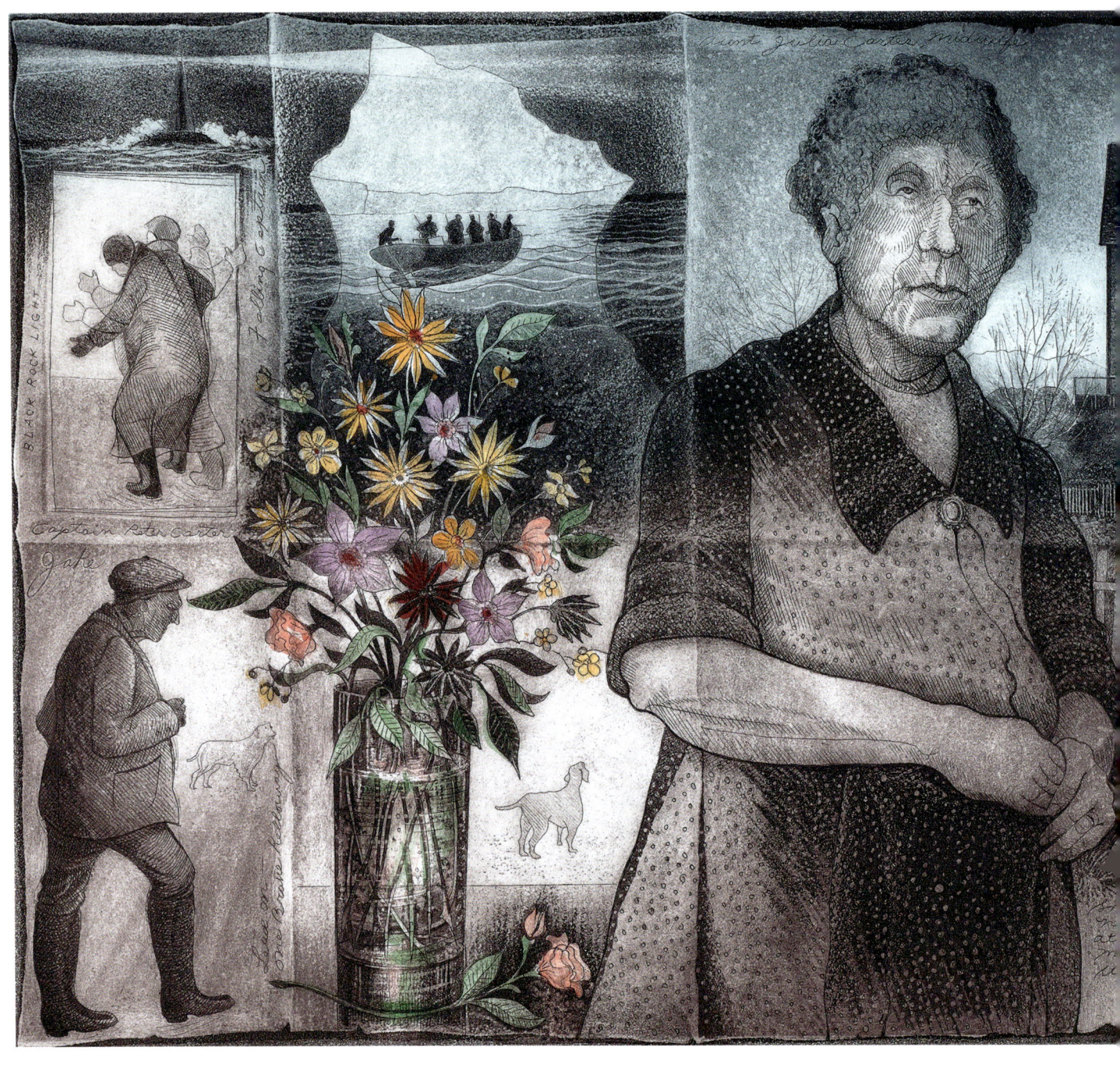

BONFIRE NIGHT ON GREENSPOND ISLAND   2002

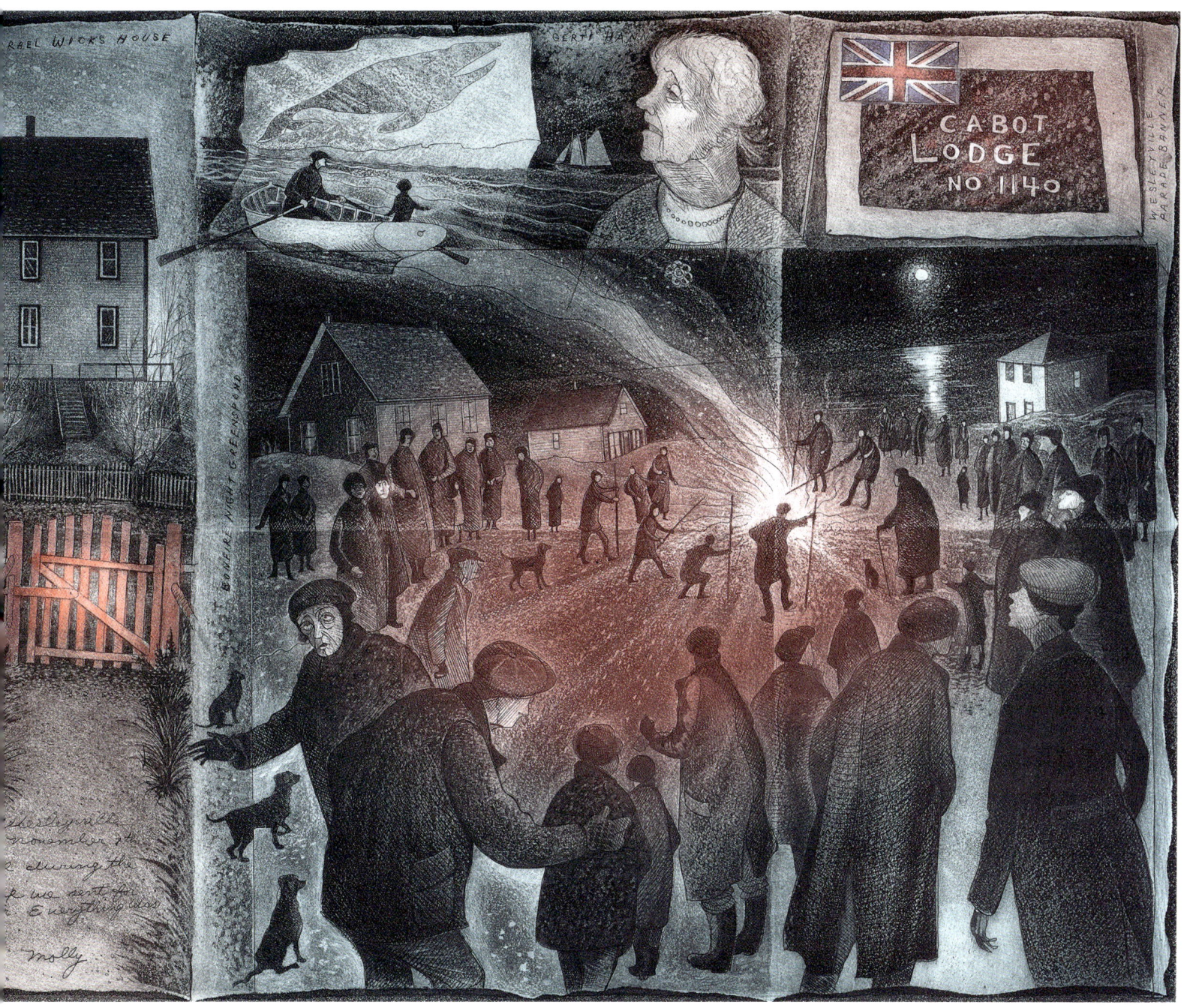

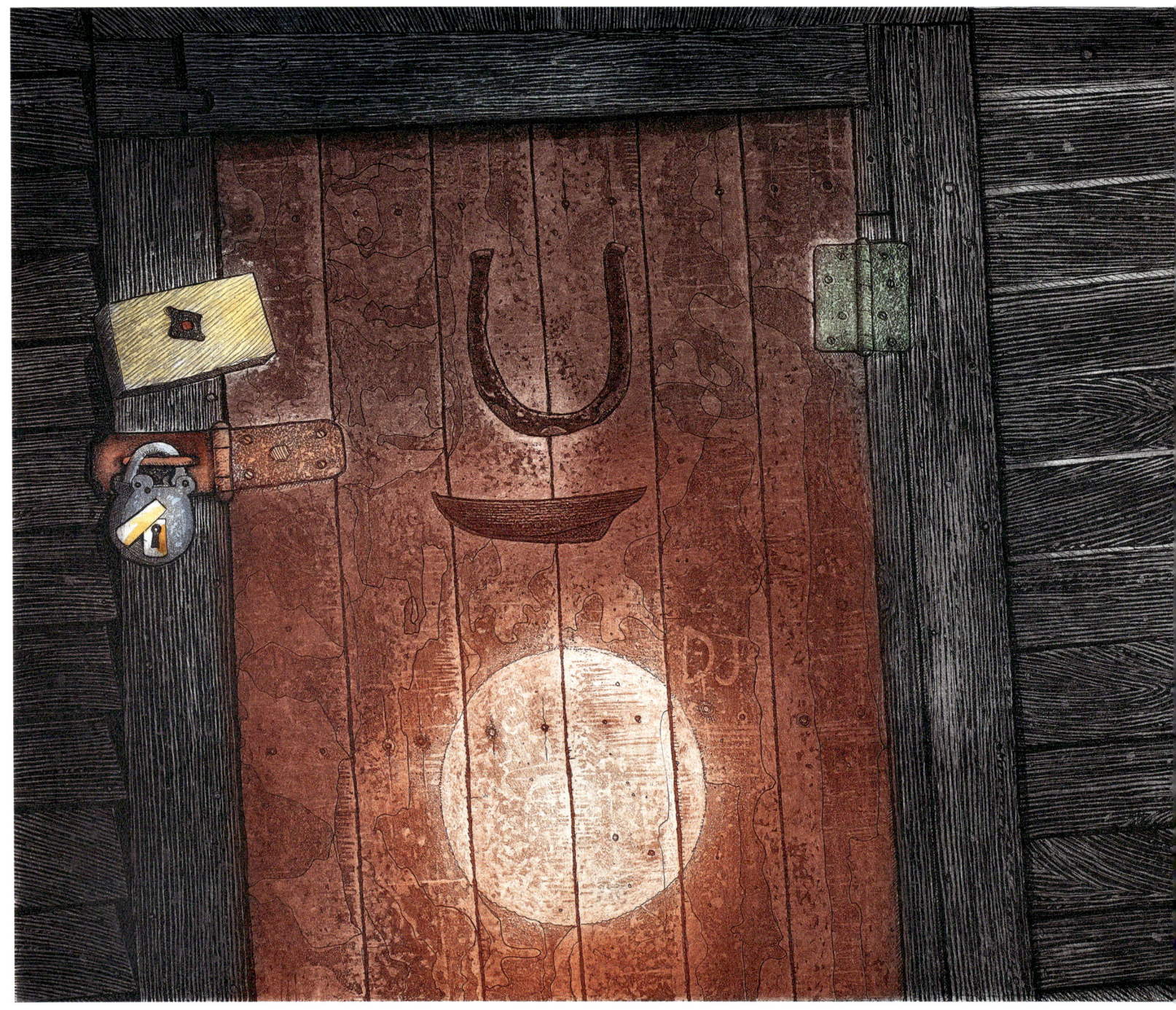

FOR DAVID JUDAH: HOME FROM BRAGG'S ISLAND   2005

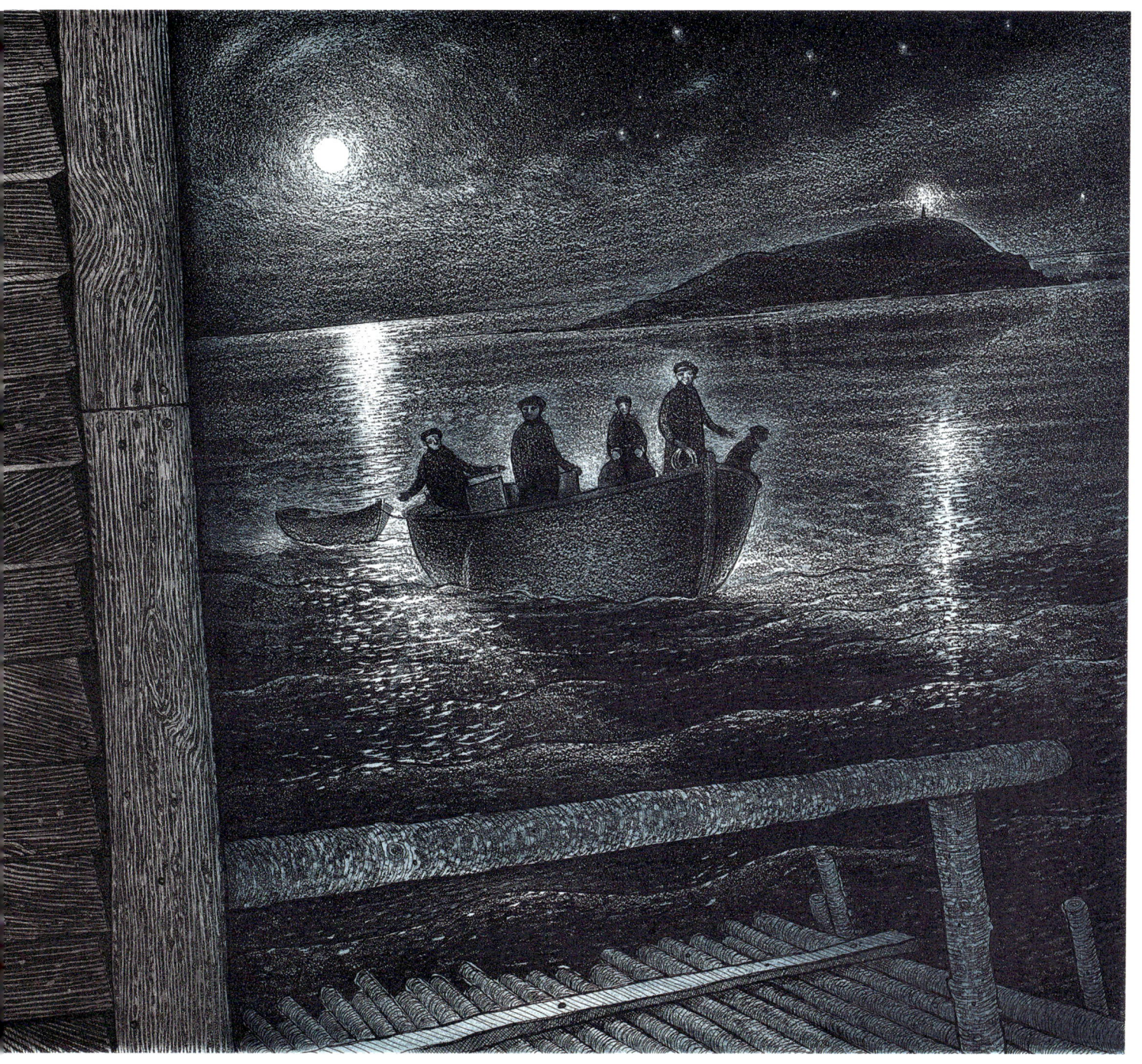

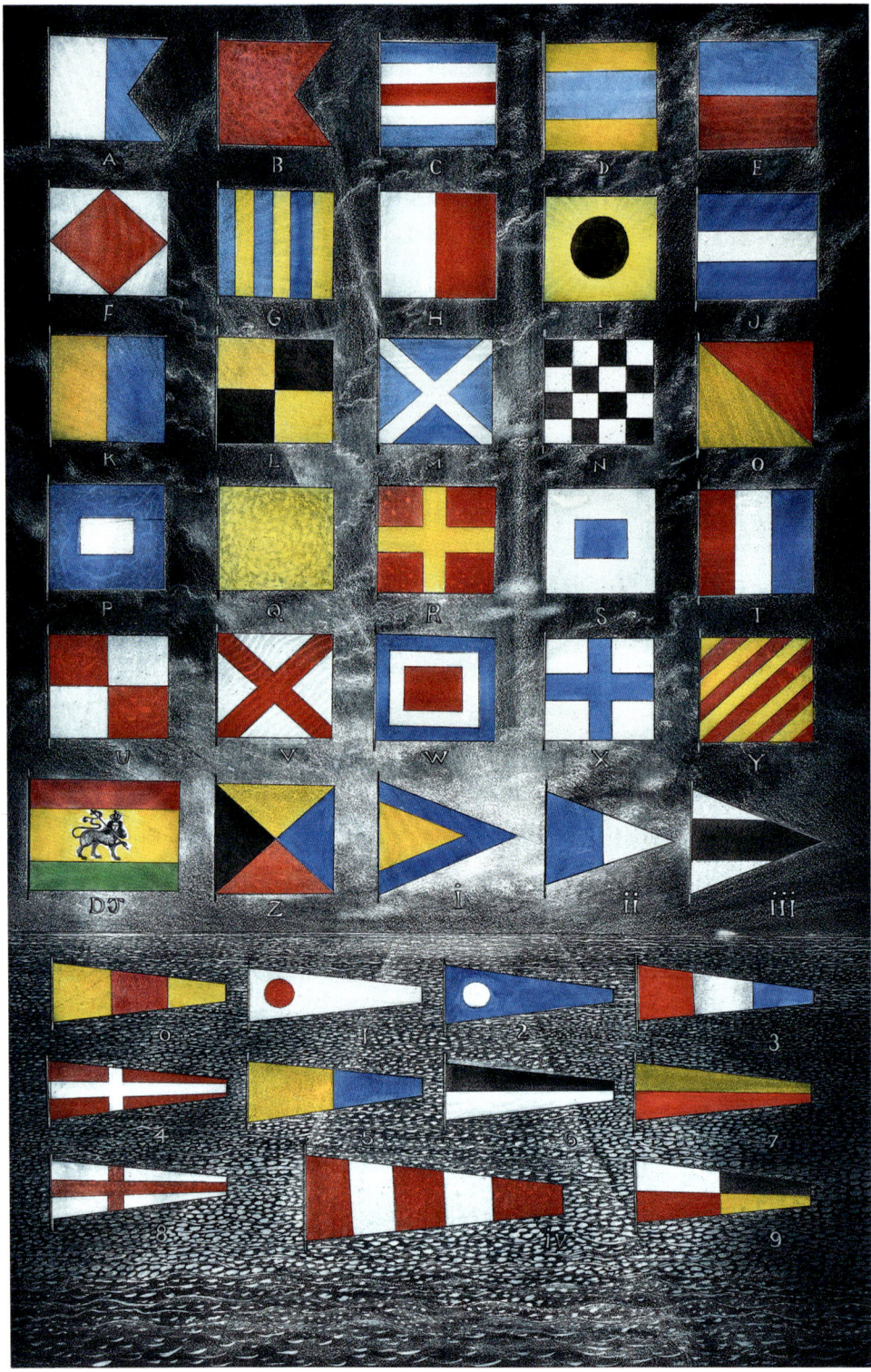

FLAGS FOR DAVID JUDAH: THE INTERNATIONAL CODE 2009

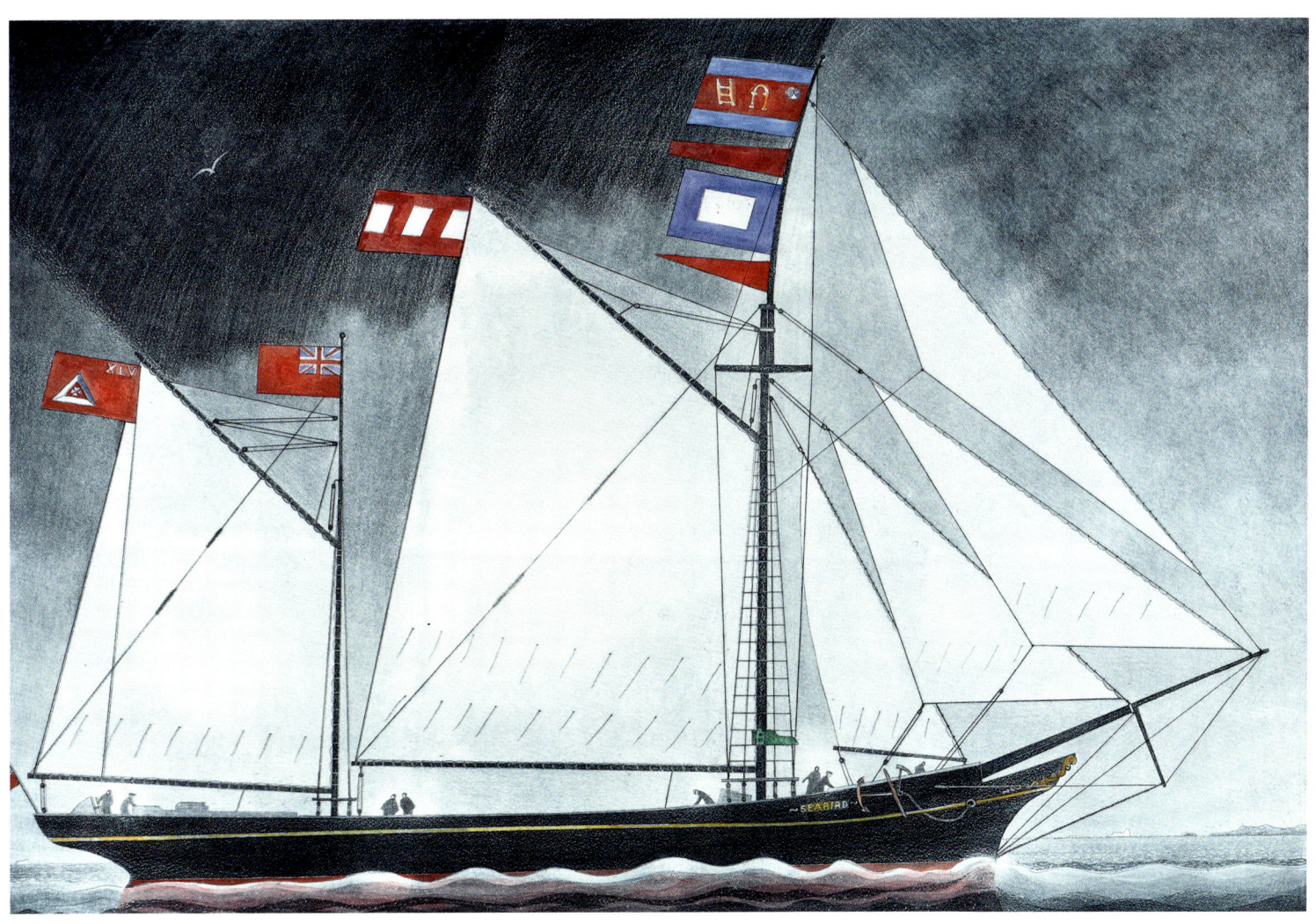

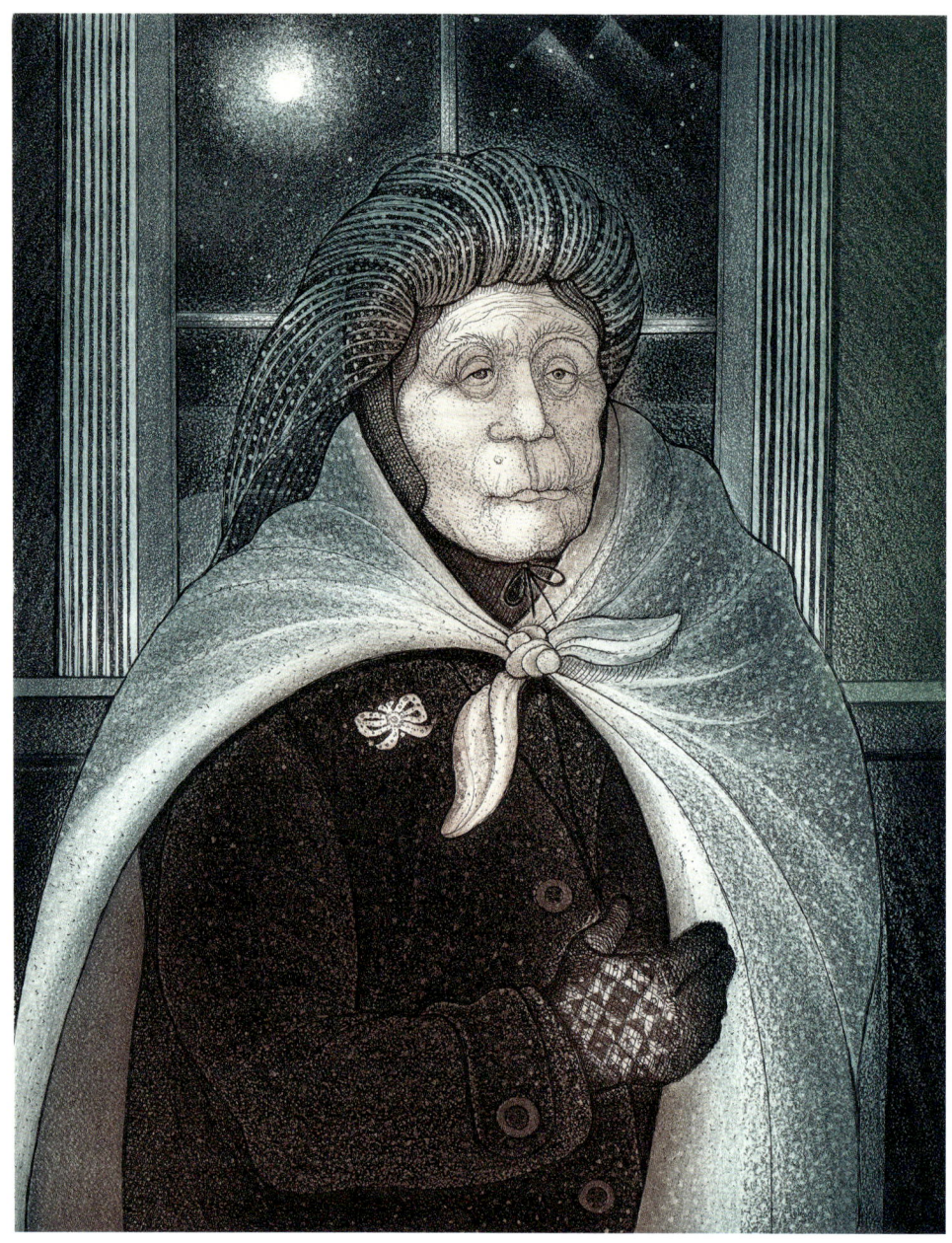

THE GREAT MUMMER EUNICE BURDERN IN WESLEY HALL 2006

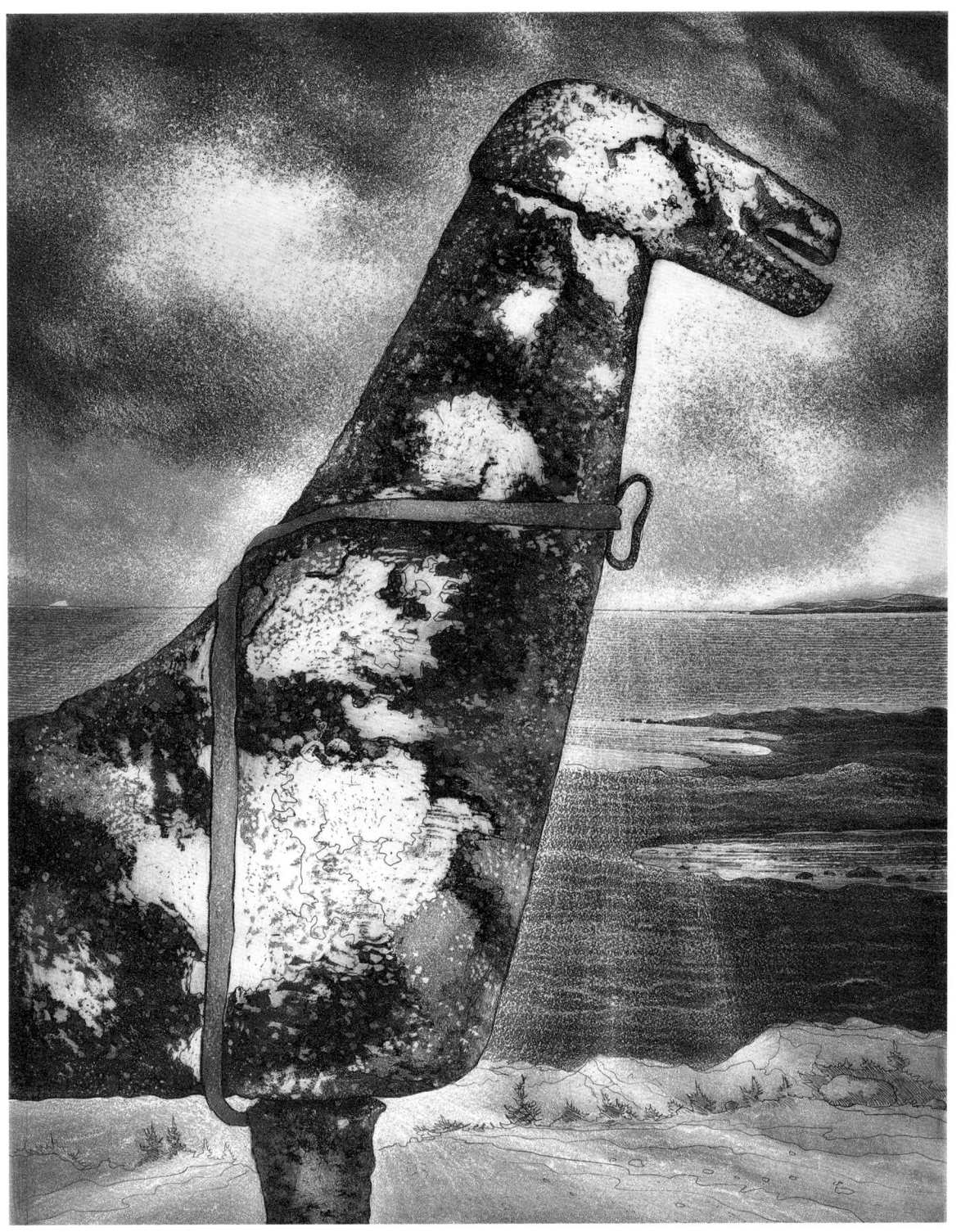

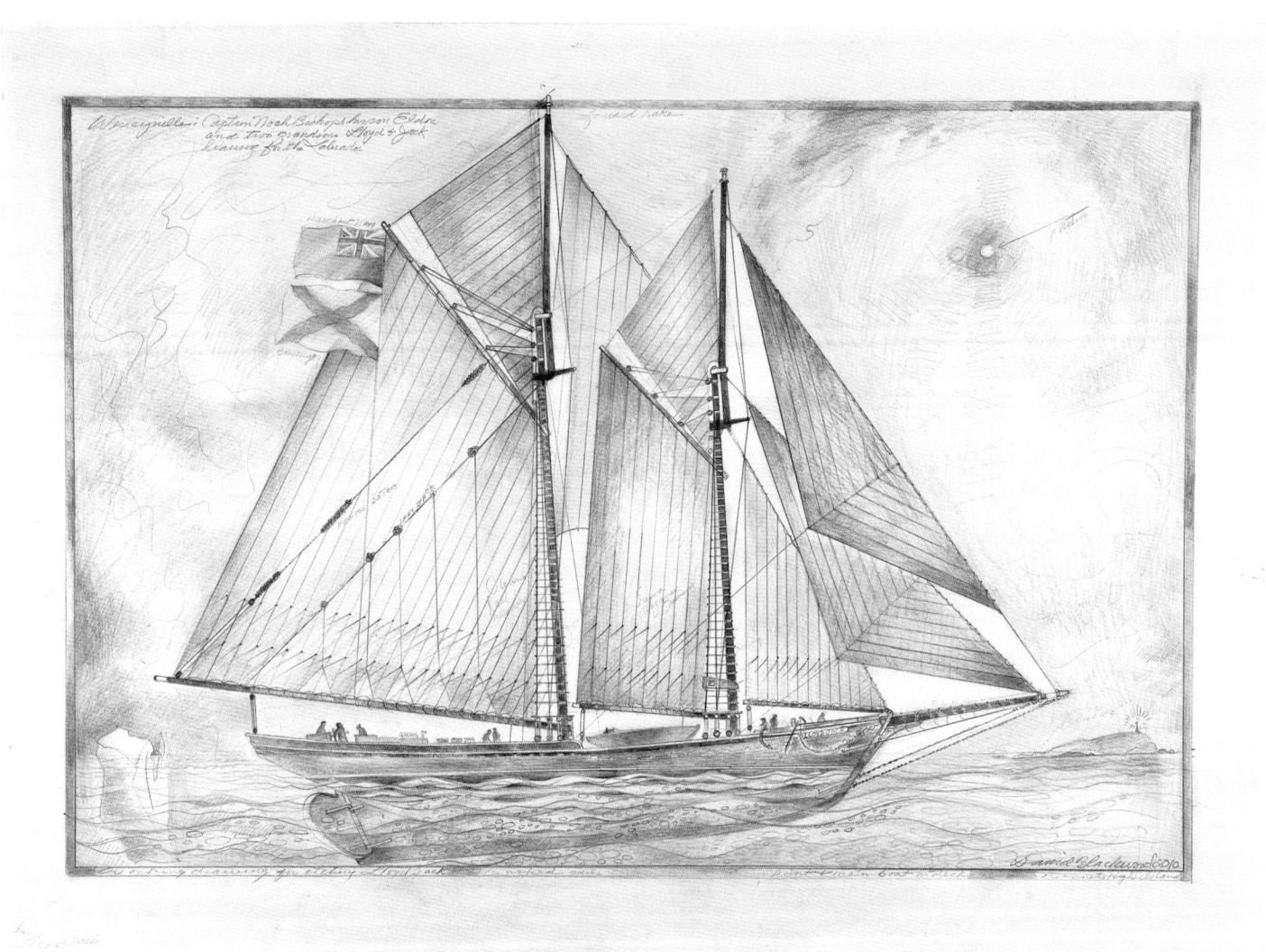

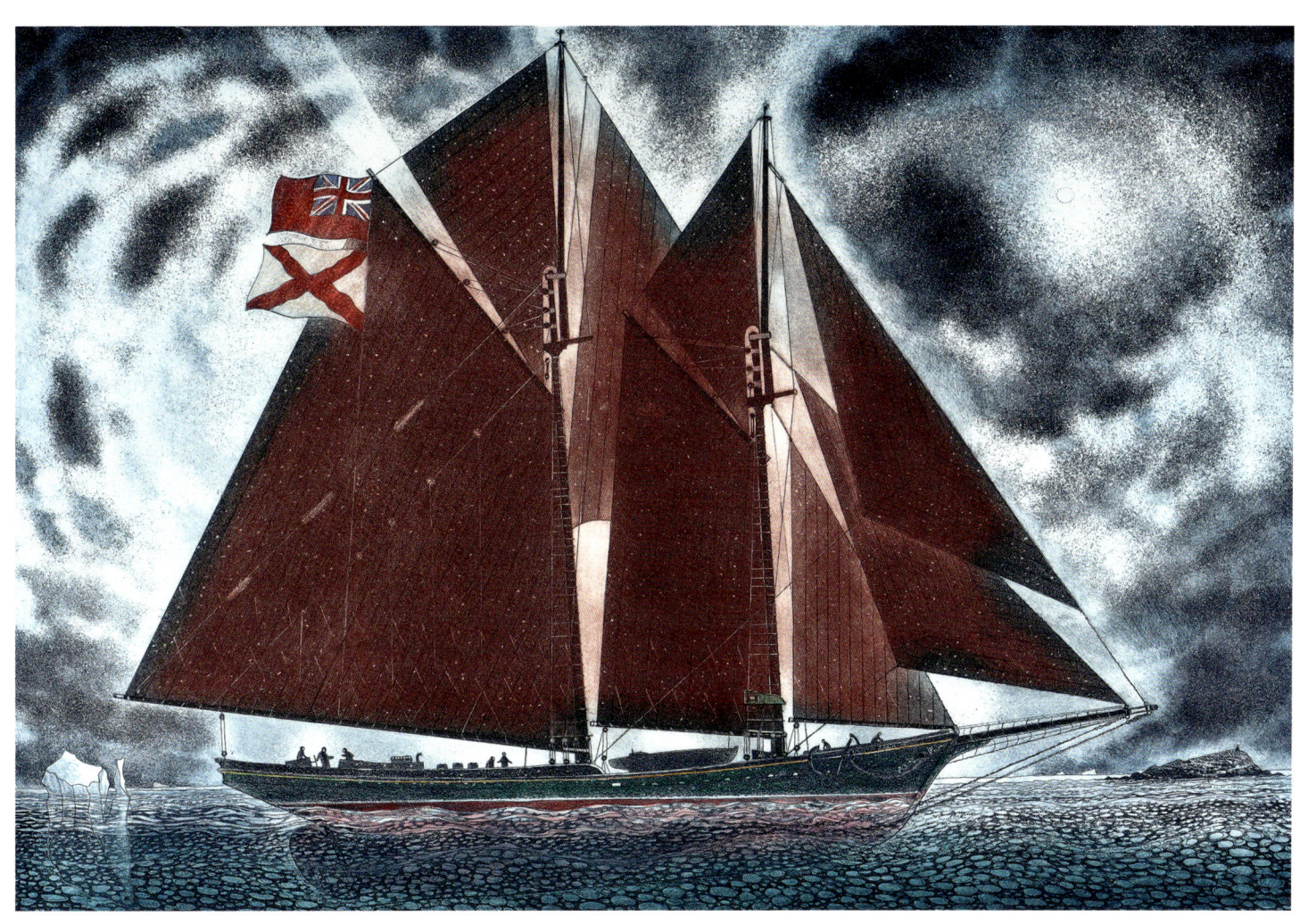

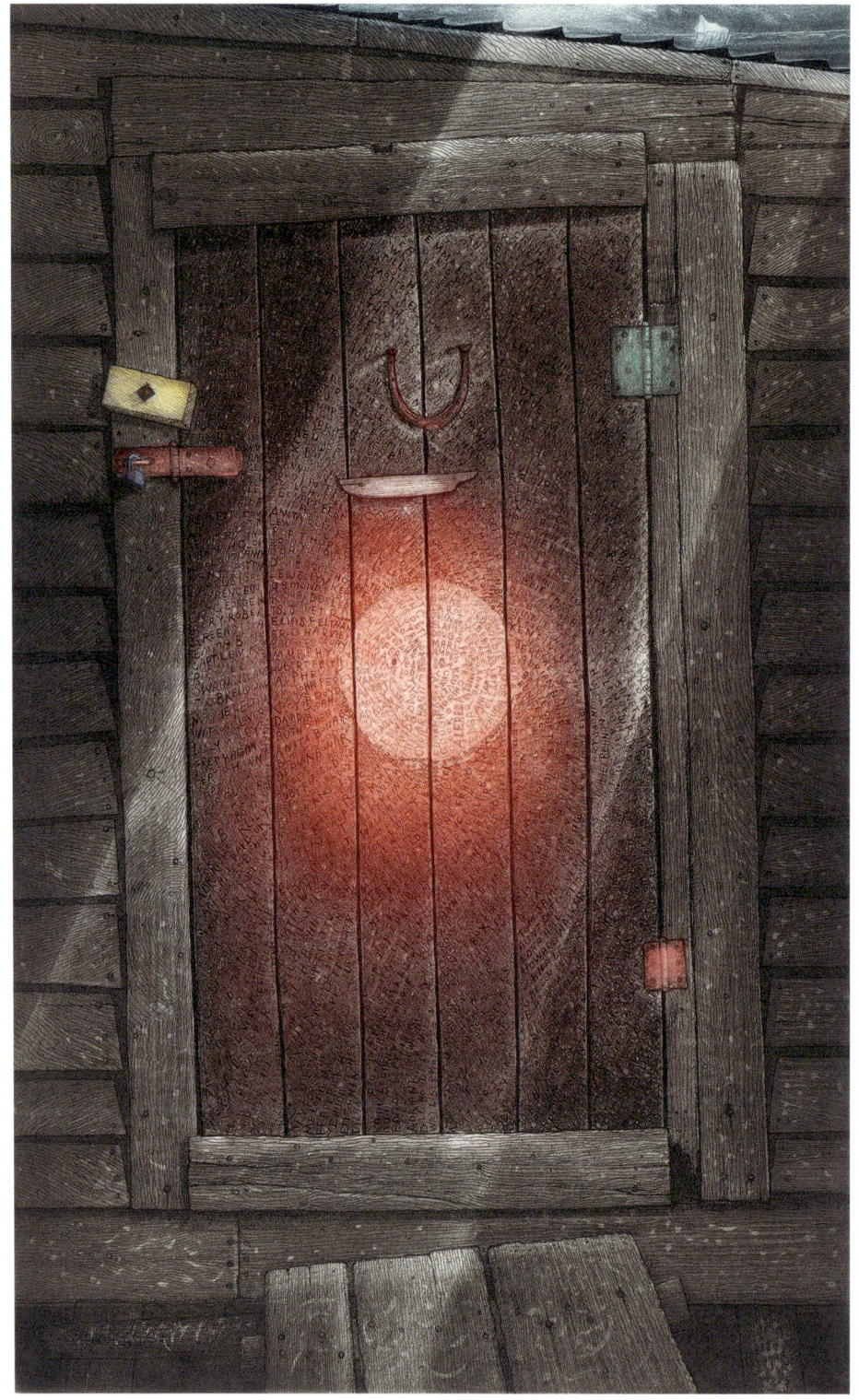

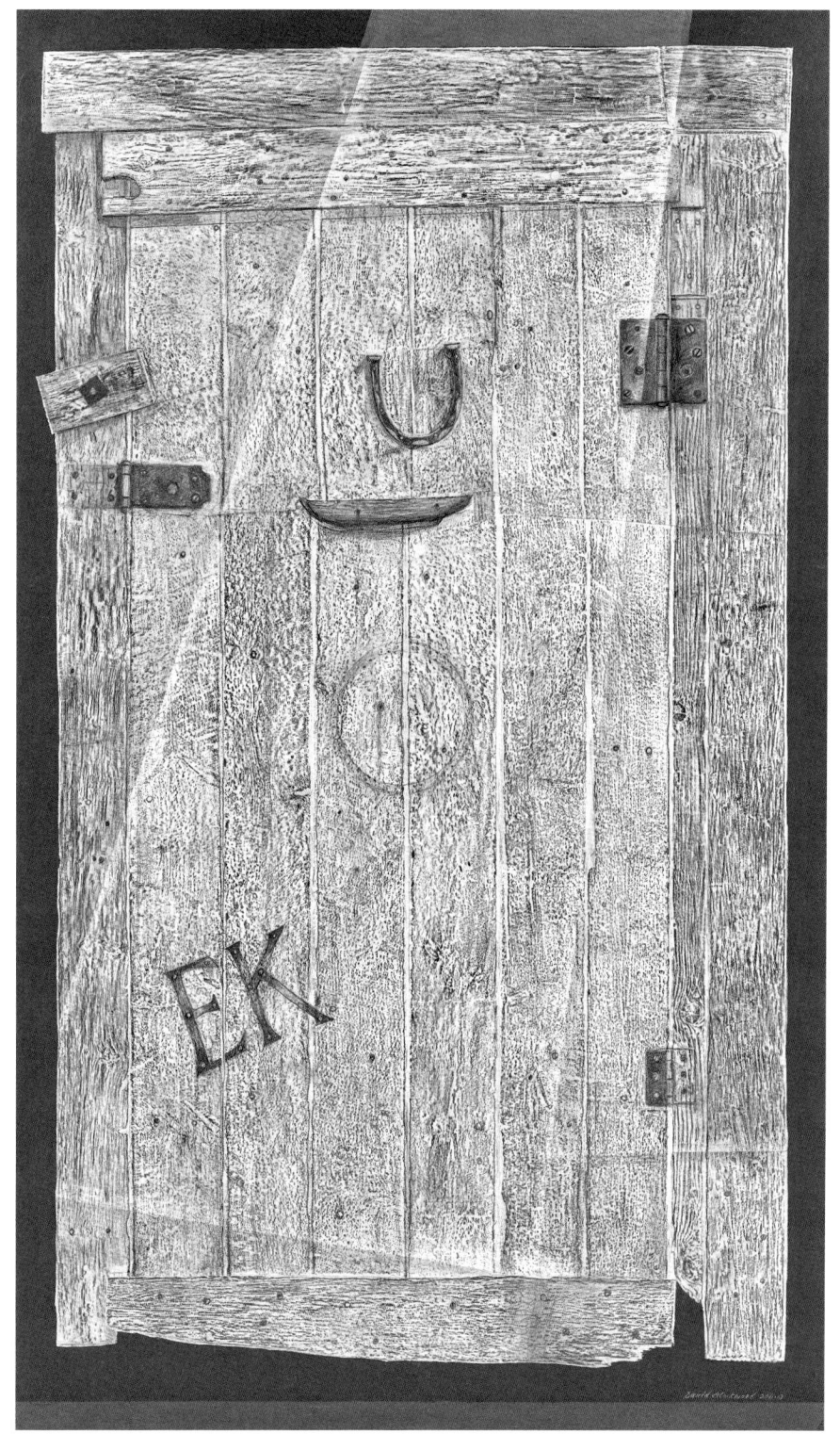

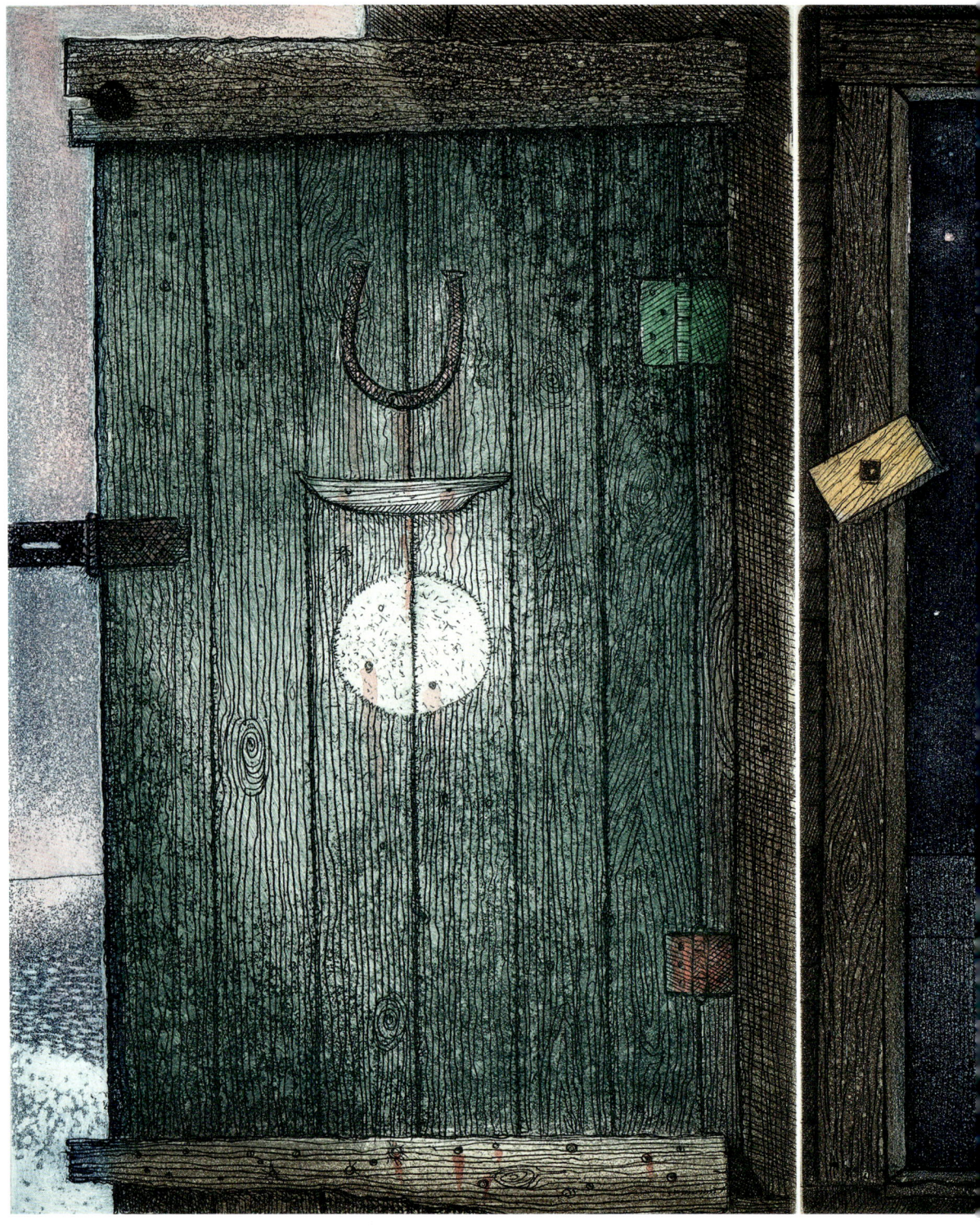

EPHRAIM KELLOWAY'S DOOR 2012

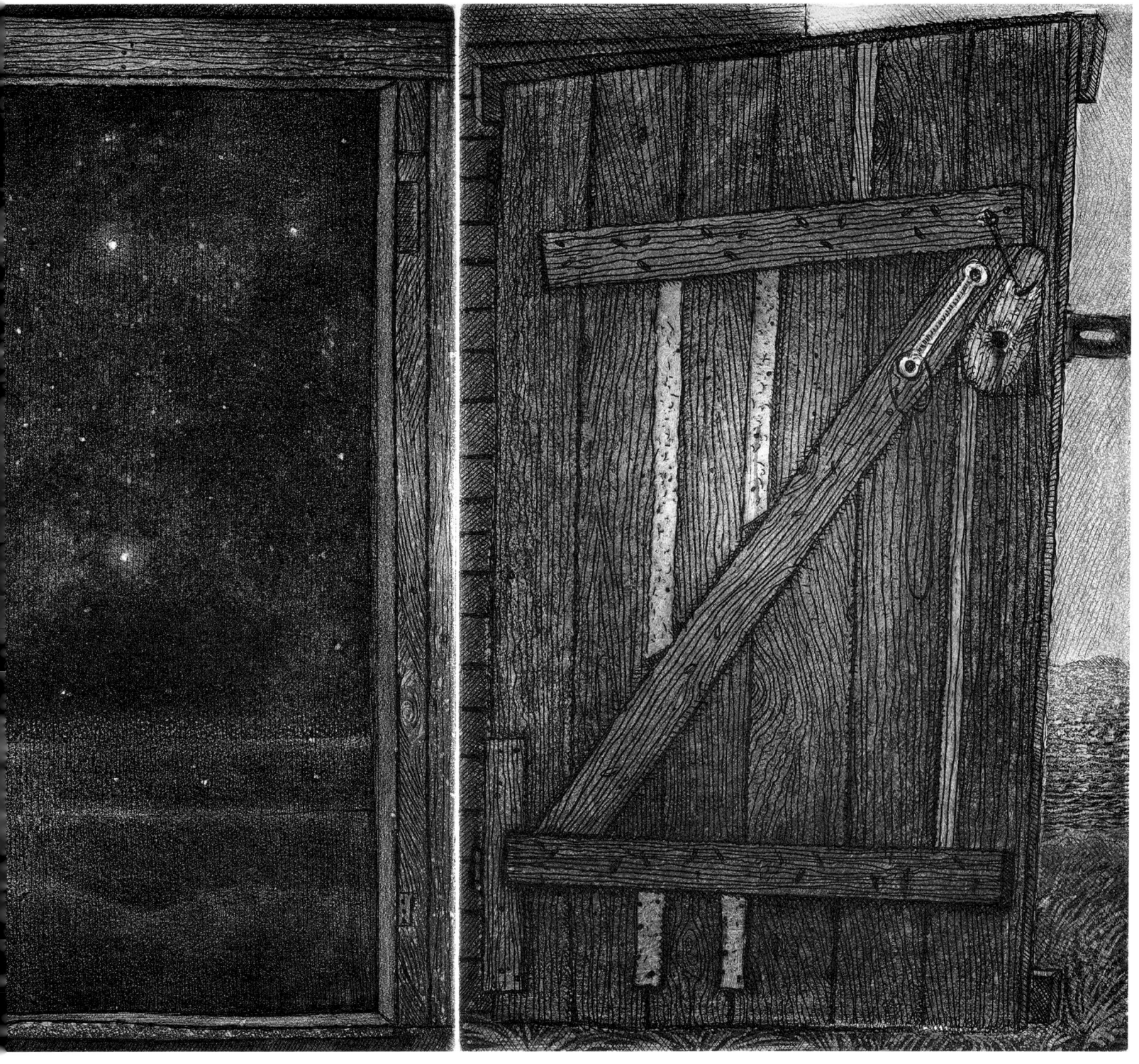

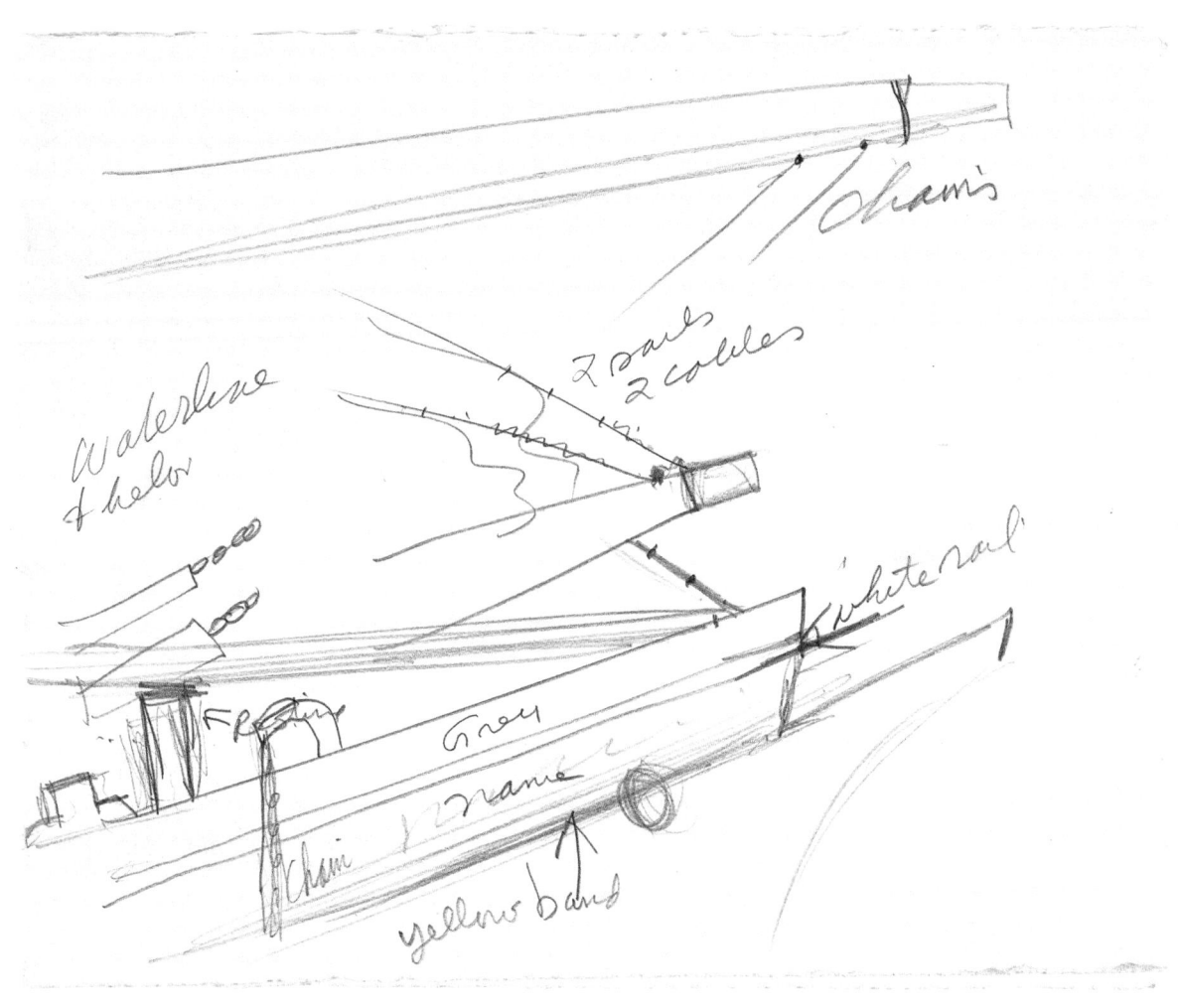

PASSING UNDER THE ROSTELLAN (RIGGING DETAIL) 2013

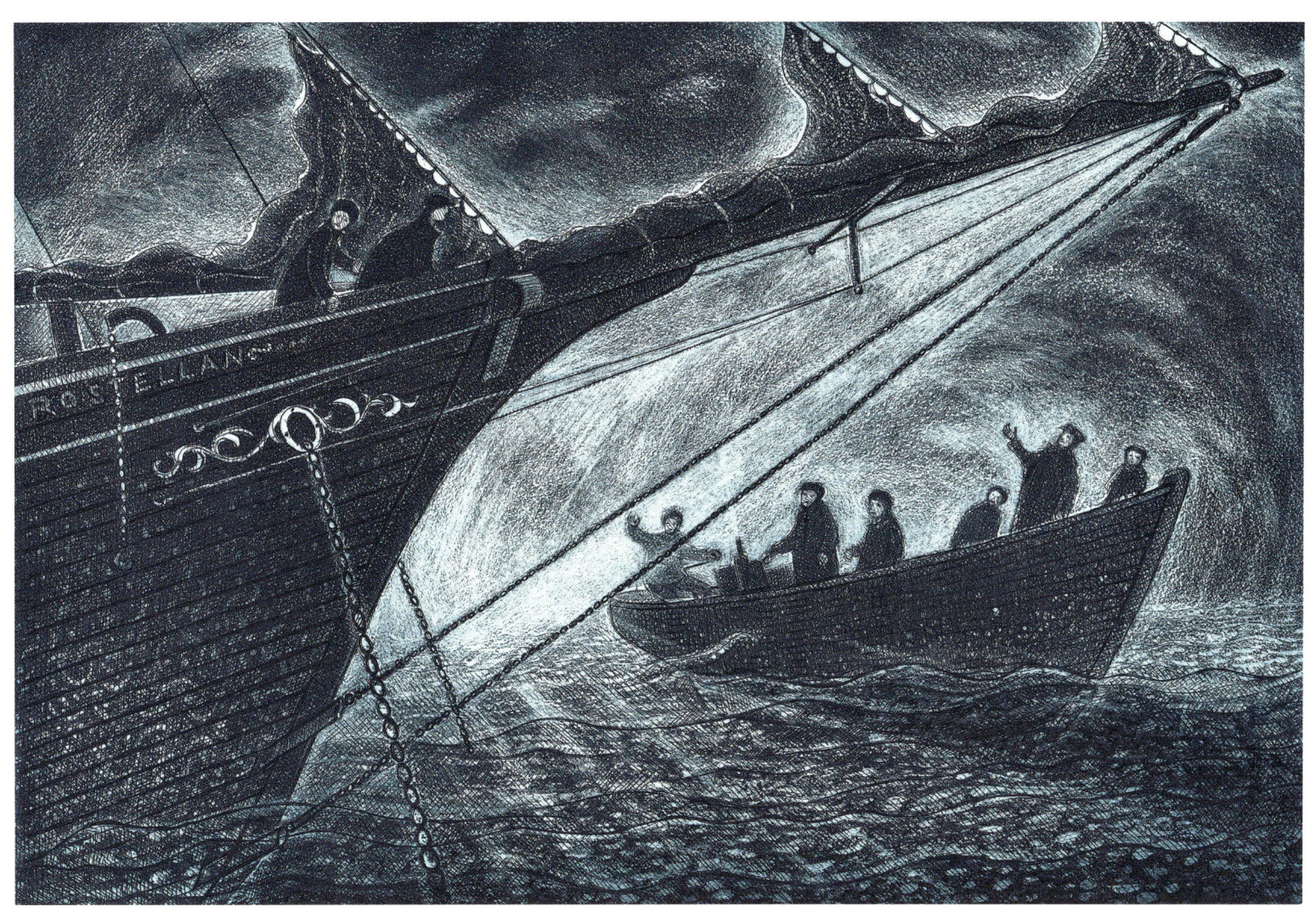

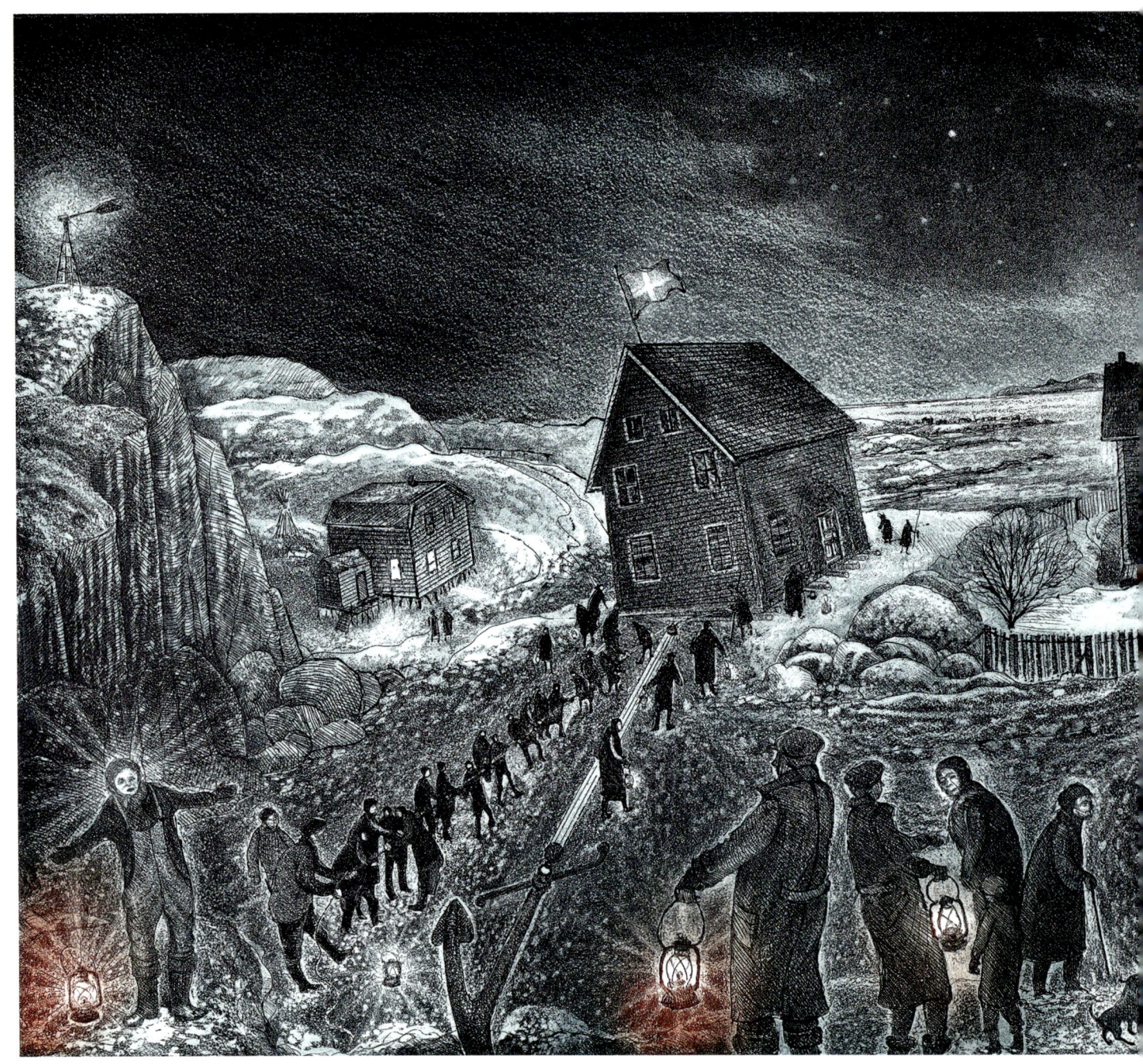

HAULING ORAM'S HOUSE 2018

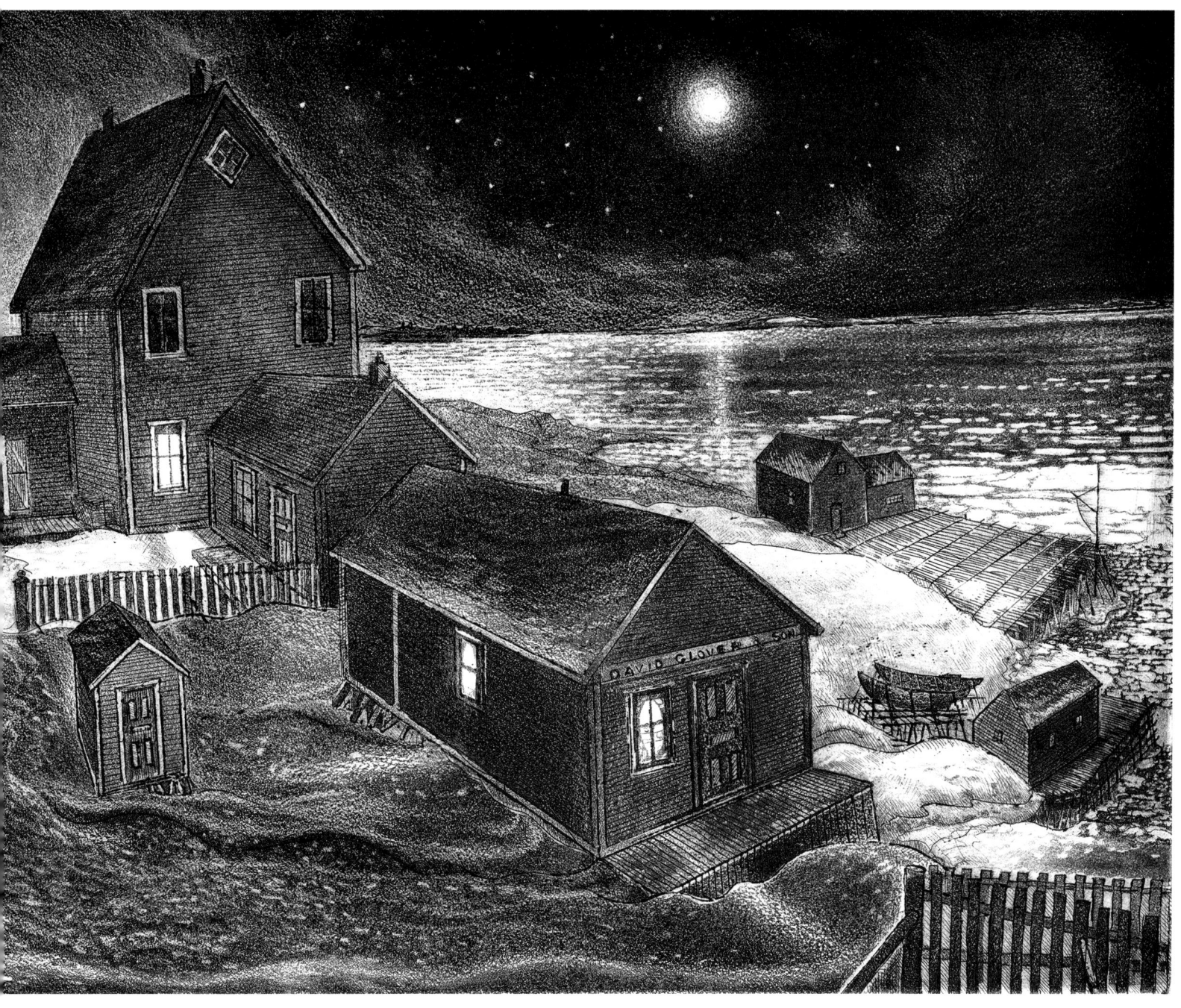

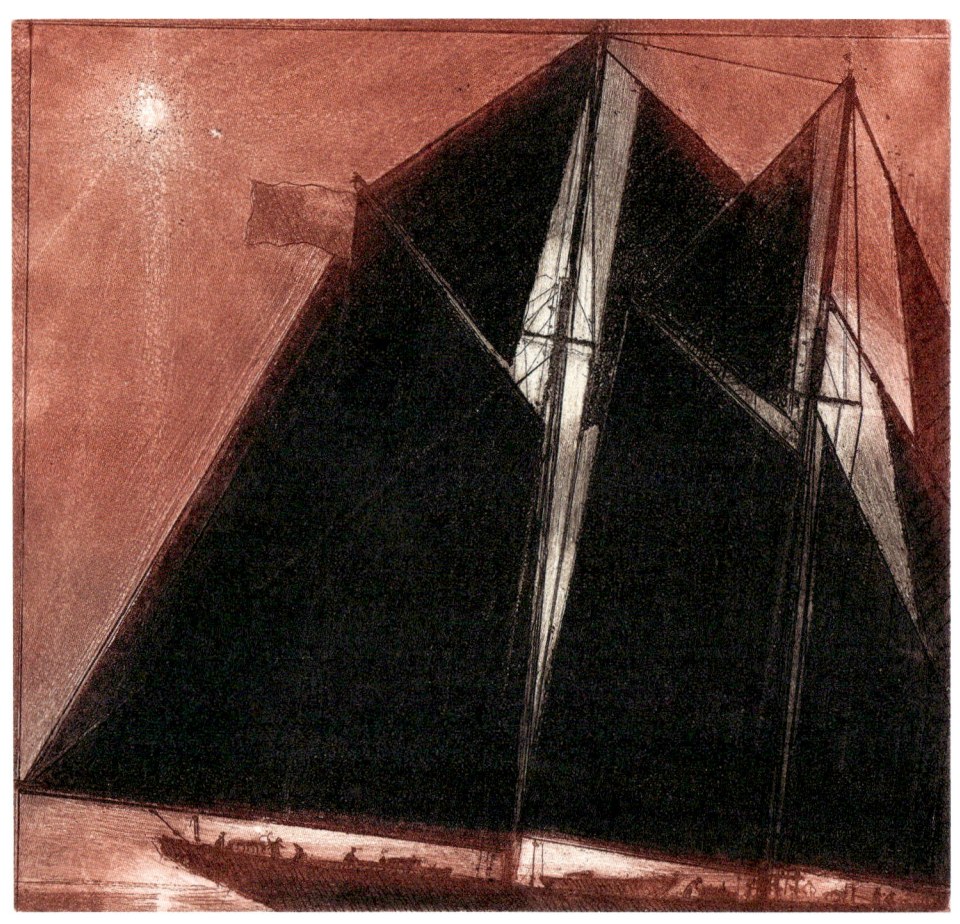

THE NICKERSON PASSING   2015

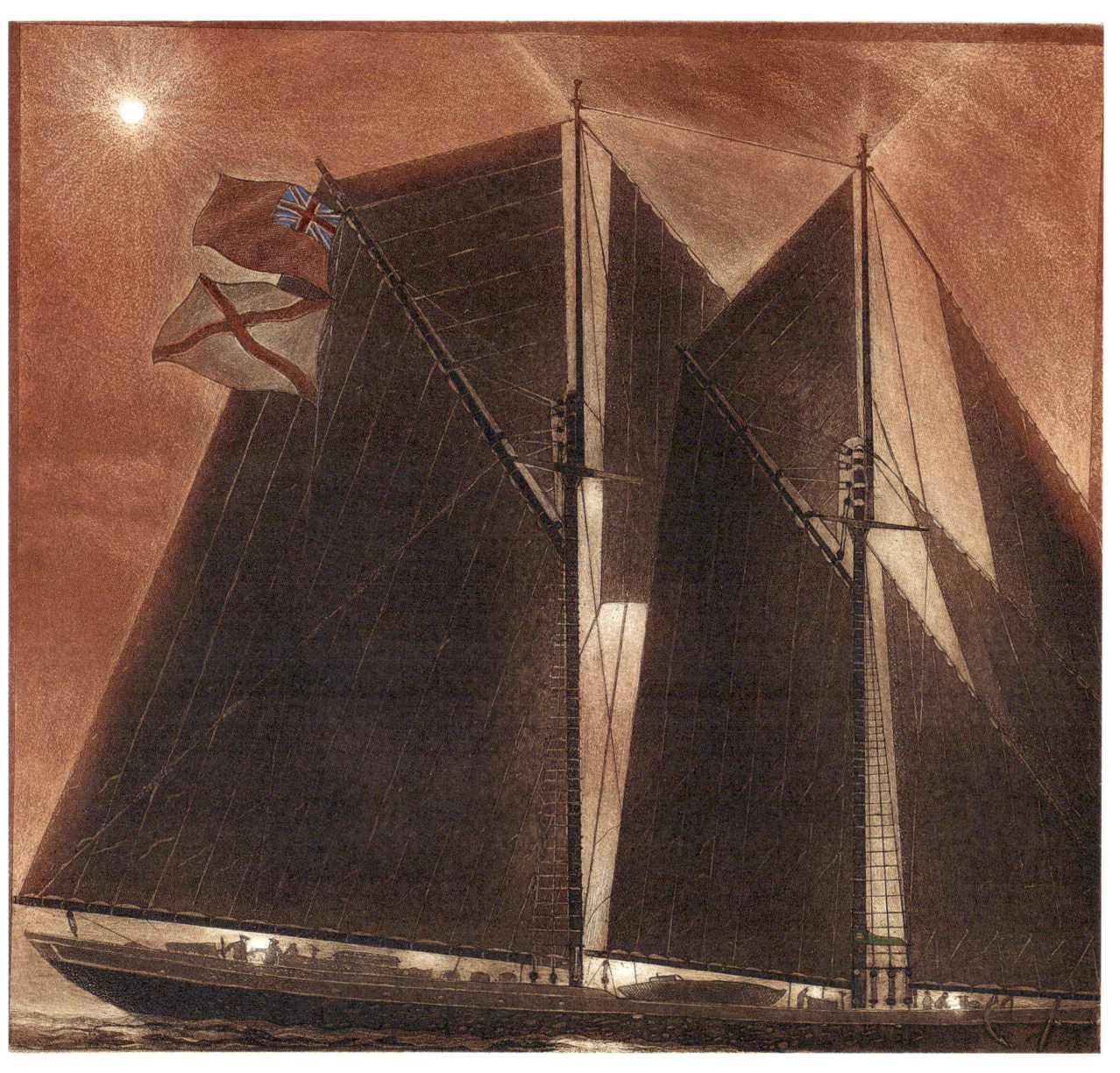

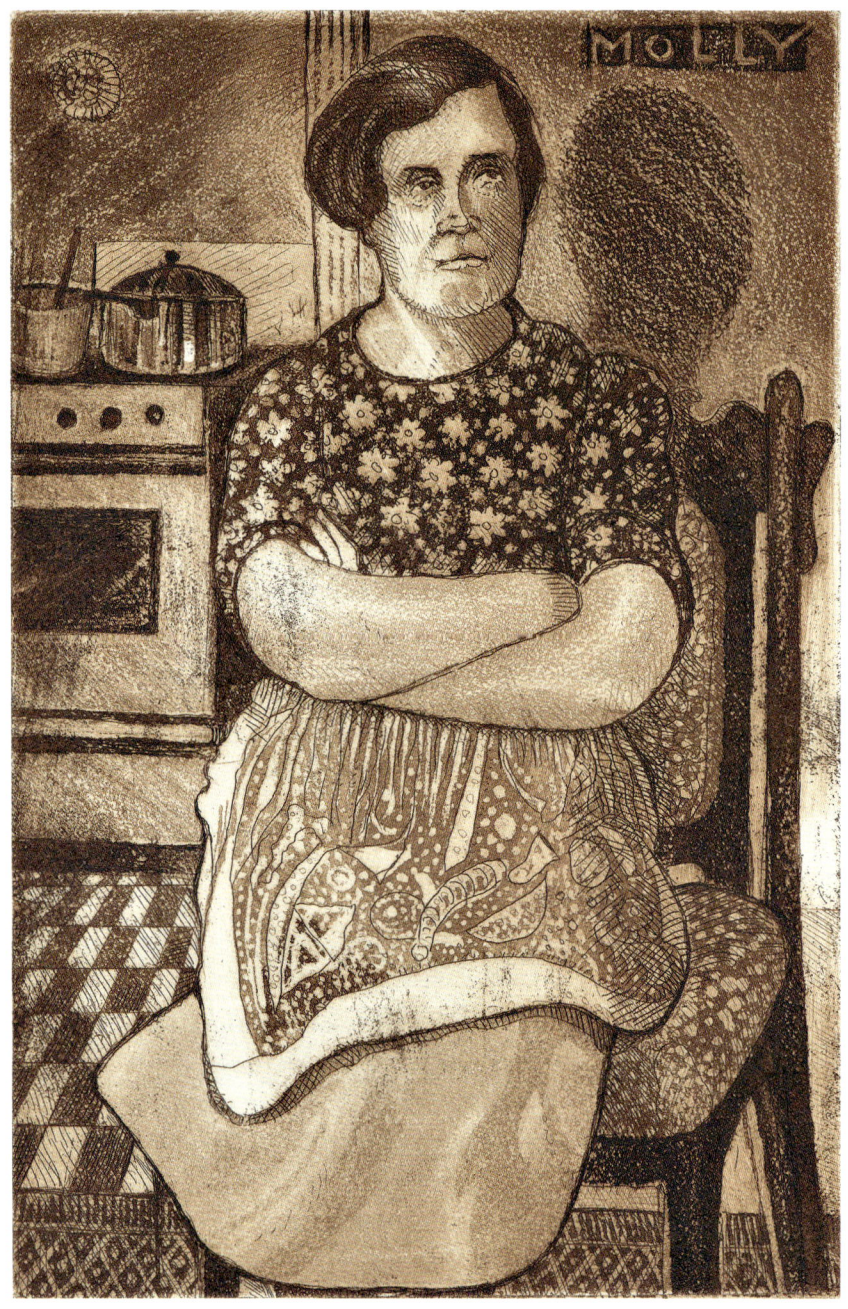

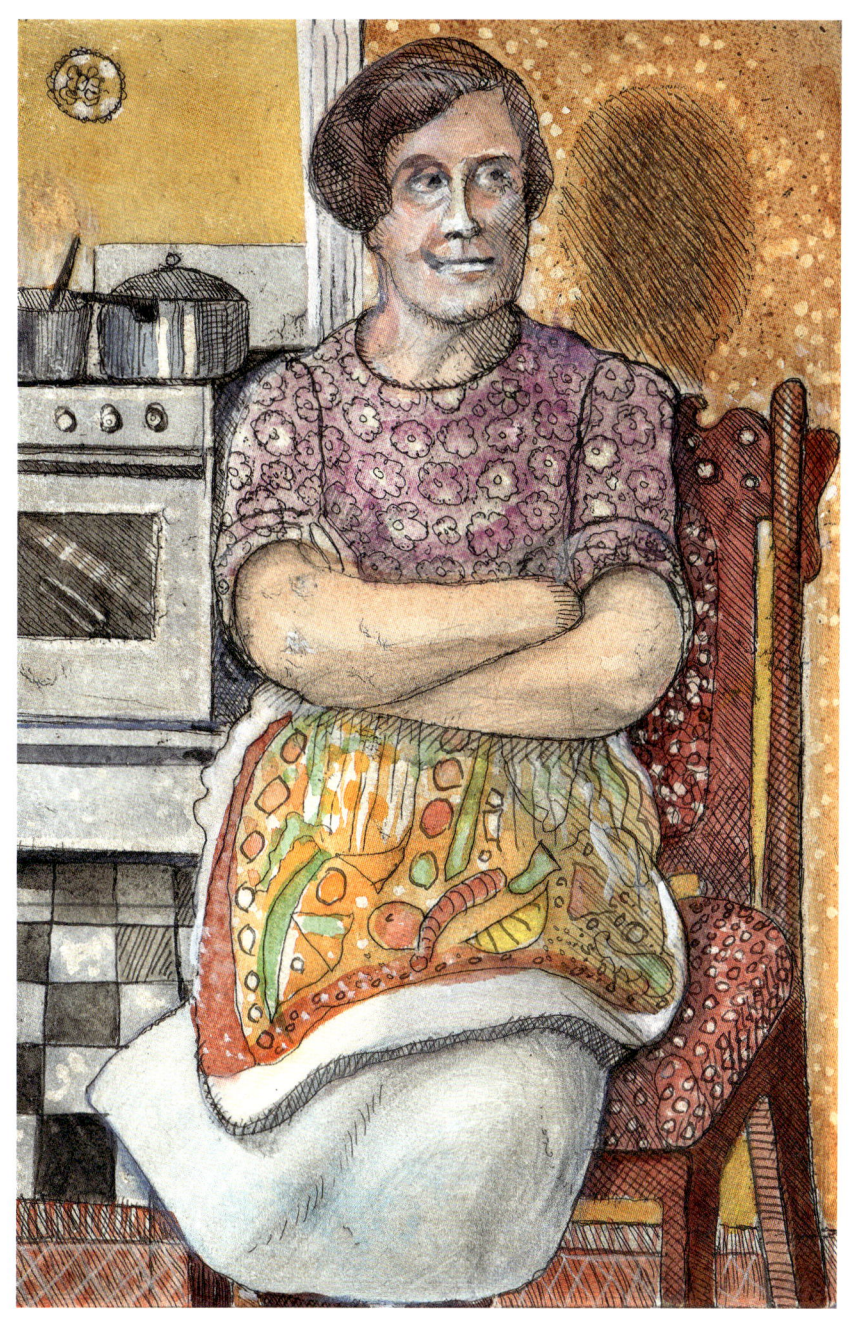

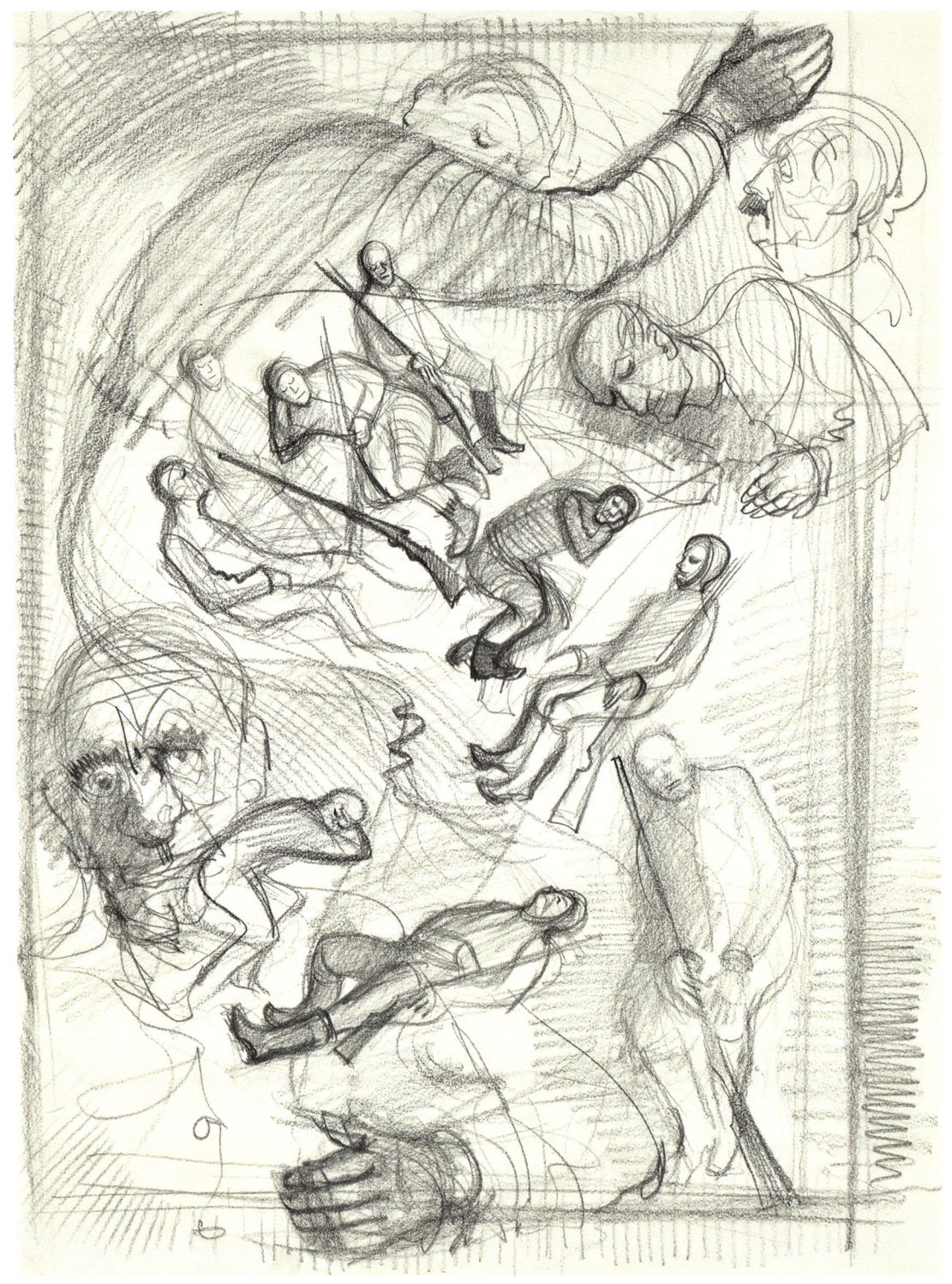

SEATED FIGURE STUDIES   date unknown

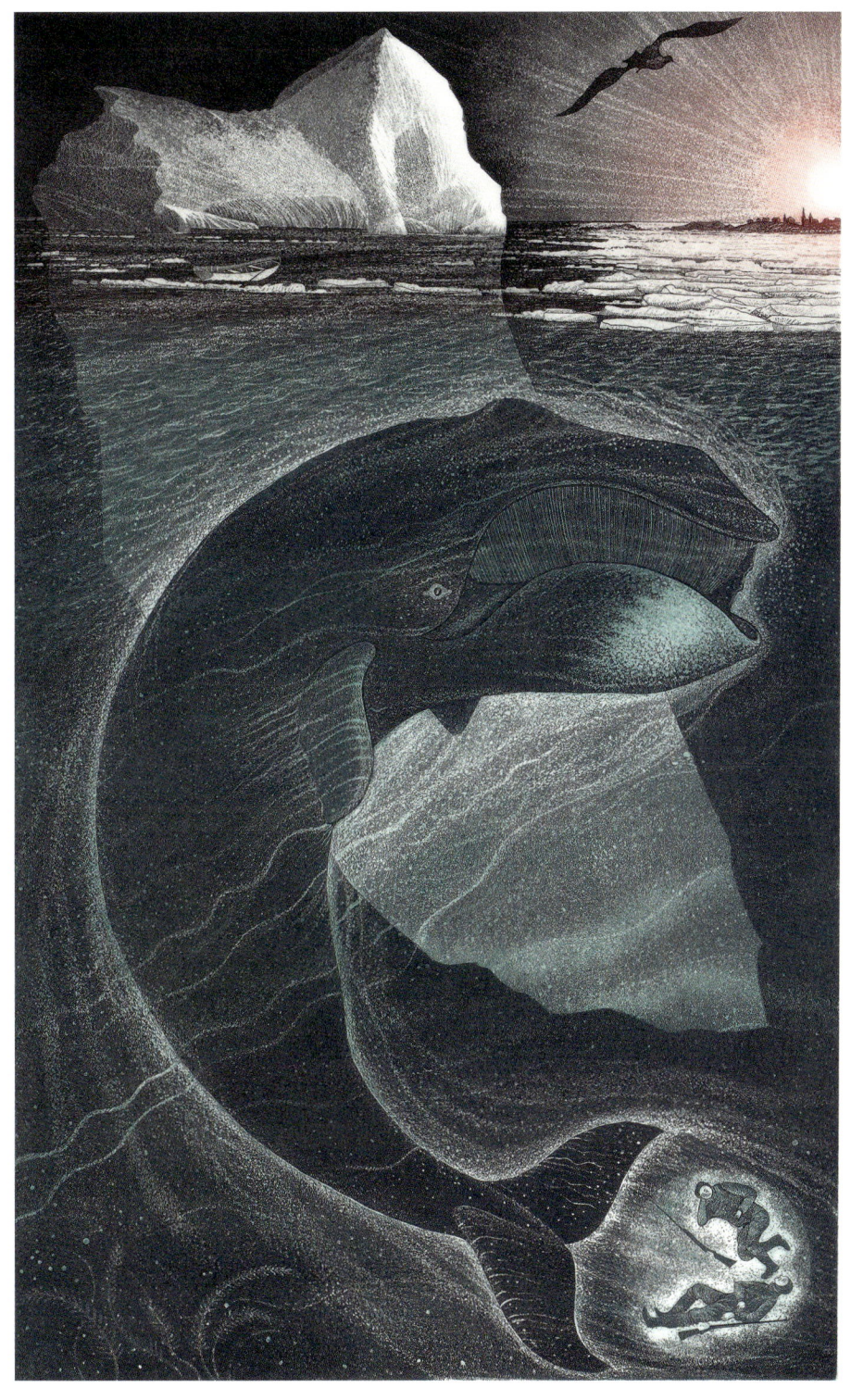

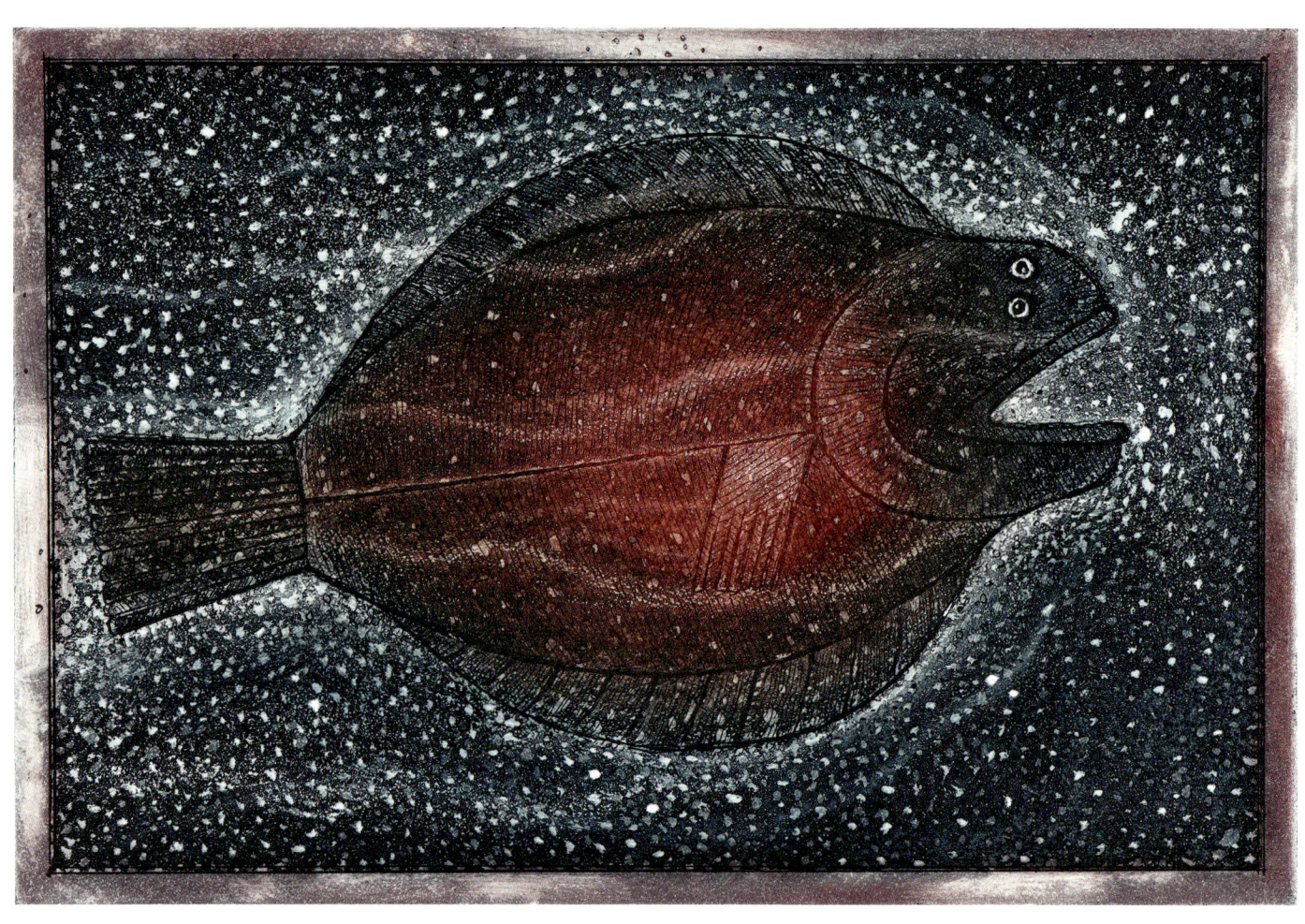

FLATTY 2015

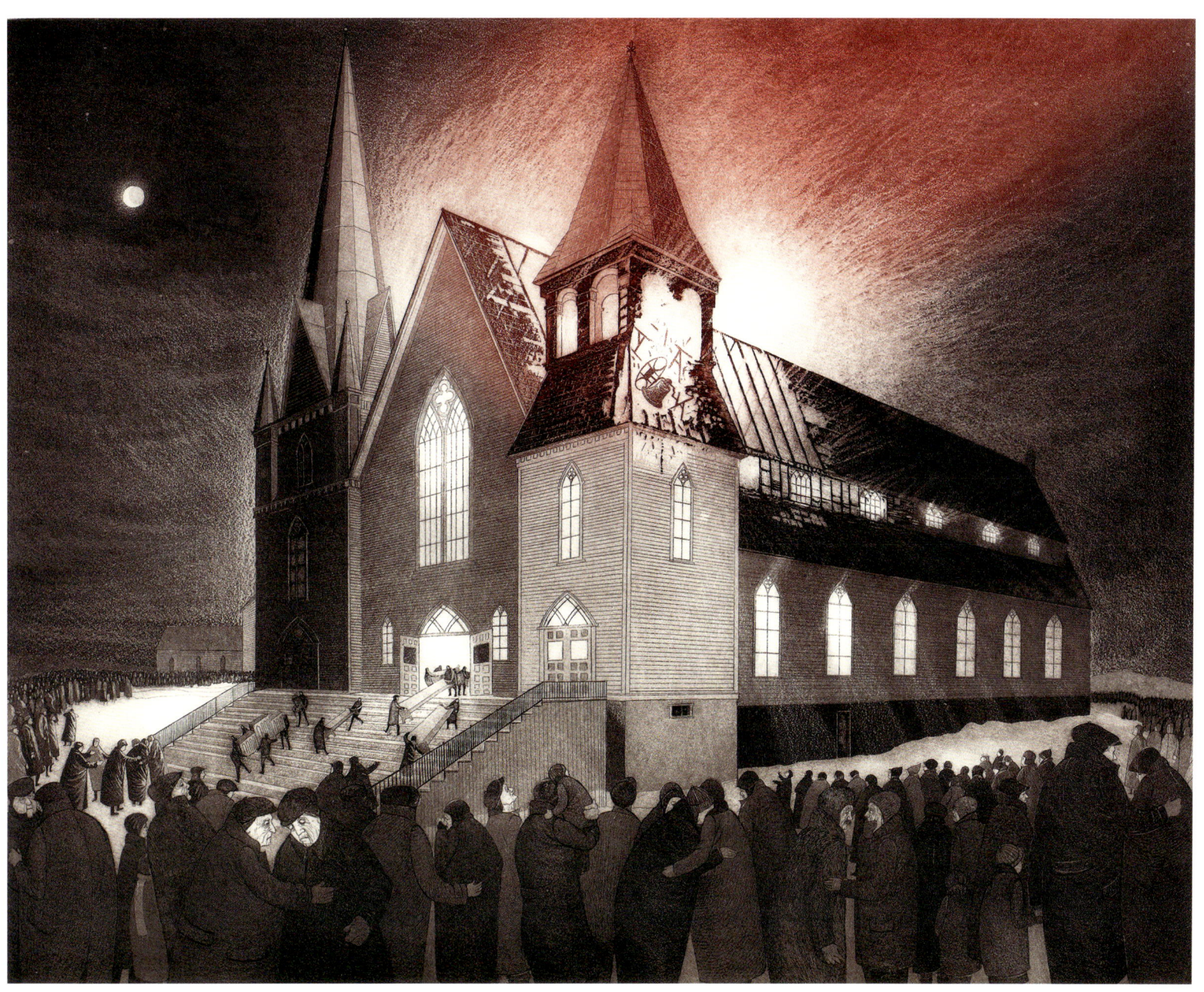

WESLEYVILLE: BURNING OF THE METHODIST CHURCH 1976   **93**

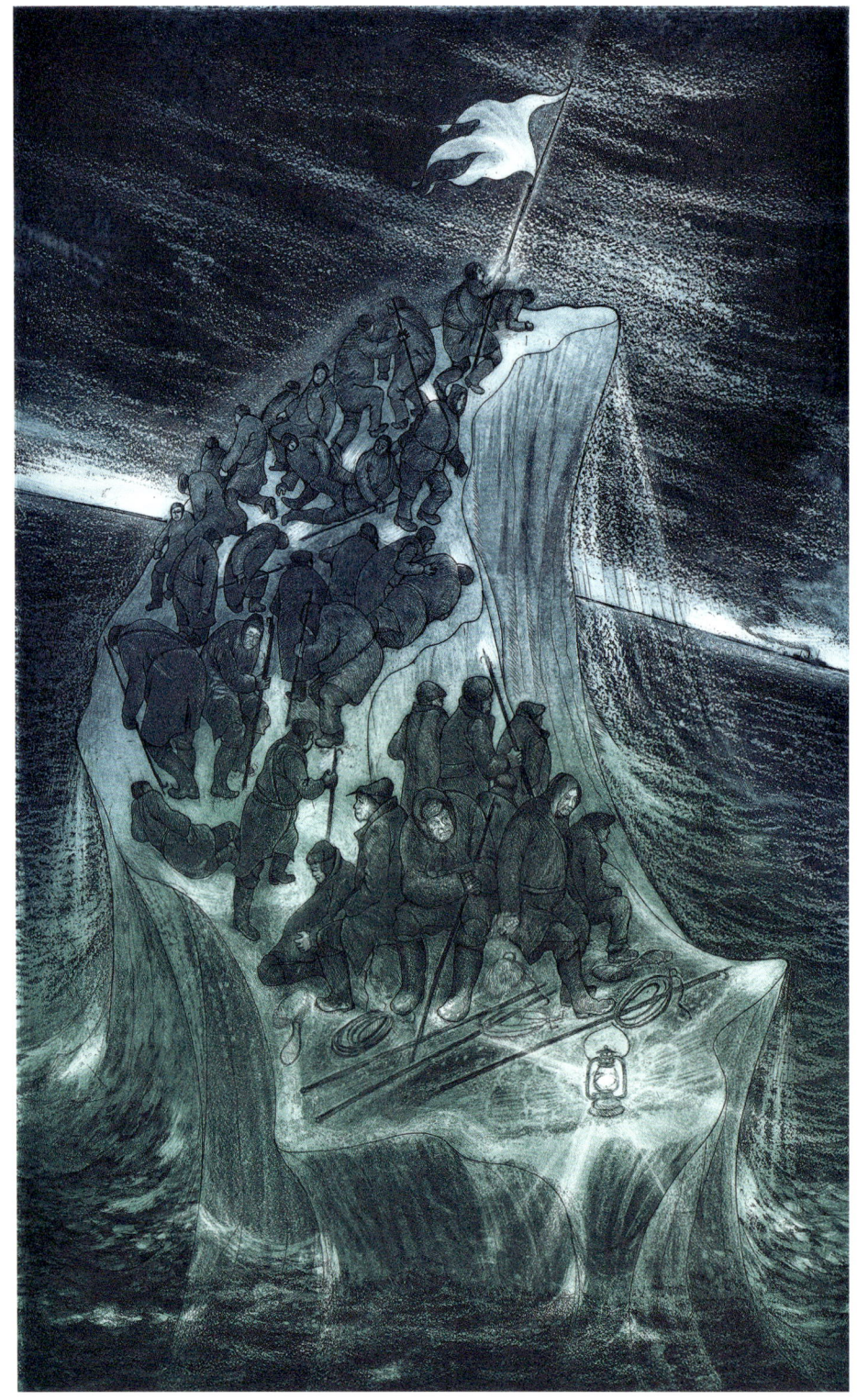

SEARCH PARTY: LOST 1970–2021

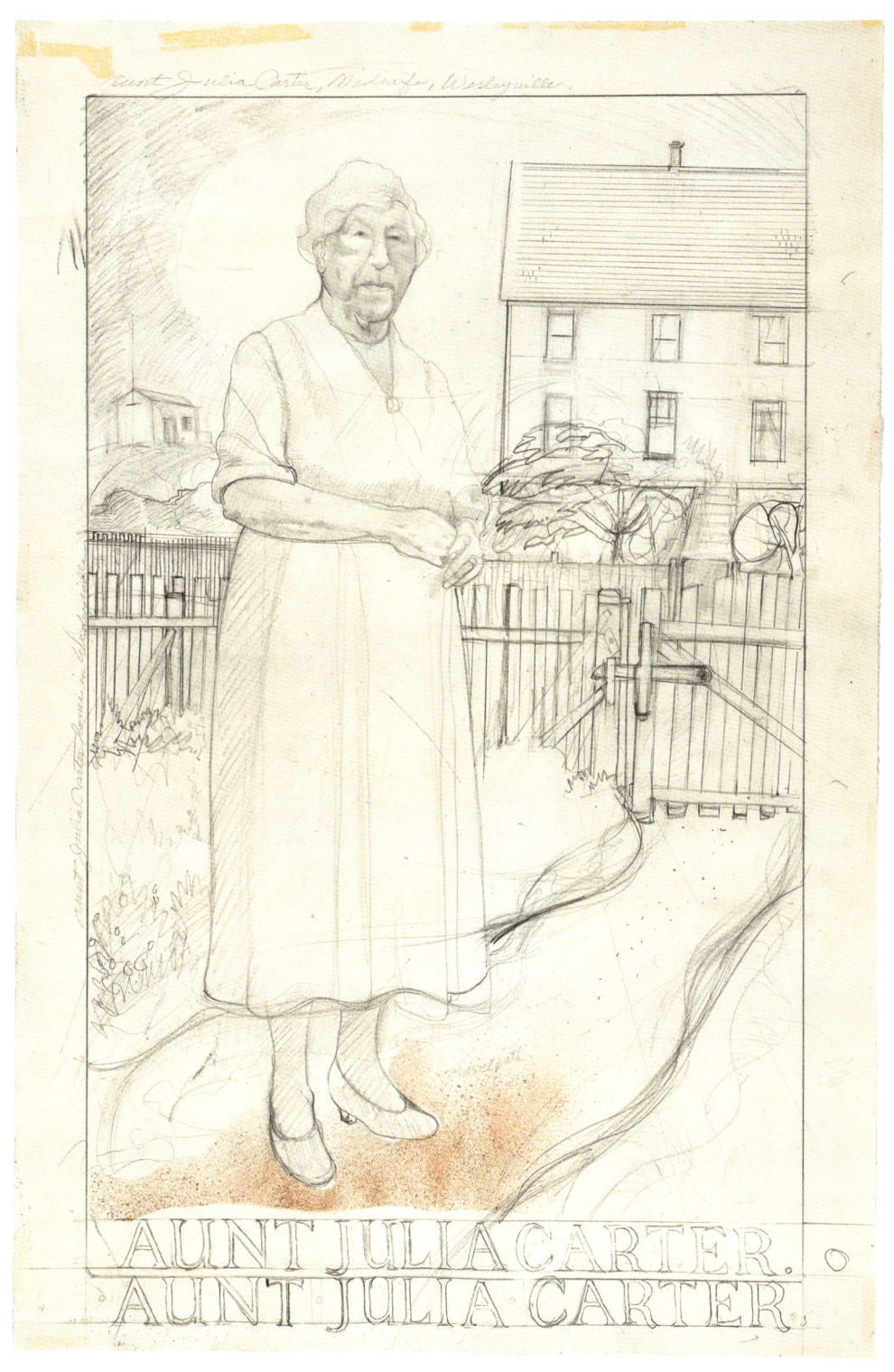

Aunt Julia Carter, Midwife, Wesleyville.

AUNT JULIA CARTER.
AUNT JULIA CARTER.

Wedding on Deer Island

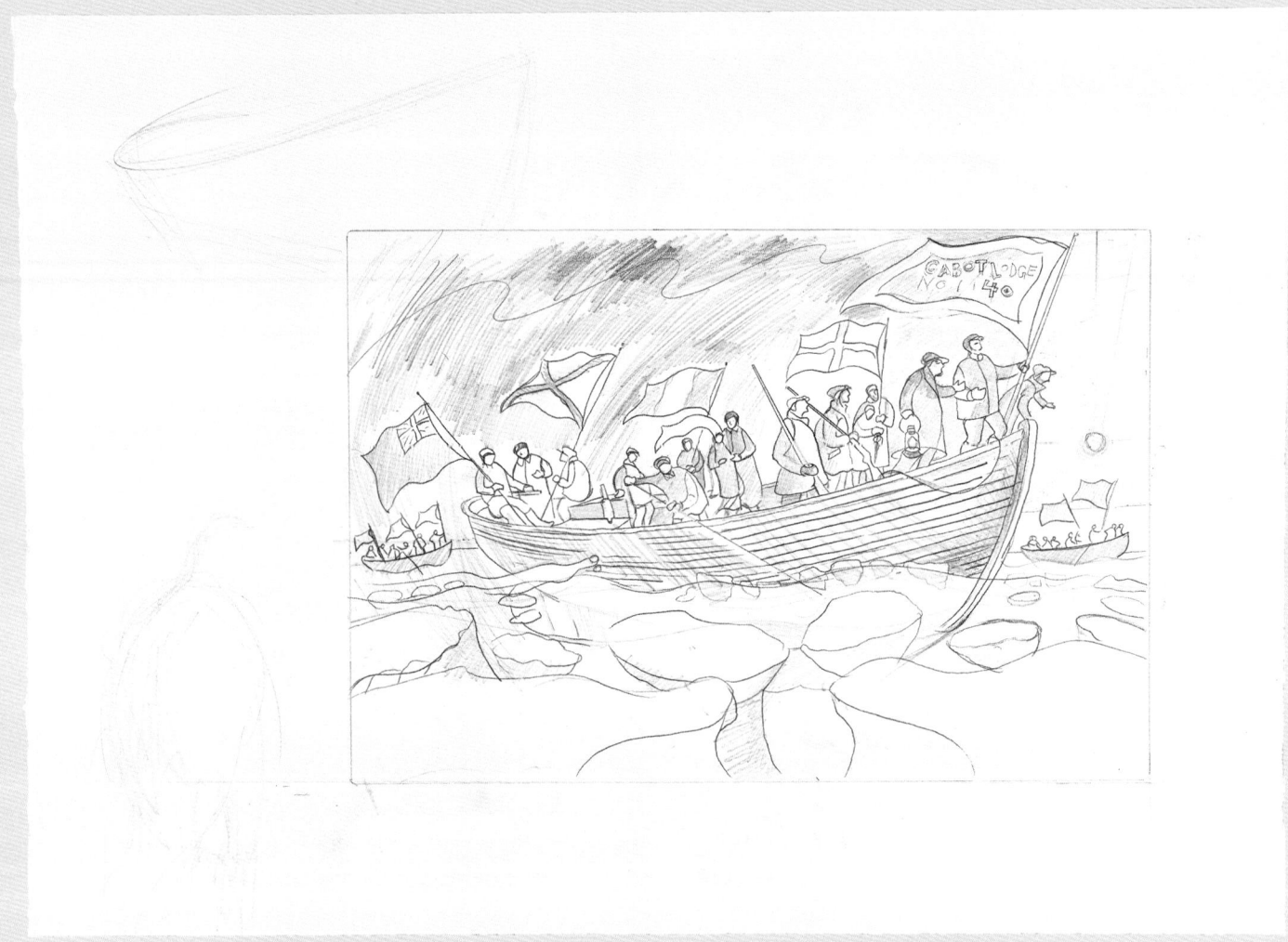

These two drawings and ten distinct proofs
capture changes made by Blackwood. Each
unique state gives us a glimpse into the artist's
printmaking process.

WEDDING ON DEER ISLAND
2020
graphite on paper

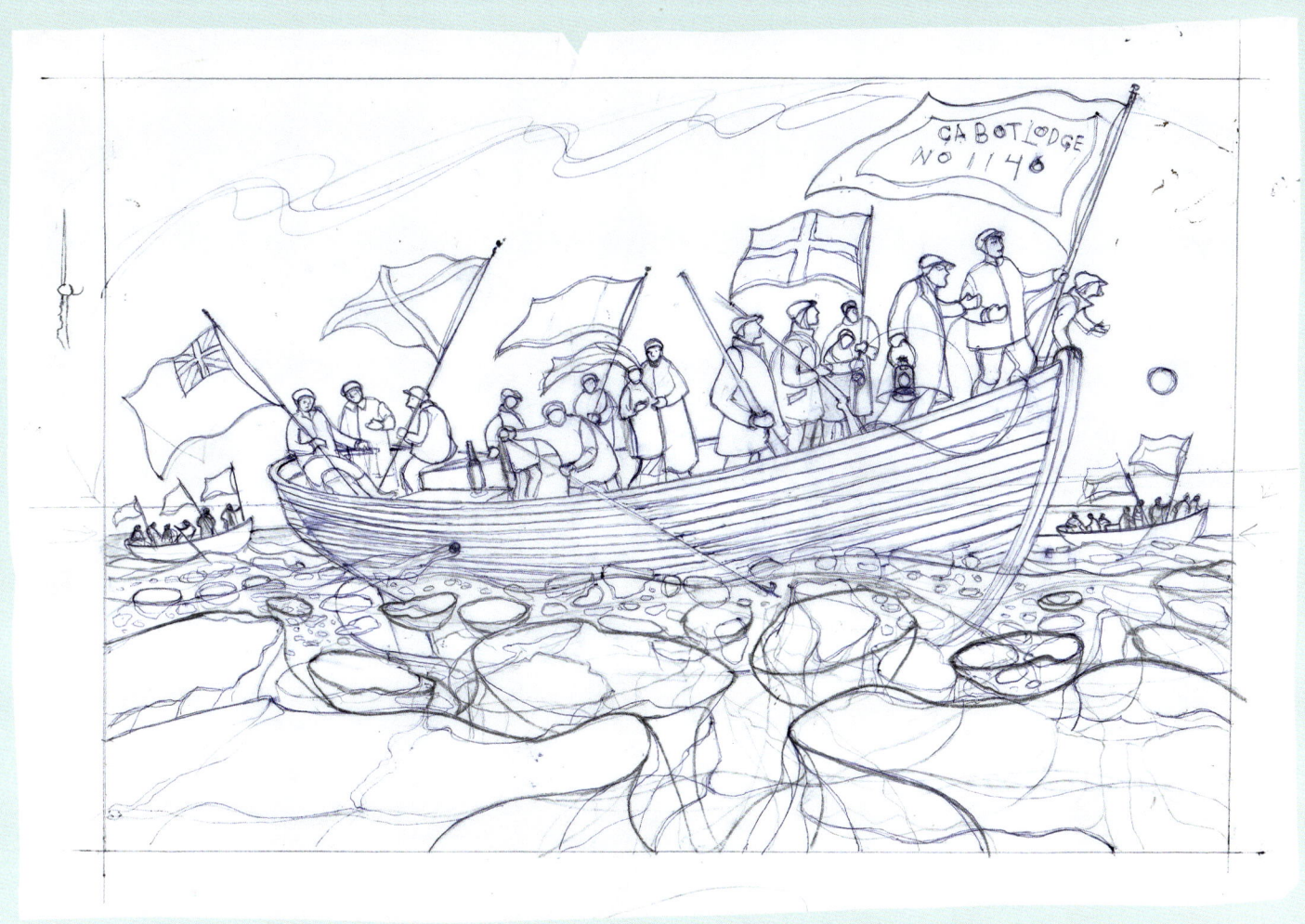

WEDDING ON DEER ISLAND
2020
graphite and ballpoint ink on tracing paper

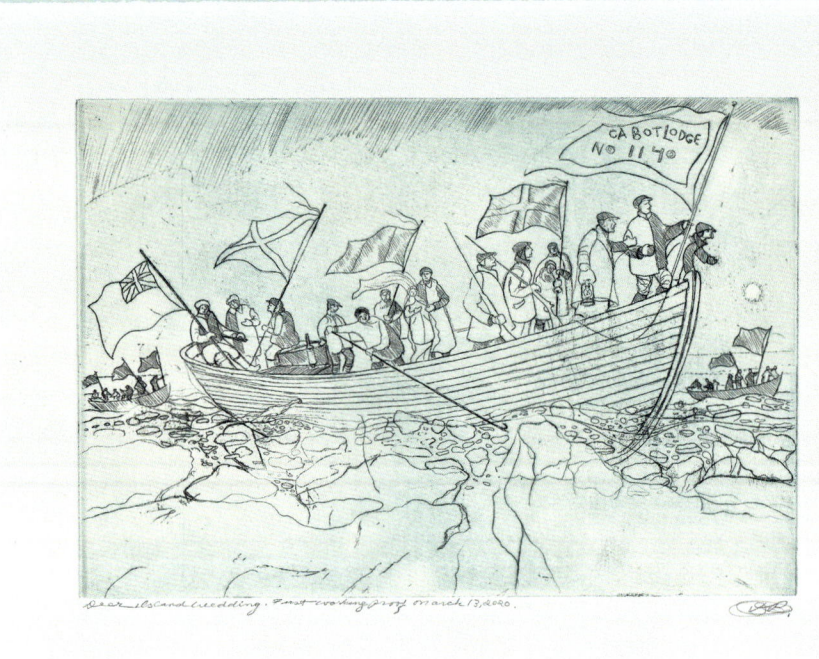

Dear Island wedding. First working proof march 13, 2020.

WEDDING ON DEER ISLAND
March 13, 2020
etching, with plate tone, and graphite on paper
WP 1

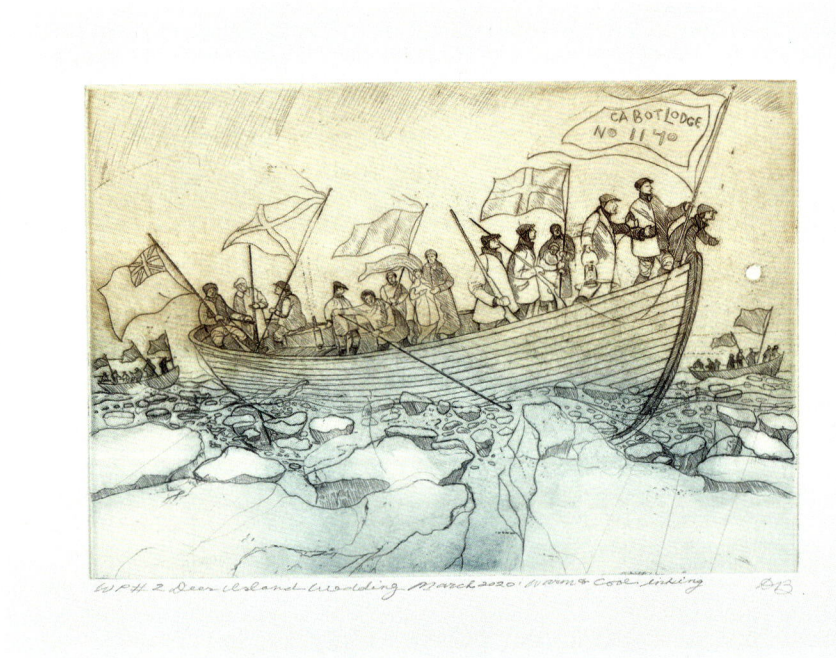

WP# 2 Deer Island wedding. March 2020. Warm & cool inking

WEDDING ON DEER ISLAND
March 2020
etching, with plate tone, and graphite on paper
WP 2

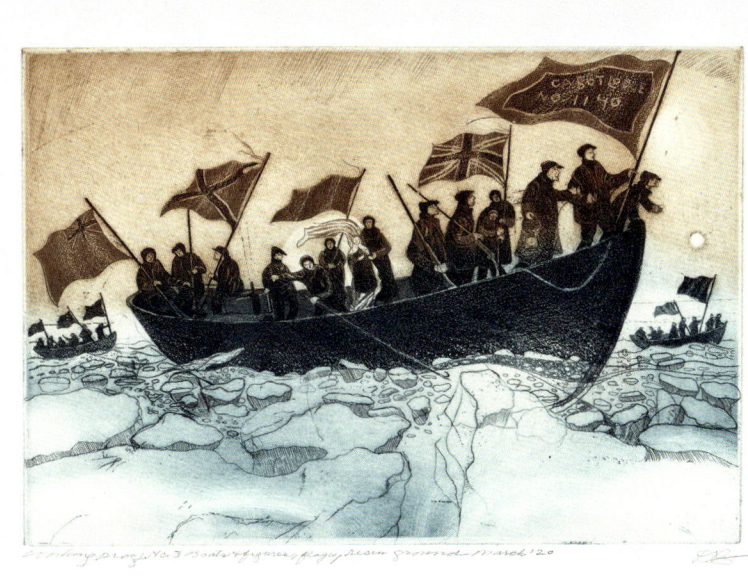

WEDDING ON DEER ISLAND
March 2020
etching and aquatint on paper
WP 3

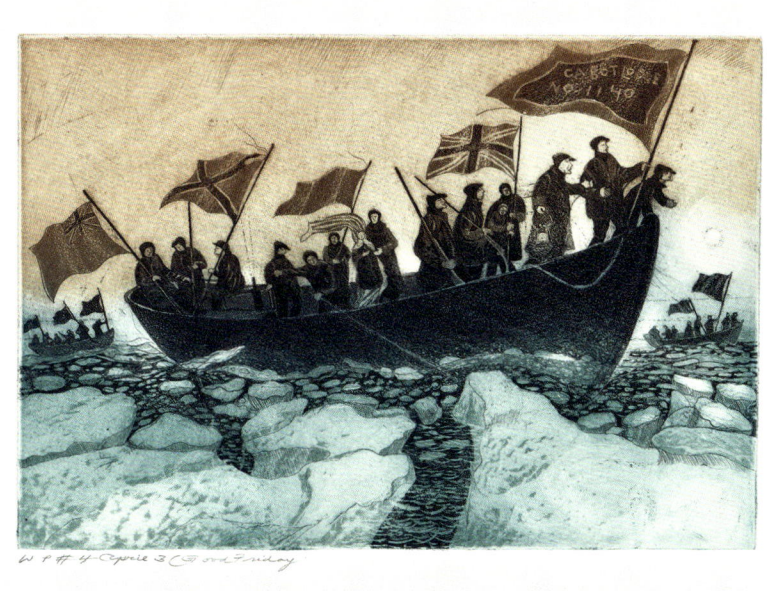

WEDDING ON DEER ISLAND
April 3, 2020
etching and aquatint on paper
WP 4

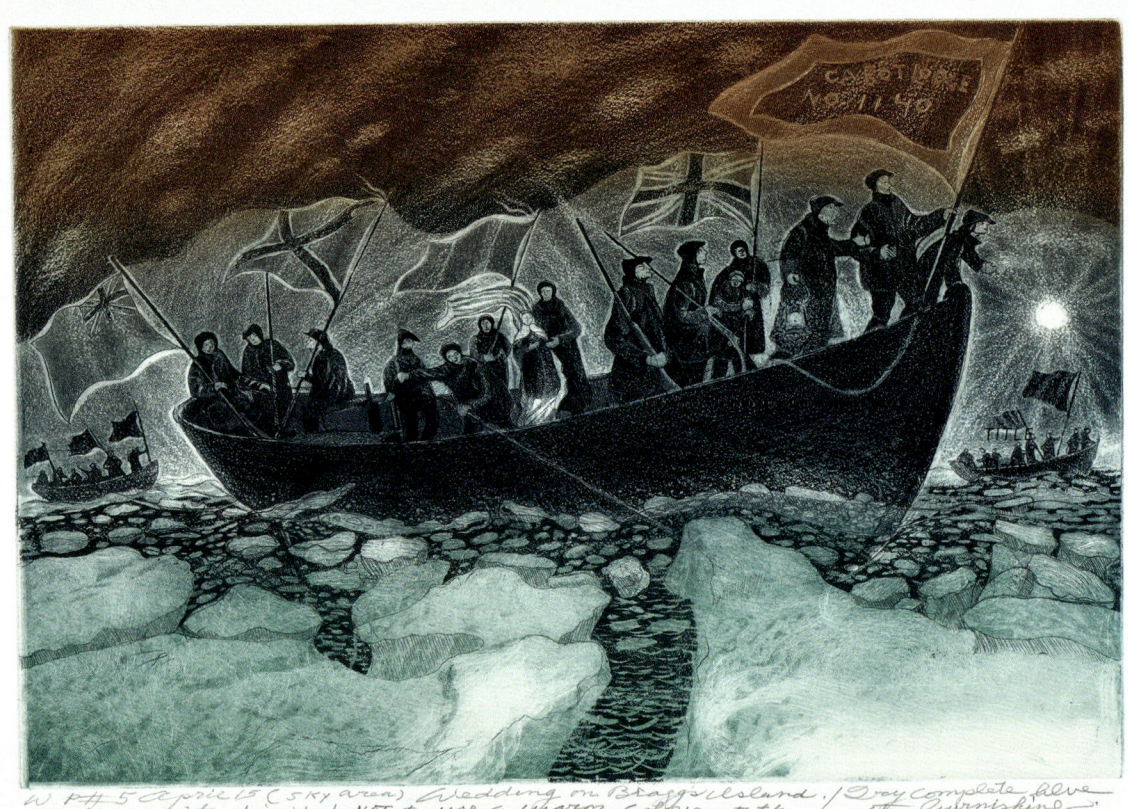

WEDDING ON DEER ISLAND
April 15, 2020
etching and aquatint on paper
WP 5

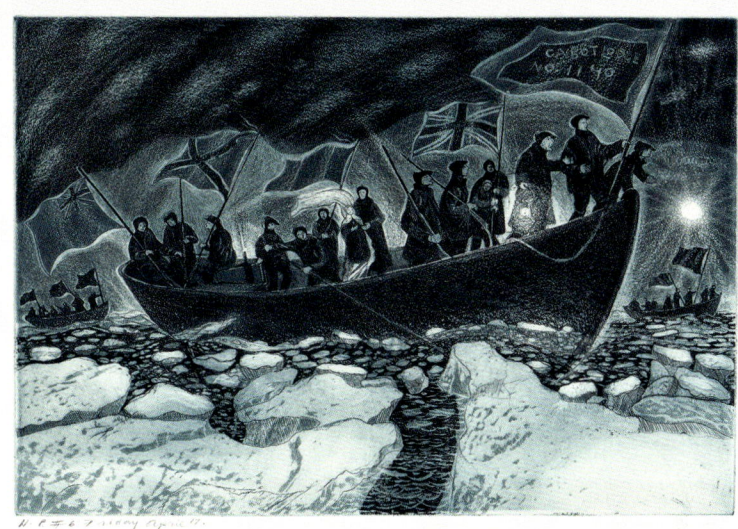

WEDDING ON DEER ISLAND
April 17, 2020
etching and aquatint on paper
WP 6

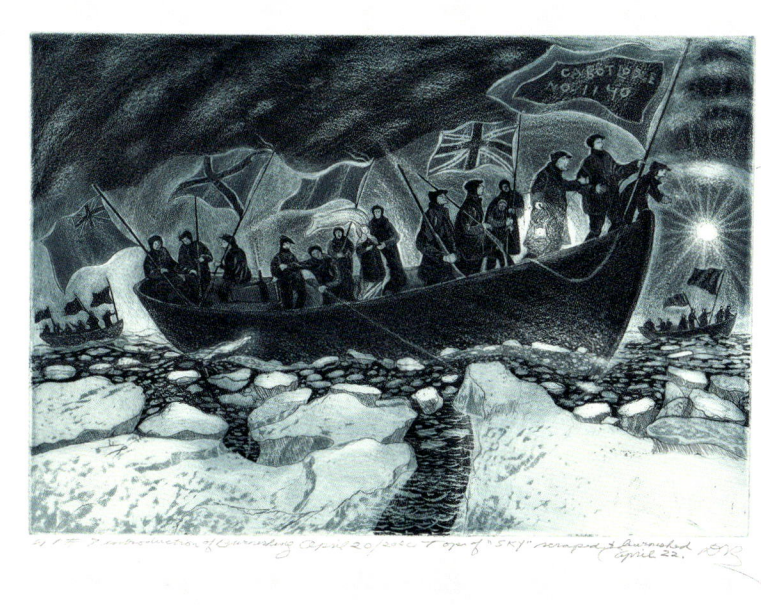

WEDDING ON DEER ISLAND
April 20 & 22, 2020
etching and aquatint on paper
WP 7

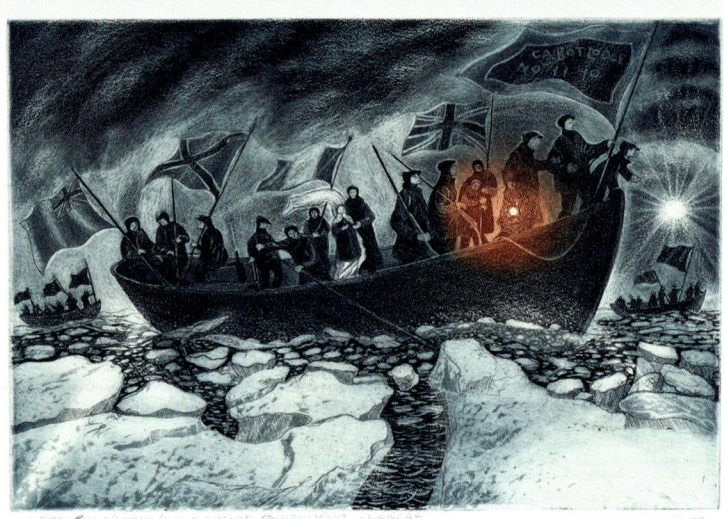

WEDDING ON DEER ISLAND
April 24, 2020
etching and aquatint on paper
WP 8

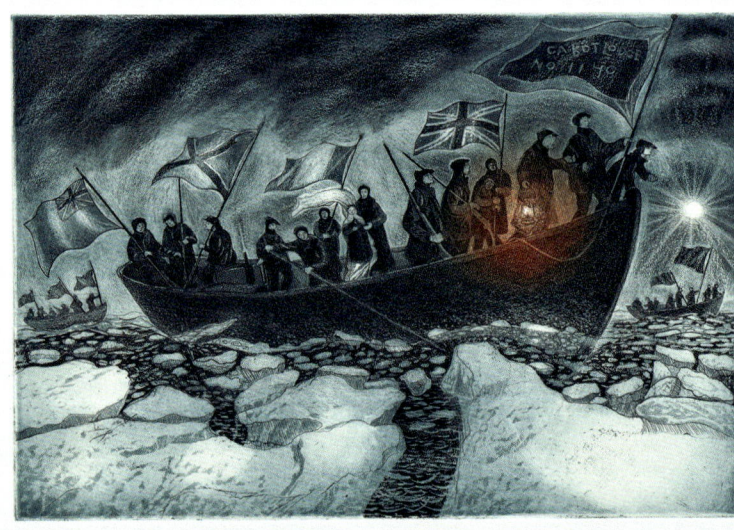

WEDDING ON DEER ISLAND
2020
etching and aquatint on paper
WP 9

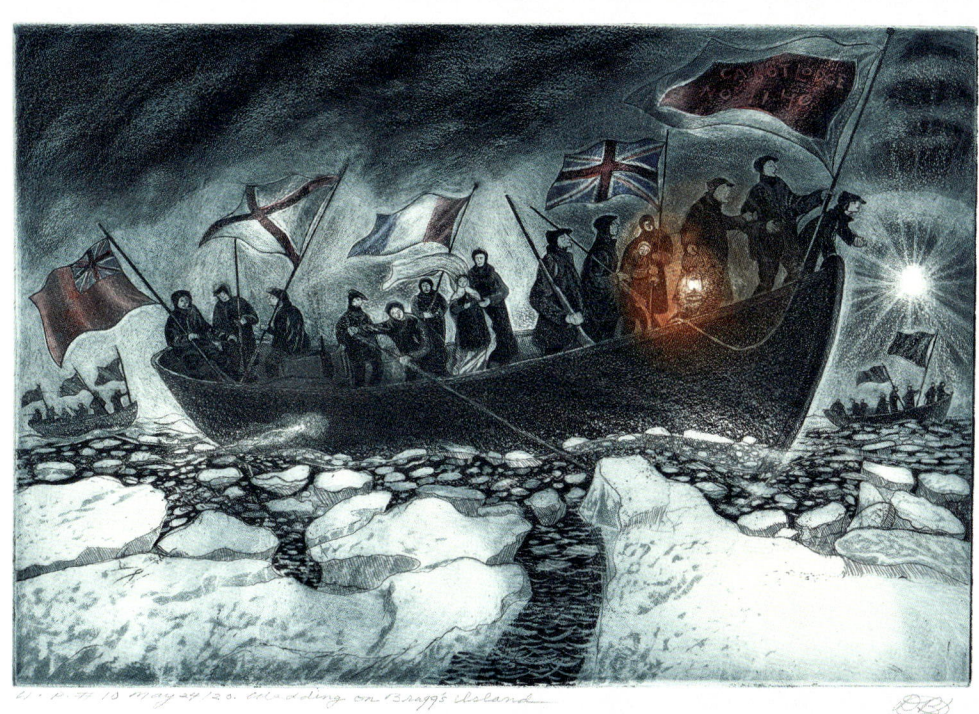

WEDDING ON DEER ISLAND
May 24, 2020
etching, aquatint, colour washes,
and white pencil on paper
WP 10

Close looking will reveal that Blackwood titled the tenth working proof *Wedding on Bragg's Island*, referring to a print of an outport wedding that he completed in 1973. He was inconsistent in his titling of prints, but this charming slip suggests a meaningful kinship between these works made almost thirty years apart.

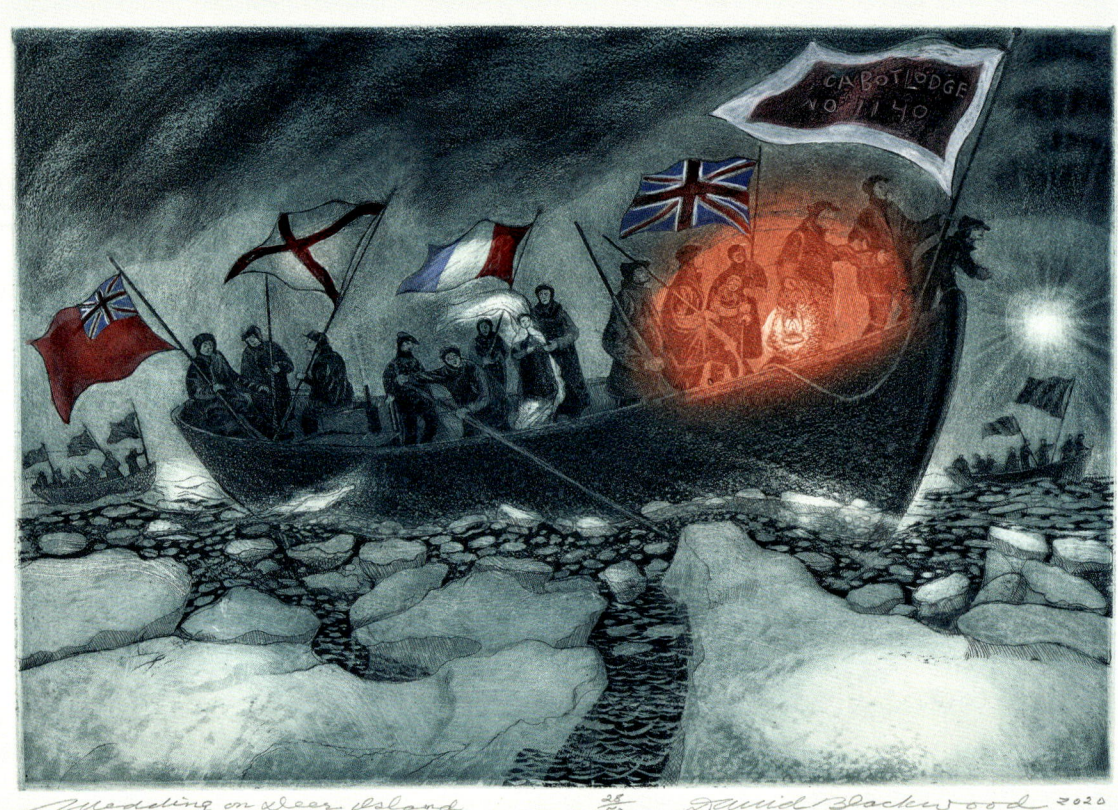

Wedding on Deer Island 28/50 David Blackwood 2020

WEDDING ON DEER ISLAND
2020
etching, aquatint, and watercolour on paper
edition 28/50

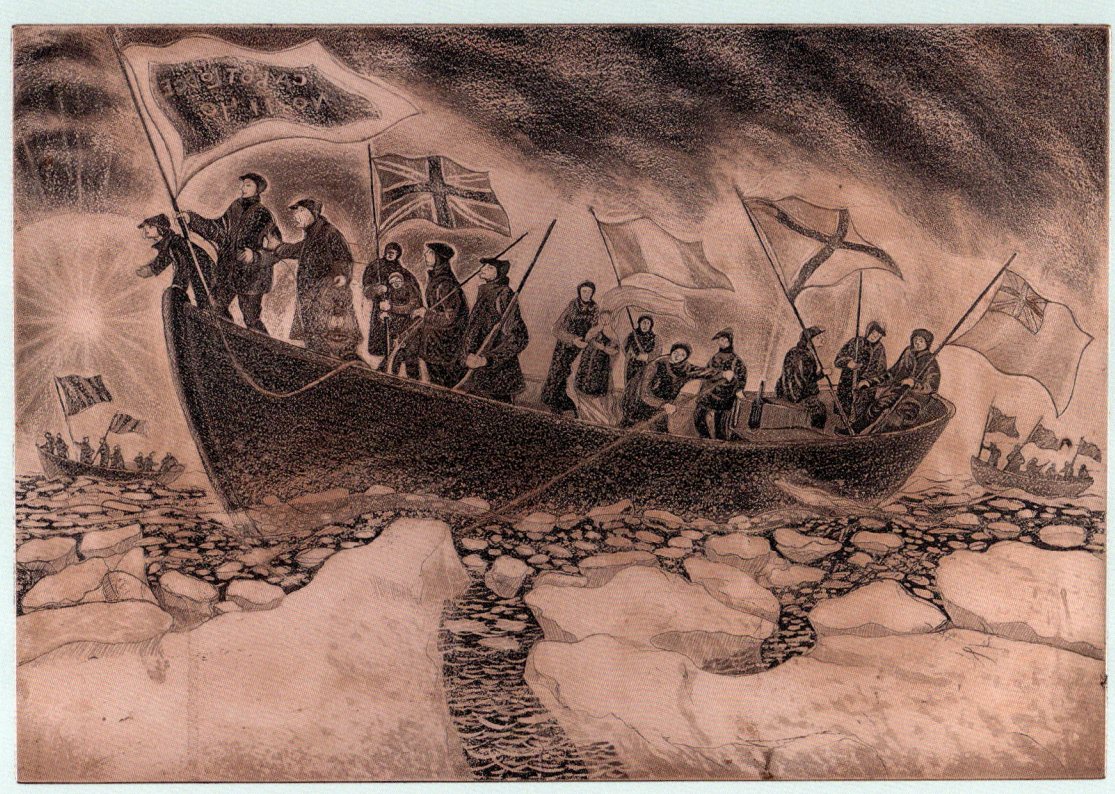

WEDDING ON DEER ISLAND
2020
copperplate

The image on the copperplate is a mirror of the final print. Blackwood used proofs to check his work as he moved toward the version of a print he would later edition.

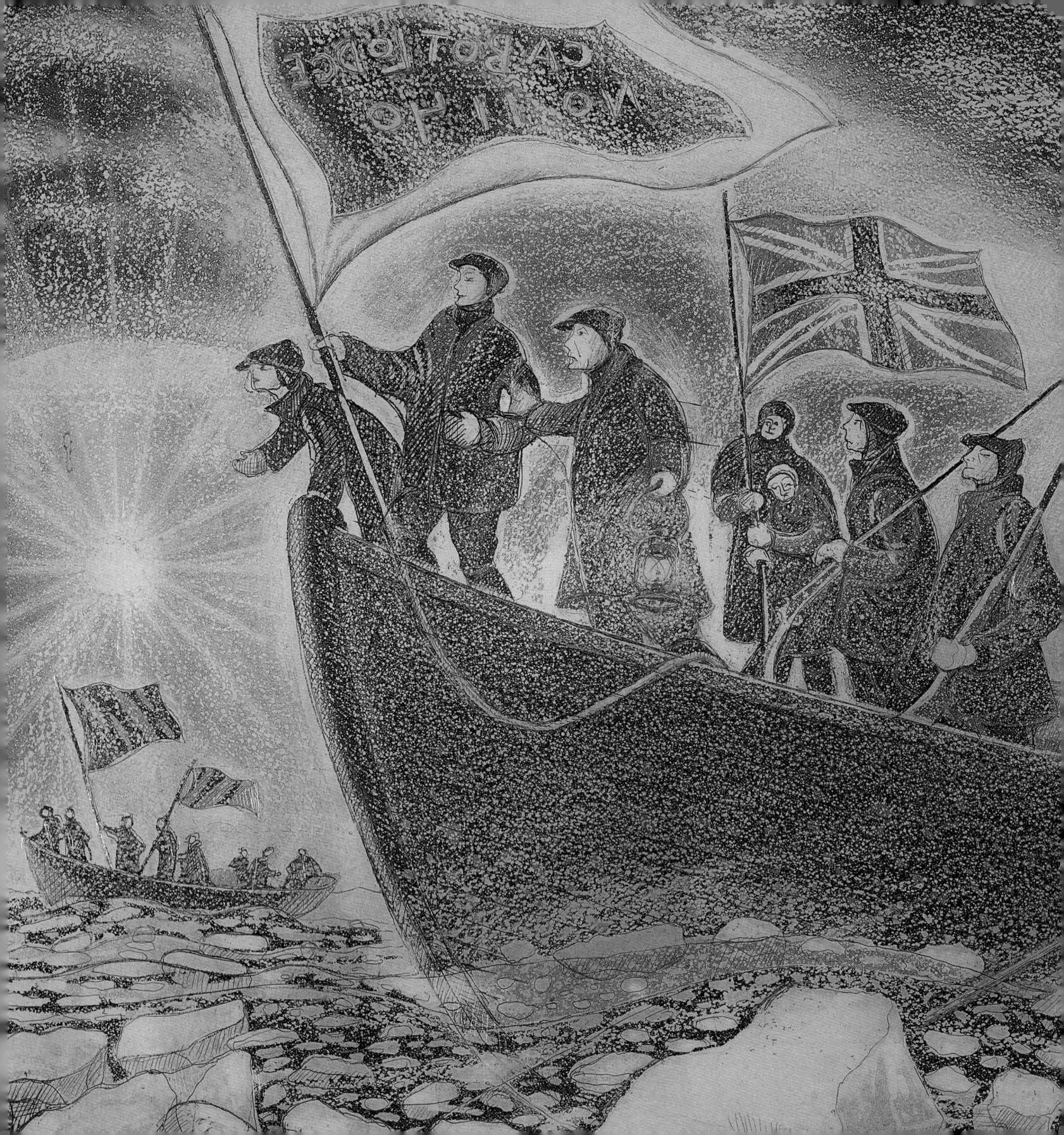

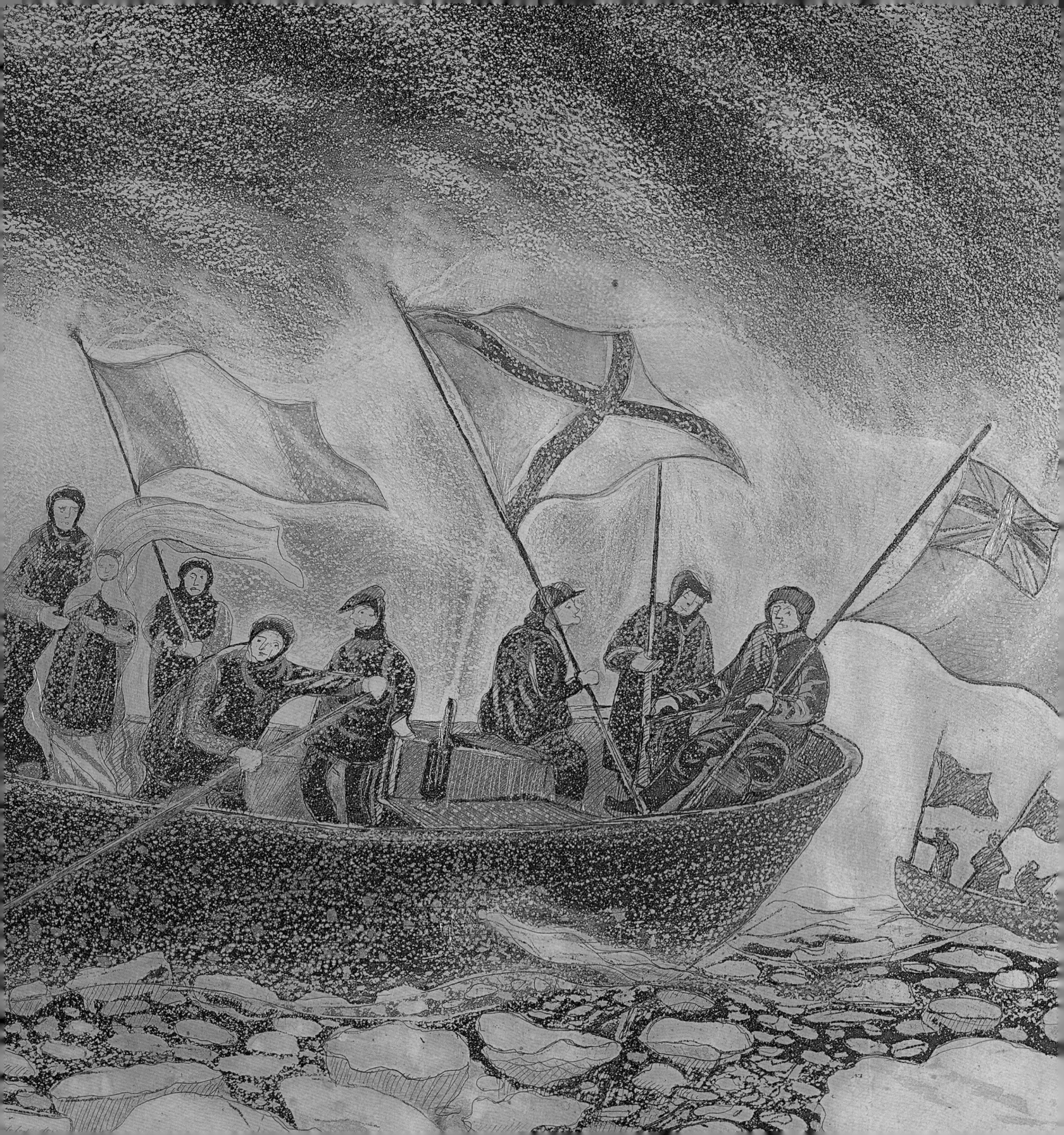

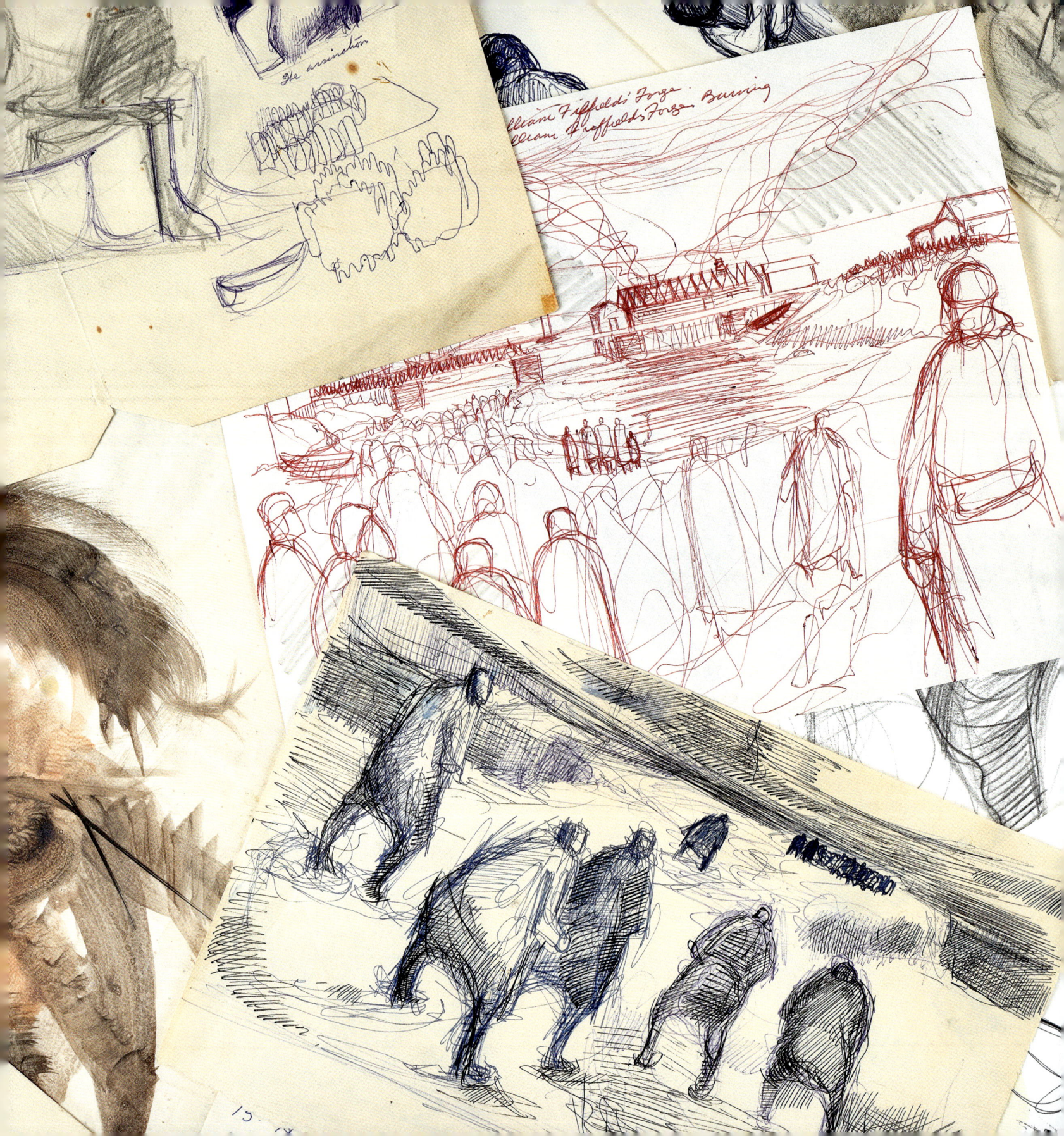

William Fiffield's Forge

William Fiffield's Forge Burning

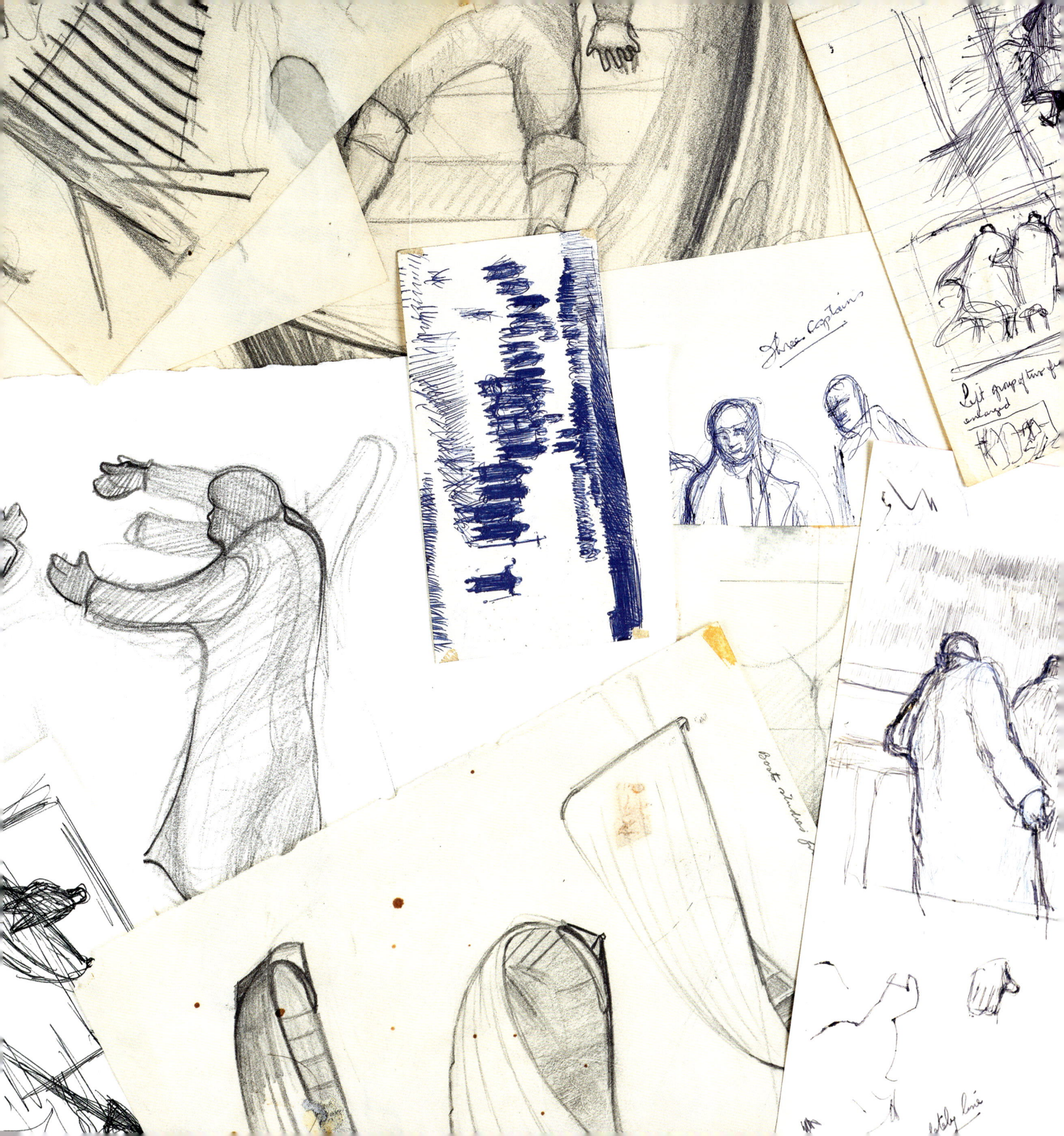

Three Captains

Left group of two f
enlarged

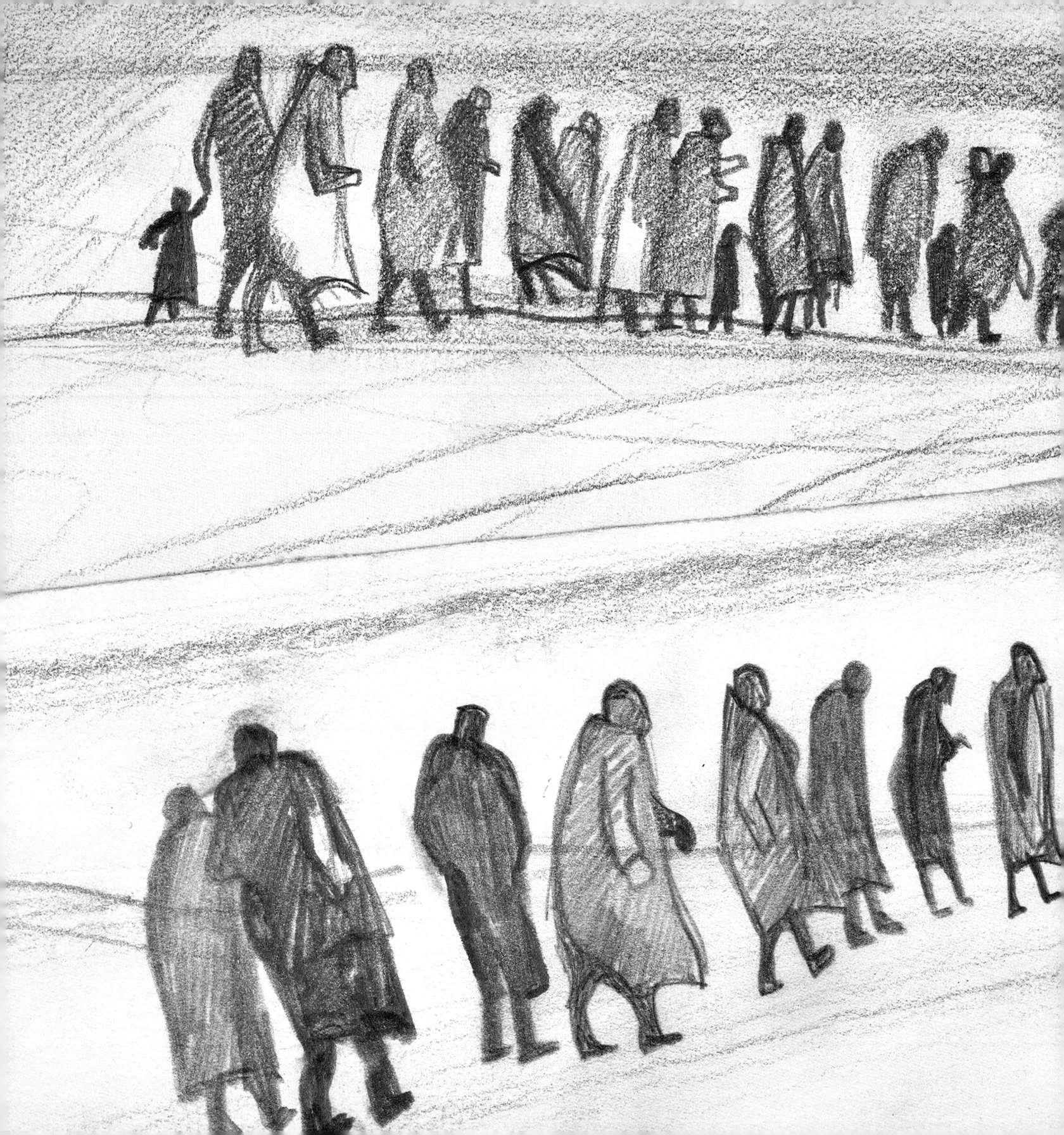

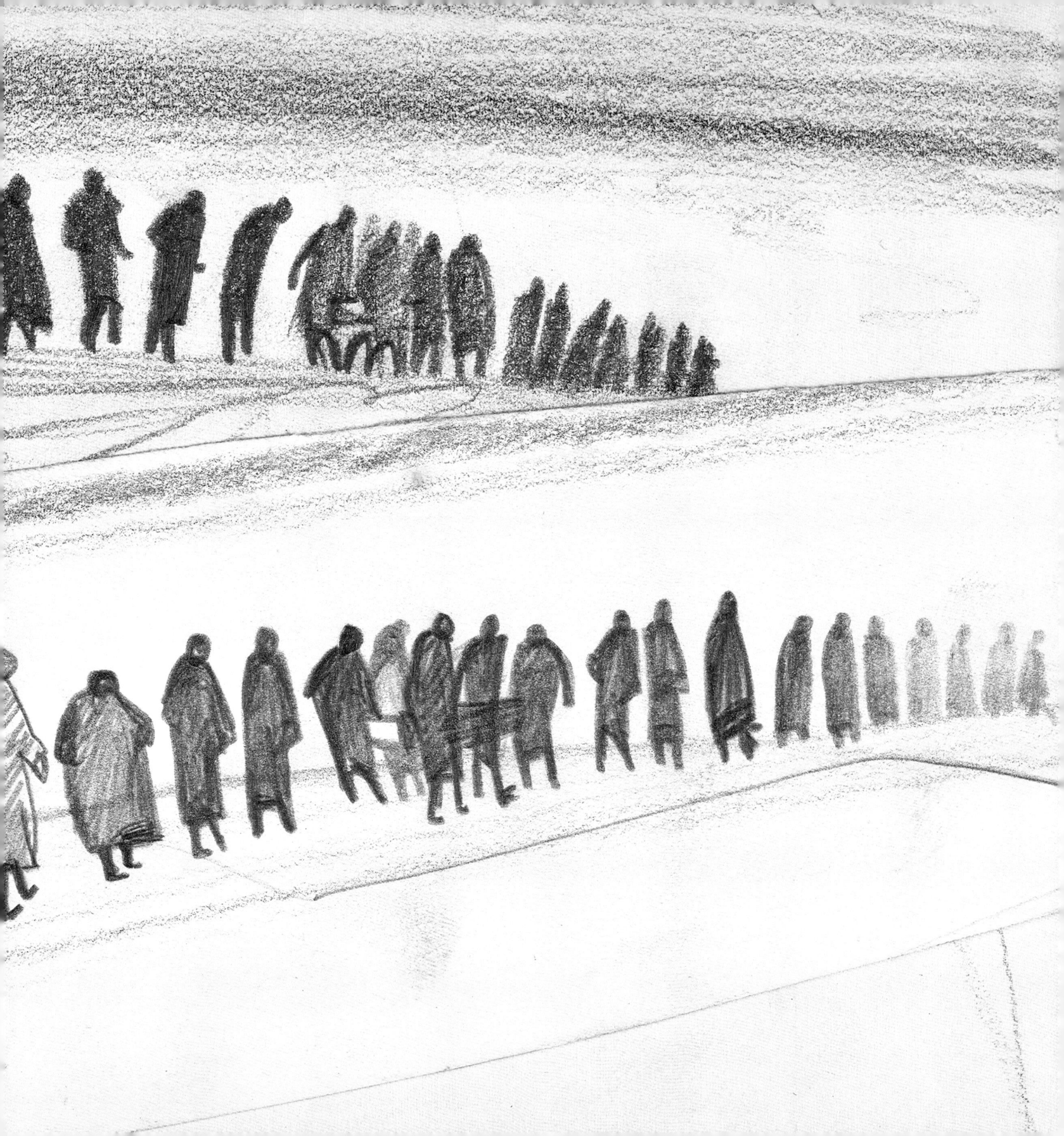

The Archive and the Storyteller

AMY MARSHALL FURNESS

Throughout the modern era, we have celebrated the artist as a personality. With that comes a certain expectation that by revealing the artist's creative process and private life, we might better understand the artwork. This is where archives come into play. Since David Blackwood's passing in 2022, curators, biographers, and researchers have worked to position the artist's legacy in the larger context of Canadian art history. The Art Gallery of Ontario is the collection of record for Blackwood, which means its holdings of his artwork are deep and definitive. This distinction also means—less obviously, but fundamental to our ability to sustain future research and exhibitions on the artist—that the organization is responsible for his archives.

And yet, collecting artists' archives is not something every art museum does. The AGO began acquiring archival material in 1918, and there are now around eighty artists substantially represented in the Special Collections of the Edward P. Taylor Library & Archives. When a museum's collections include archives, it means that part of the artist's studio lives on in the same institution as the artwork; while no longer animated by creative work, it becomes safeguarded and available for discovery.

A personal archive requires the time and the means to create documentation and to keep it safe—to preserve the written pages, the snapshots, the evidence, and the treasures through all the doubts and upheavals of a lifetime. Throughout Blackwood's archive are traces of his belief that someday this would matter to his future self—and more than that, to other people, and to the greater story of a culture.

For an archive to survive an artist (or any other creator of a personal archive), there might need to be a spouse, a child, or a niece or nephew who believes the archive matters as well. There might be a curator, a student, or a literary friend who takes an interest and tells the artist to keep going, asking some critical questions along the way. Then there's an archivist who might become involved much later, maybe even after the lifetime of the artist. The archivist selects, filters, organizes, preserves, and attempts to represent, in detached and accessible language, the resulting files. Finally, the archive is ready for reading.

This institutionalized archive is not a simple life narrative but rather the work of many hands. It is a space where stories are captured indefinitely. Holding Blackwood's archive makes it possible to reveal these histories and answer questions in greater depth. This includes the raw materials for the stories Blackwood retold through his art as well as the stories of the life of the artist himself. The archive waits for a future reader and new questions that we can't yet frame from our present moment. The narrative paths through it might be infinite.

opposite

Assembled journals of
David Blackwood, 1955–1960s.

Blackwood's archive holds the story of a sensitive and brilliant boy who travelled far from home, worked hard, and found love, success, and tragedy. It's a story that the artist has not exactly written for himself, but he has made sure that we have all the pieces. The archive contains a strong throughline of Newfoundland stories—a historical arc in which the artist situated himself, even from his earliest diary entries.

The nineteen volumes of Blackwood's diary form the core of his archive. He kept the diary going his entire life, starting with a five-year journal that he obtained shortly before his fifteenth birthday. In that first volume, Blackwood declared his ambition to restore his family's position in their community through his art: "I am glad that I have a talent and I pray that I will grow up to develop it and build up our reputation that has died down since my good grandfather died."

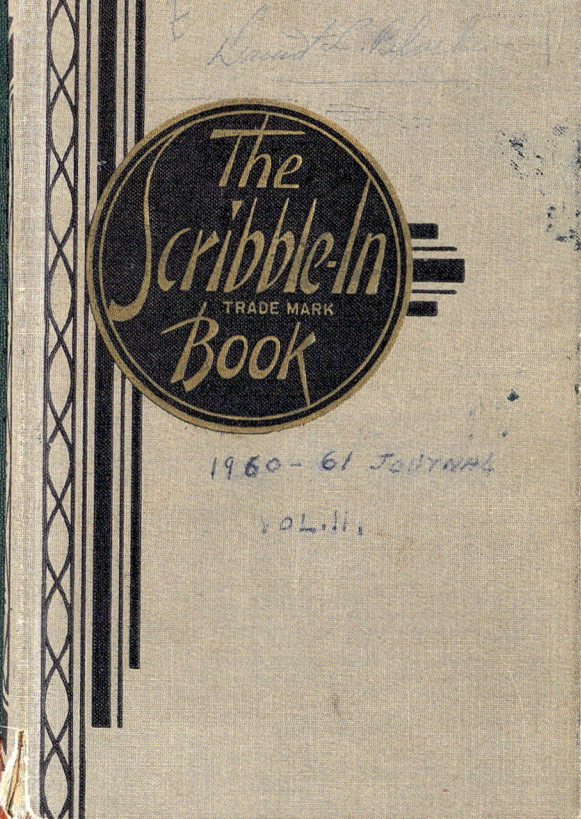

The Scribble-In Book
TRADE MARK

1960-61 JOURNAL
VOL. III.

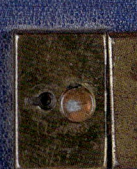

Five Year Diary

RECORD

RECORD

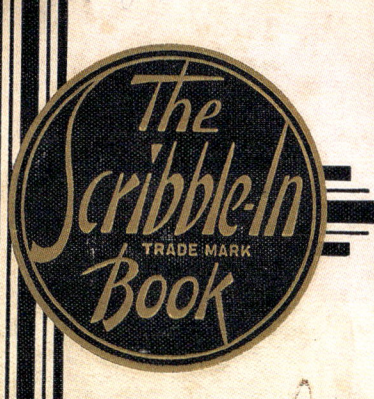

The Scribble-In Book
TRADE MARK

Journal

1959-1960.
1960-1961

A THIRD YEAR
AT
O.C.A.

RECORD

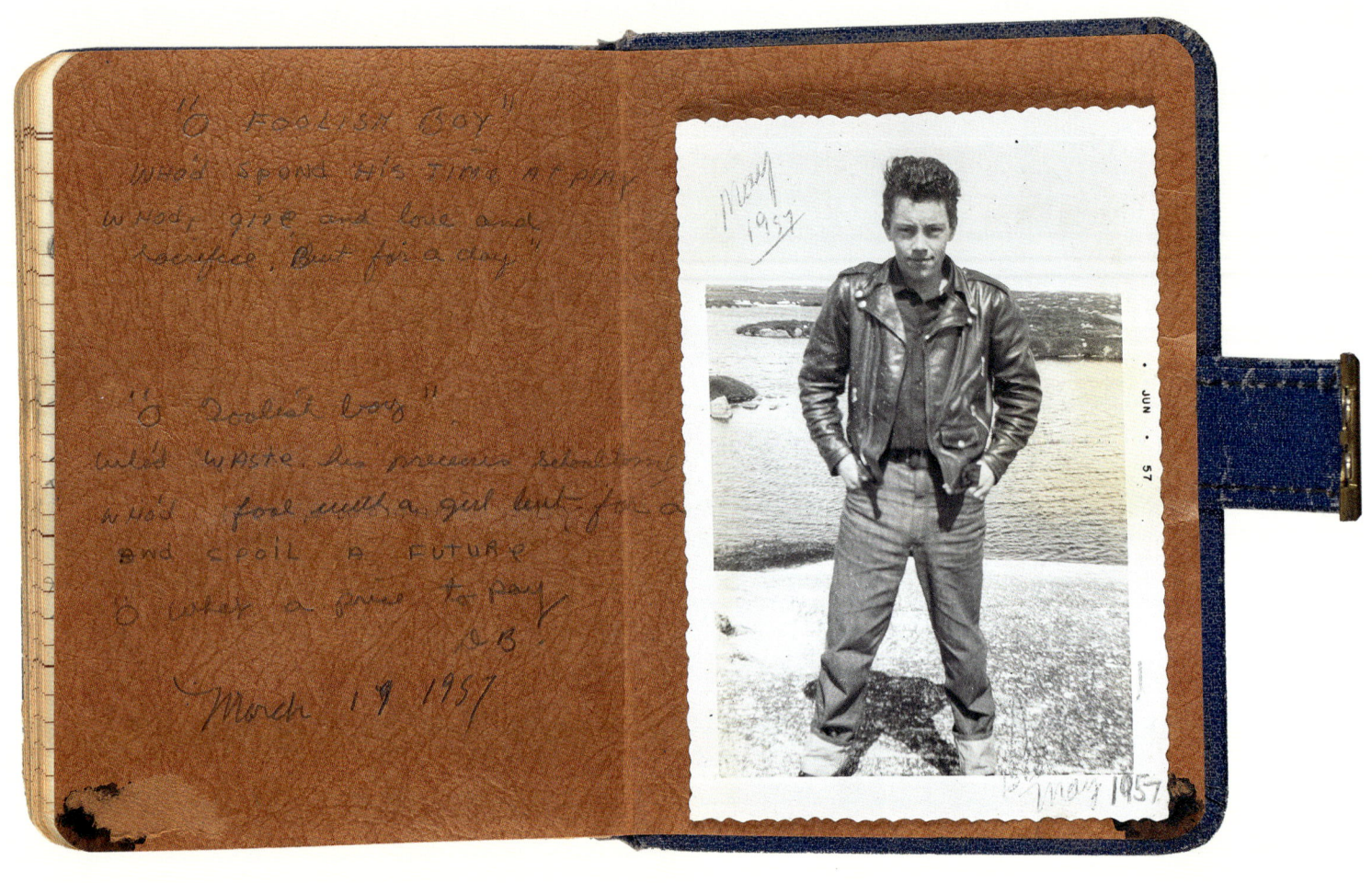

Back endsheets from first journal with
photograph of a young David Blackwood,
January 2, 1955 – December 31, 1958.

New Years Eve
HUTCHINGS & PATRICK LTD.
Printed in Canada
Dec 31/1955

19 __During the past year many happy and sad things happened. Only God knows what the New Year will bring.__

19

During the past year many a Joyful + Sad things happen of which the worst was that gram died, Business was good during 1956.

1957 Today ends another year, in which I witnessed the launching of the first man made moon During 1957 I made great strides in art completing a record no. of pictures and winning a great award in art.

1958 Today ends another year a most successful one because of the great Steps I made in Art. I look forward and even greater achievements in that field

1959.

my mother who is not very well because of mental health cannot work very well.

Money at the pleasures of life are robbed from us because of this, but I cannot complain because of the many things we have that others don't

I am glad that I have a talent and I pray that I will grow up to develope it and build up our reputation that has died down since my good grandfather died

Dec 4th /1955.

David F. Blackwood 15

Page spread from first journal with entries
on December 4 and 31, 1955, and recurring on
December 31 from 1956 through 1958.

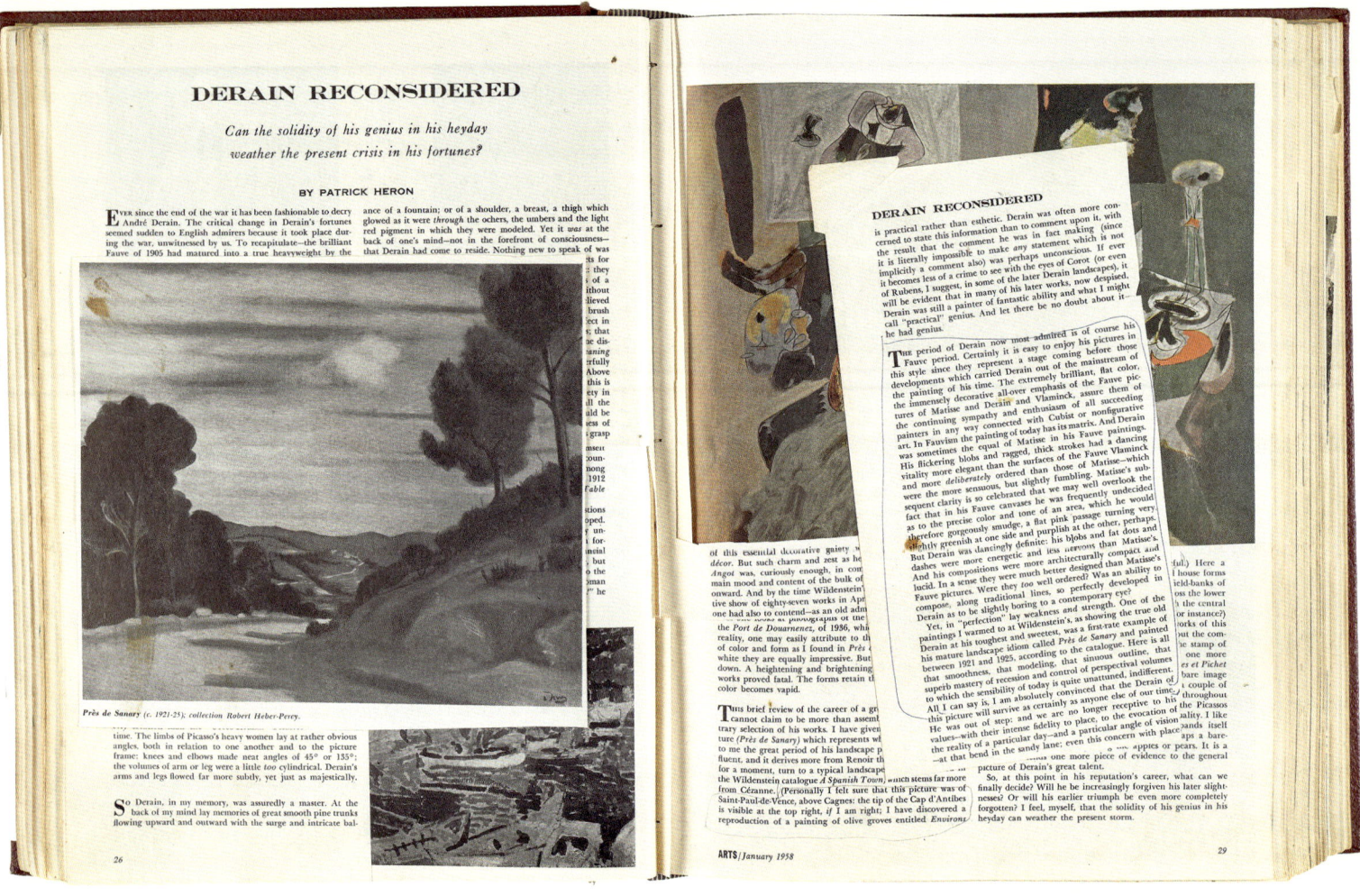

In his early teens, Blackwood subscribed to *Arts Magazine*, hungry to learn about an art world far beyond his small community of Wesleyville. He annotated the pages and cut out illustrations that he found particularly inspiring, such as the work of modern French painter André Derain. Before leaving his hometown to attend art college in Toronto, Blackwood had the collected issues bound into one volume.

above and opposite

David Blackwood's bound copies of *Arts Magazine* (1950s) with explanatory note (2011).

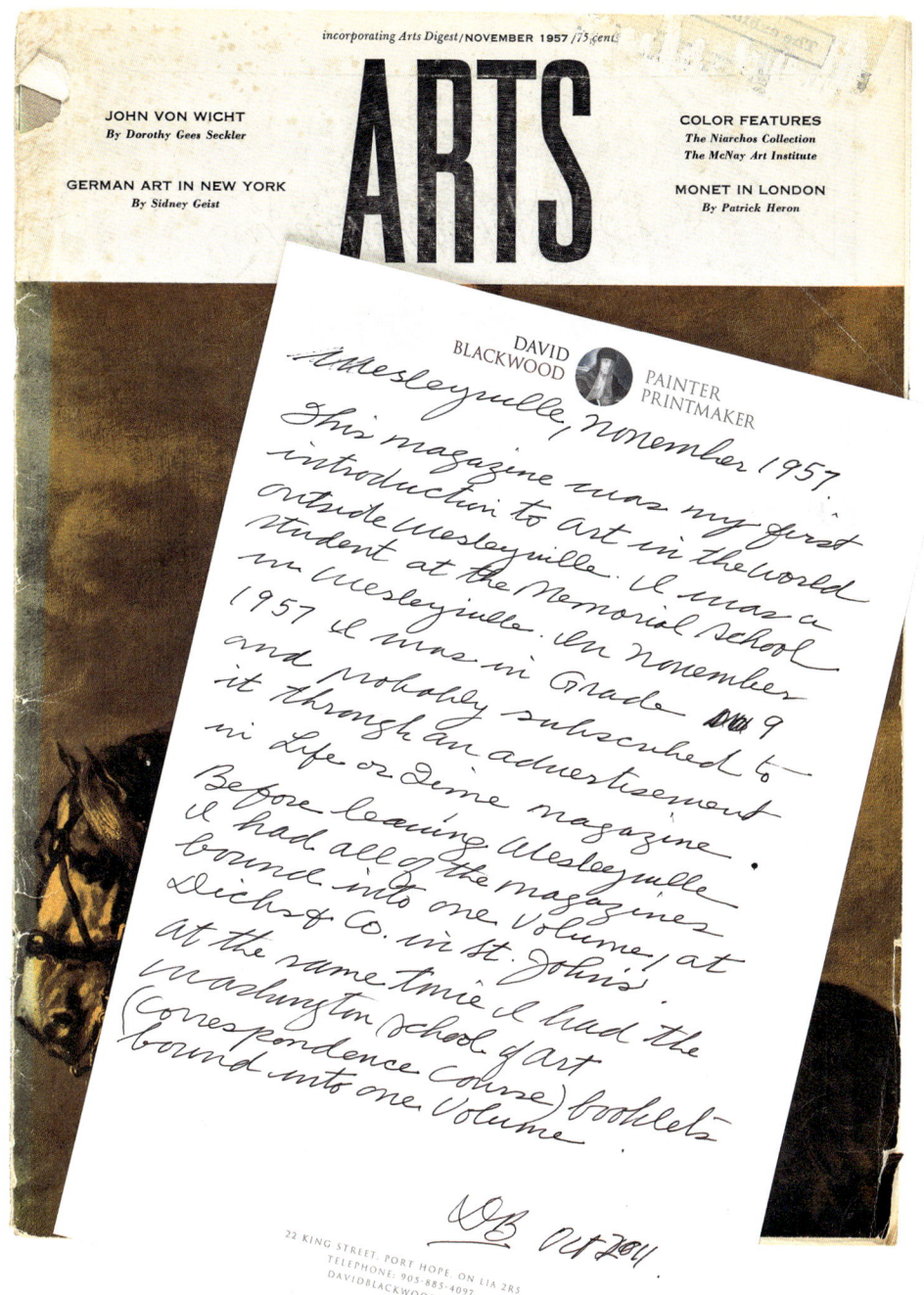

incorporating Arts Digest/NOVEMBER 1957/75 cents

ARTS

JOHN VON WICHT
By Dorothy Gees Seckler

GERMAN ART IN NEW YORK
By Sidney Geist

COLOR FEATURES
The Niarchos Collection
The McNay Art Institute

MONET IN LONDON
By Patrick Heron

DAVID
BLACKWOOD   PAINTER
PRINTMAKER

Wesleyville, November 1957.

This magazine was my first
introduction to Art in the world
outside Wesleyville. I was a
student at the Memorial School
in Wesleyville. In November
1957 I was in Grade 9
and probably subscribed to
it through an advertisement
in Life or Time magazine.
Before leaving Wesleyville
I had all of the magazines
bound into one Volume, at
Dicks & Co. in St. John's.
At the same time I had the
Washington School of Art
(correspondence course) booklets
bound into one Volume

DB Oct 2011.

22 KING STREET, PORT HOPE, ON L1A 2R5
TELEPHONE: 905-885-4097
DAVIDBLACKWOOD.COM

As a student at the Ontario College of Art, Blackwood was intensely self-disciplined and determined to make the most of what he recognized as a tremendous opportunity, given his family's scant financial means. He revered his instructors, particularly Carl Schaefer, John Alfsen, and Frederick Hagan. His OCA sketchbooks reflect his studiousness and early recognition that the stories of his Newfoundland community would be the focus of his art.

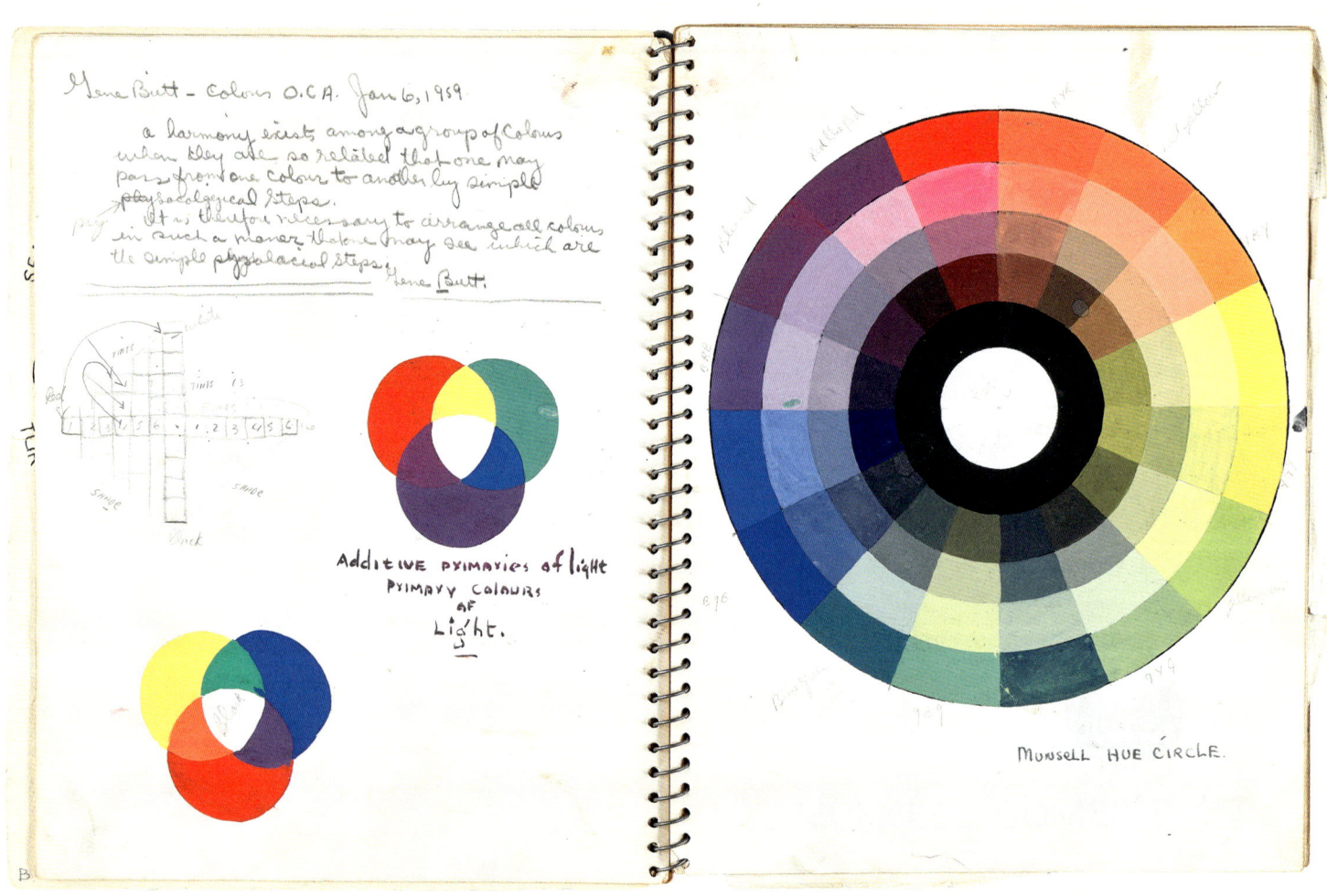

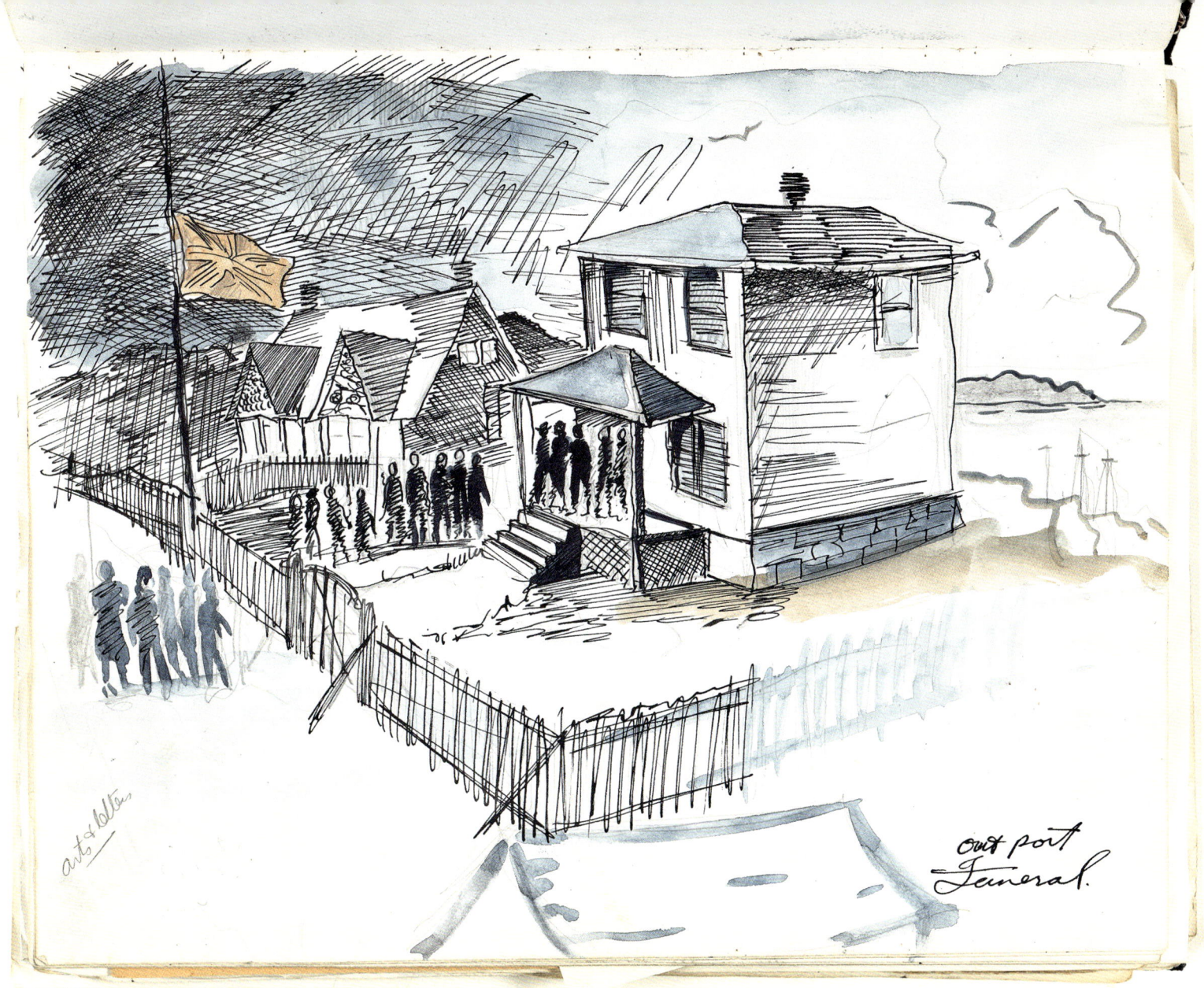

opposite

Ontario College of Art sketchbook with additive primaries of light and Munsell Hue Circle, 1959.

above

Sketchbook page with *Outport Funeral* drawing, 1960.

Blackwood's research files contain reproductions of historical photographs, genealogical documentation, news clippings, and contemporary photographs of locations on the Bonavista Peninsula—many by his brother Edgar Blackwood.

Research file on Bragg's Island, 1963–2013.

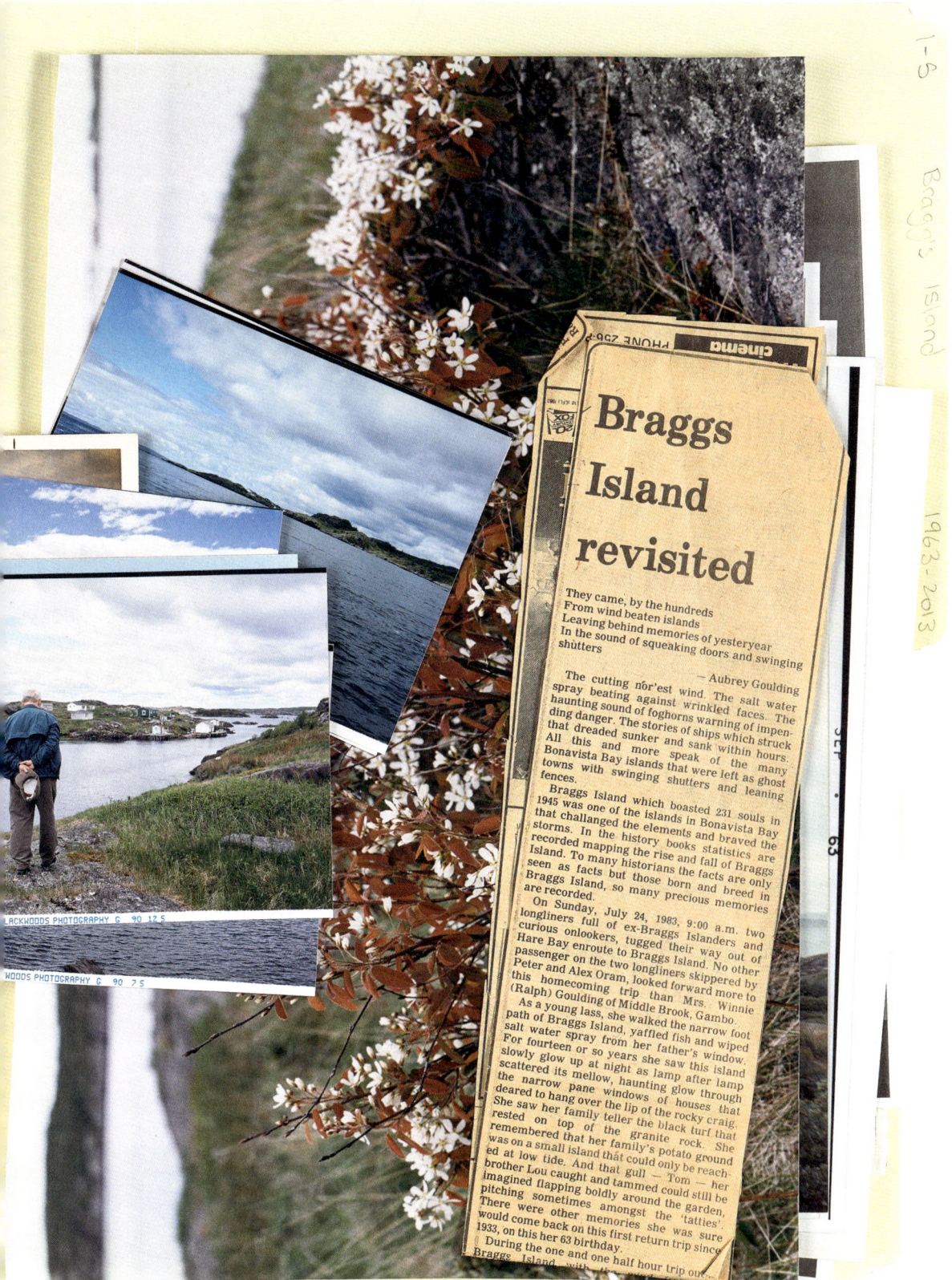

Braggs Island revisited

They came, by the hundreds
From wind beaten islands
Leaving behind memories of yesteryear
In the sound of squeaking doors and swinging shutters

— Aubrey Goulding

The cutting nôr'est wind. The salt water spray beating against wrinkled faces. The haunting sound of foghorns warning of impending danger. The stories of ships which struck that dreaded sunker and sank within hours. All this and more speak of the many Bonavista Bay islands that were left as ghost towns with swinging shutters and leaning fences.

Braggs Island which boasted 231 souls in 1945 was one of the islands in Bonavista Bay that challanged the elements and braved the storms. In the history books statistics are recorded mapping the rise and fall of Braggs Island. To many historians the facts are only seen as facts but those born and breed in Braggs Island, so many precious memories are recorded.

On Sunday, July 24, 1983, 9:00 a.m. two longliners full of ex-Braggs Islanders and curious onlookers, tugged their way out of Hare Bay enroute to Braggs Island. No other passenger on the two longliners skippered by Peter and Alex Oram, looked forward more to this homecoming trip than Mrs. Winnie (Ralph) Goulding of Middle Brook, Gambo. As a young lass, she walked the narrow foot path of Braggs Island, yaffled fish and wiped salt water spray from her father's window. For fourteen or so years she saw this island slowly glow up at night as lamp after lamp scattered its mellow, haunting glow through the narrow pane windows of houses that deared to hang over the lip of the rocky craig. She saw her family teller the black turf that rested on top of the granite rock. She remembered that her family's potato ground was on a small island that could only be reached at low tide. And that gull — Tom — her brother Lou caught and tammed could still be imagined flapping boldly around the garden, pitching sometimes amongst the 'tatties' There were other memories she was sure would come back on this first return trip since 1933, on this her 63 birthday.

During the one and one half hour trip out Braggs Island will

Notes for a Biography.

Bragg's Island (ref Feltham)

The settlement of Bragg's Is.
occured around 1885 when *
~~Greenspond Island he~~
(* when the shoreline of Greenspond
Island became crowded)
a family named Bragg started
to fish in the area, before
the days of motor boats. Bragg's
Island was close by the
fishing grounds and provided
shelter when the weather
was bad. It was also very
convenient place to unload,
clean and salt their catch.
This resulted in the building
of stages, flakes and in a
short time houses. *
The very first shelters were
constructed from logs covered
with sods. These "huts" were
temporary until more substantial
dwellings could be constructed.
Bragg's Island had many
ideal sheltered coves and
with an abundance of
firewood on the island and
the nearby mainland.
My grandfather David Glover

(* on Greenspond it was
referred to as "the place
where the Braggs fished"
Other people moved from
Greenspond to the Island
including Glovers. My grandfather

In one of his later sketchbooks, Blackwood wrote several pages titled "Notes for a Biography," one of many autobiographical passages woven throughout the archive. The story begins long before his own birth, with the origins of the Bragg's Island community and his maternal grandfather's life. His narrative speaks of resourcefulness, steady hard work, and Methodist values and traditions.

Sketchbook page with "Notes for a biography," early 2000s.

Blackwood's maternal grandparents' house on Bragg's Island and their fish-drying apparatus, or "flake," remained vivid, lifelong memories for the artist. An undated drawing traces the floorplan of the house, noting the bedroom where the artist slept as a small boy ("me").

Floorplan of Glover house on Bragg's Island drawn from memory, early 2000s.

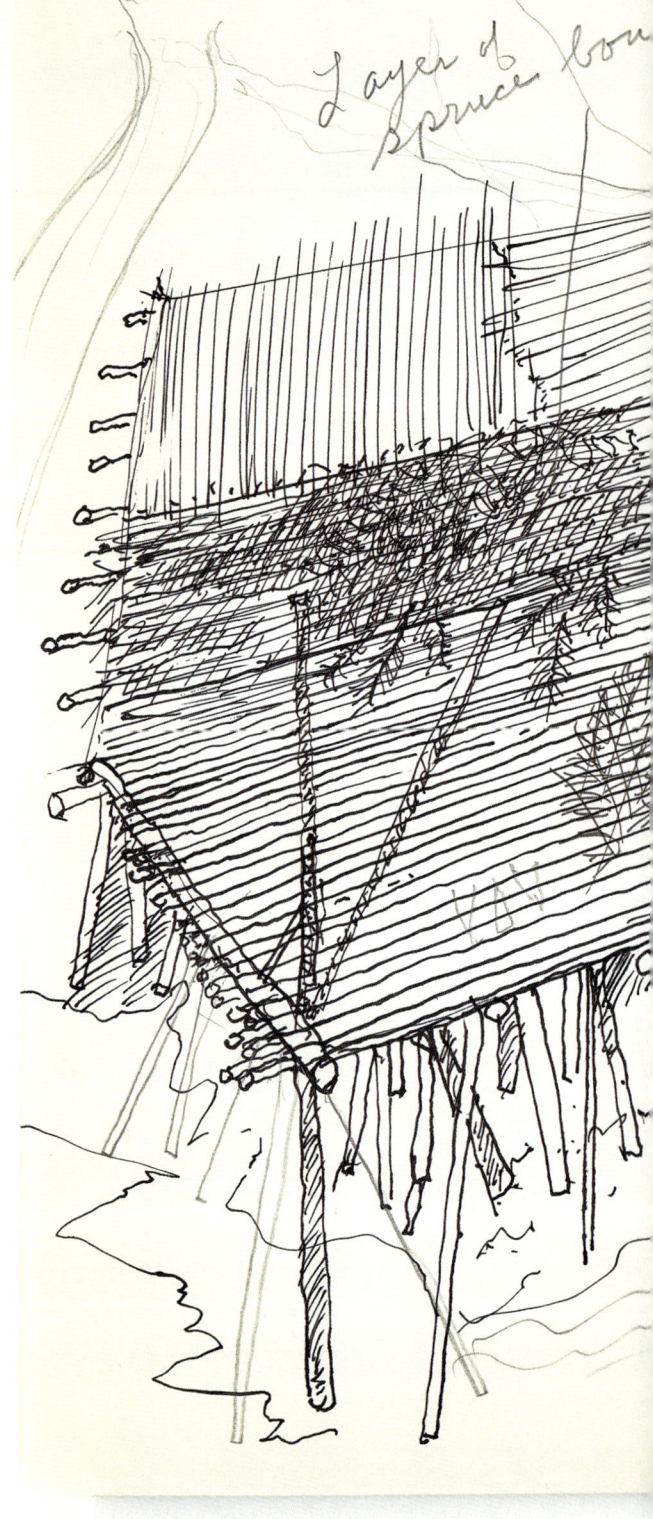

Sketchbook page with drawing
of his grandfather Glover's flake
on Bragg's Island, early 2000s.

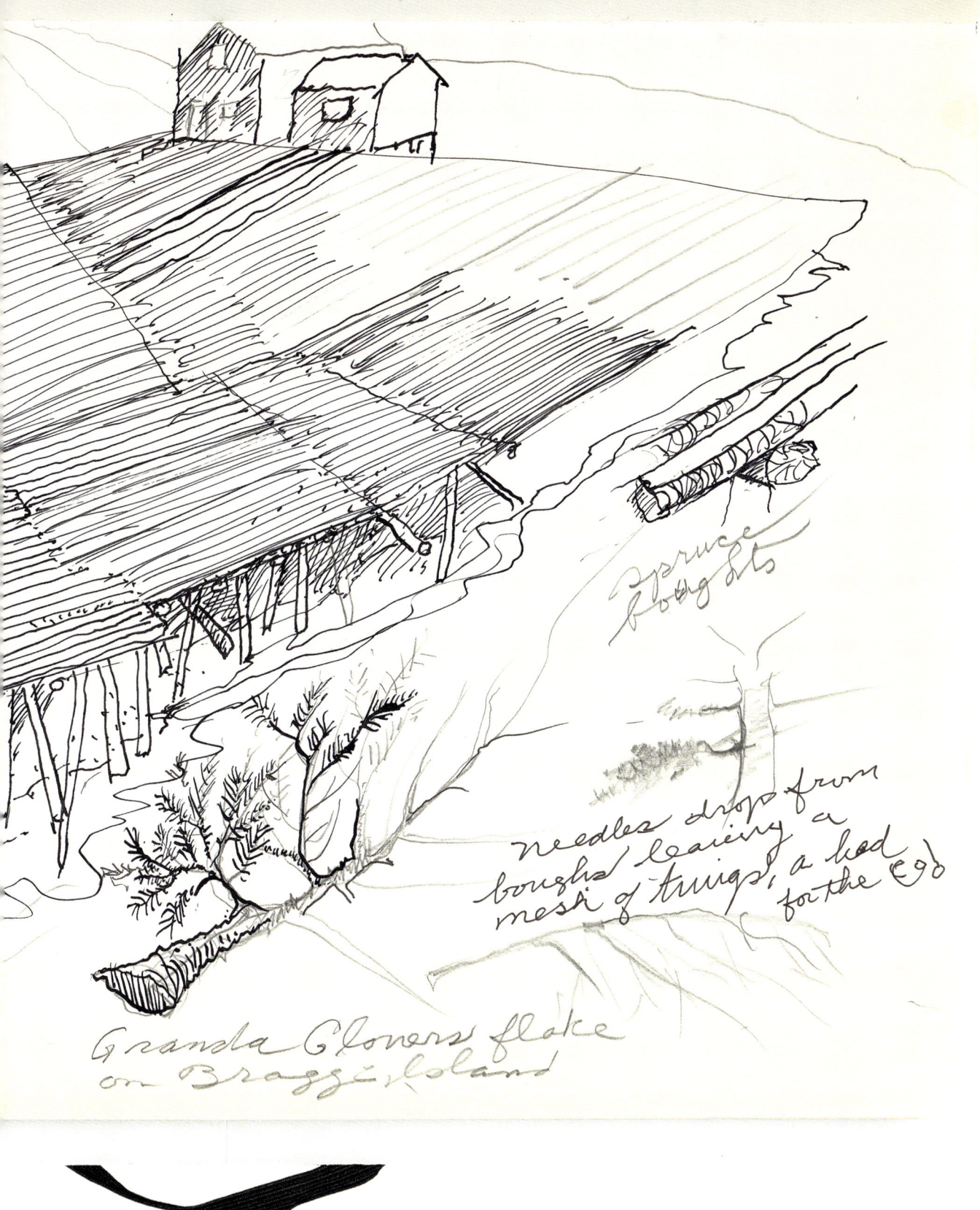

spruce
boughs

needles drop from
boughs leaving a
mesh of twigs, a bed
for the Egg

Granda Glovers flake
on Braggs Island

127

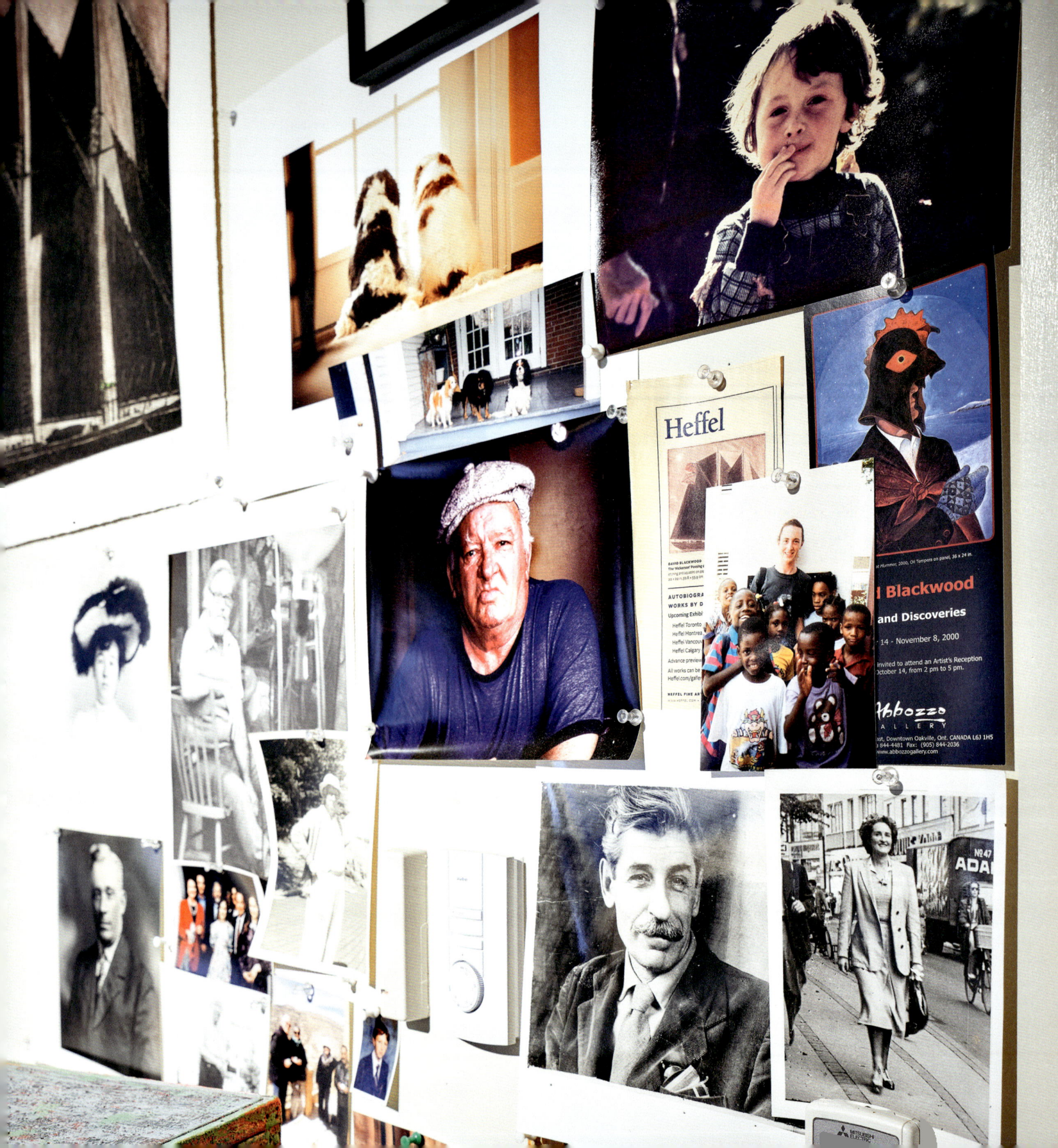

Blackwood's studio was the natural habitat of much of his archive—the space where sketchbooks and drawings fulfilled their purpose, and where source images and beloved objects were close at hand as sources of inspiration. On the wall next to the entrance door, there is a constellation of photographs, news clippings, and sketches pinned up where the artist could see them most often. There are the faces of his greatest teachers, his family elders, and his beloved dogs. Alongside storytelling and memory, a profound sense of loss echoes throughout Blackwood's oeuvre, from lost culture to mourning those closest to him. Amid the photos is one of a small, merry-eyed boy with a halo of sunlight behind him: the artist's son, David Judah, who died of cancer as a young man.

David Blackwood's studio wall, Port Hope, Ontario.

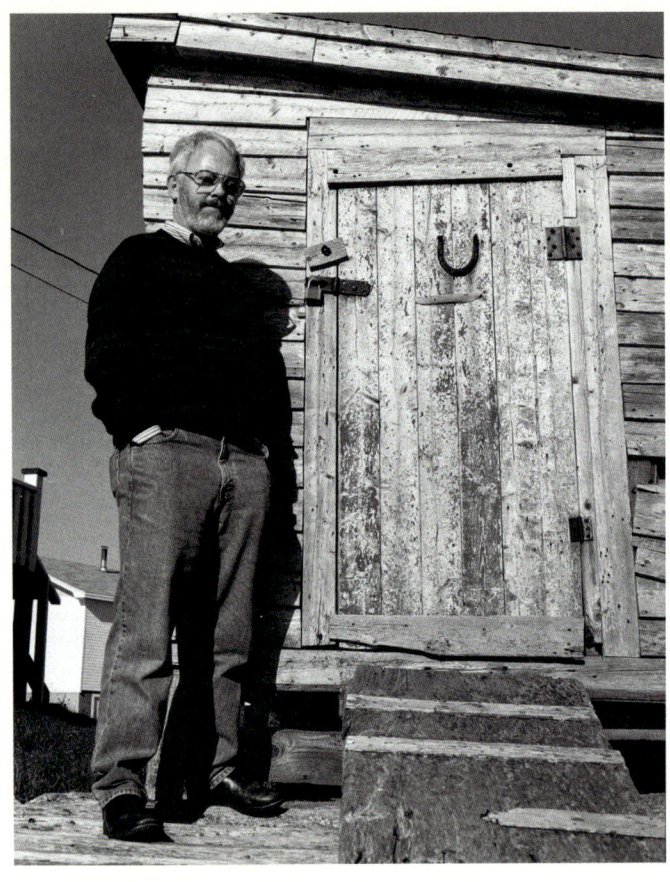

In the 2010 print *Autobiography*, Blackwood recorded the names of all the people whose lives touched his own, as if carved into a rustic wooden door. The artist's inspiration for the image is an ordinary shed door that once belonged to a Wesleyville neighbour named Ephraim Kelloway. Covered in weathered layers of colourful paint worn away by time, the door held great meaning for Blackwood; a humble and mysterious portal to the eternal truths that he strove to reach through his art. He would return to this subject repeatedly over the course of his career, laying the groundwork for infinite entry points into his body of work years later. ⚓

above

David Blackwood with Ephraim Kelloway's door in Wesleyville, photographed by Edgar Blackwood, October 19, 1990. David Blackwood fonds, Edward P. Taylor Library & Archives, Art Gallery of Ontario, Gift of David and Anita Blackwood, 2018 (LA.SC152).

opposite

Autobiography (detail), 2010

next spread

Ephraim Kelloway's Door (detail), 2012

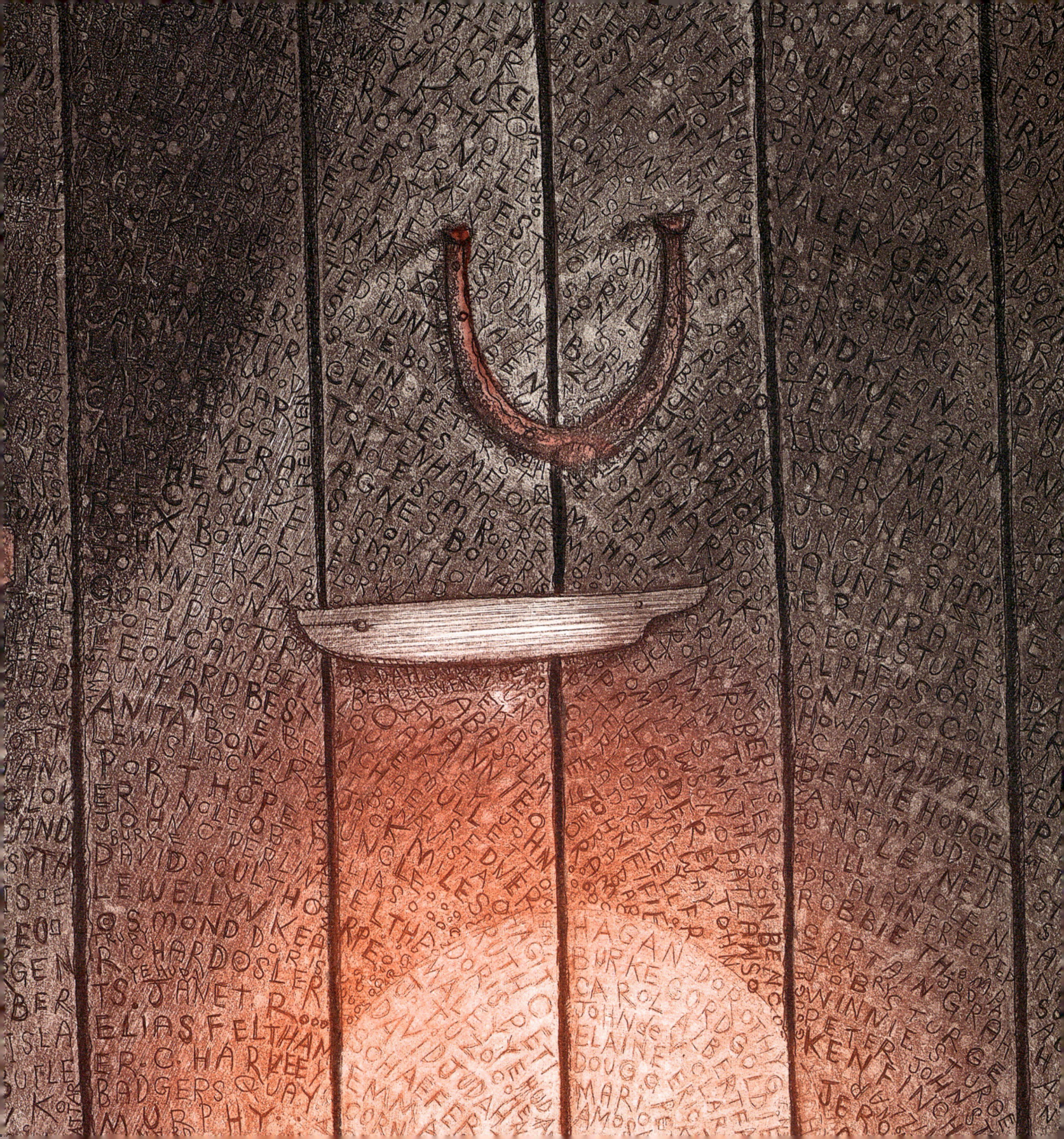

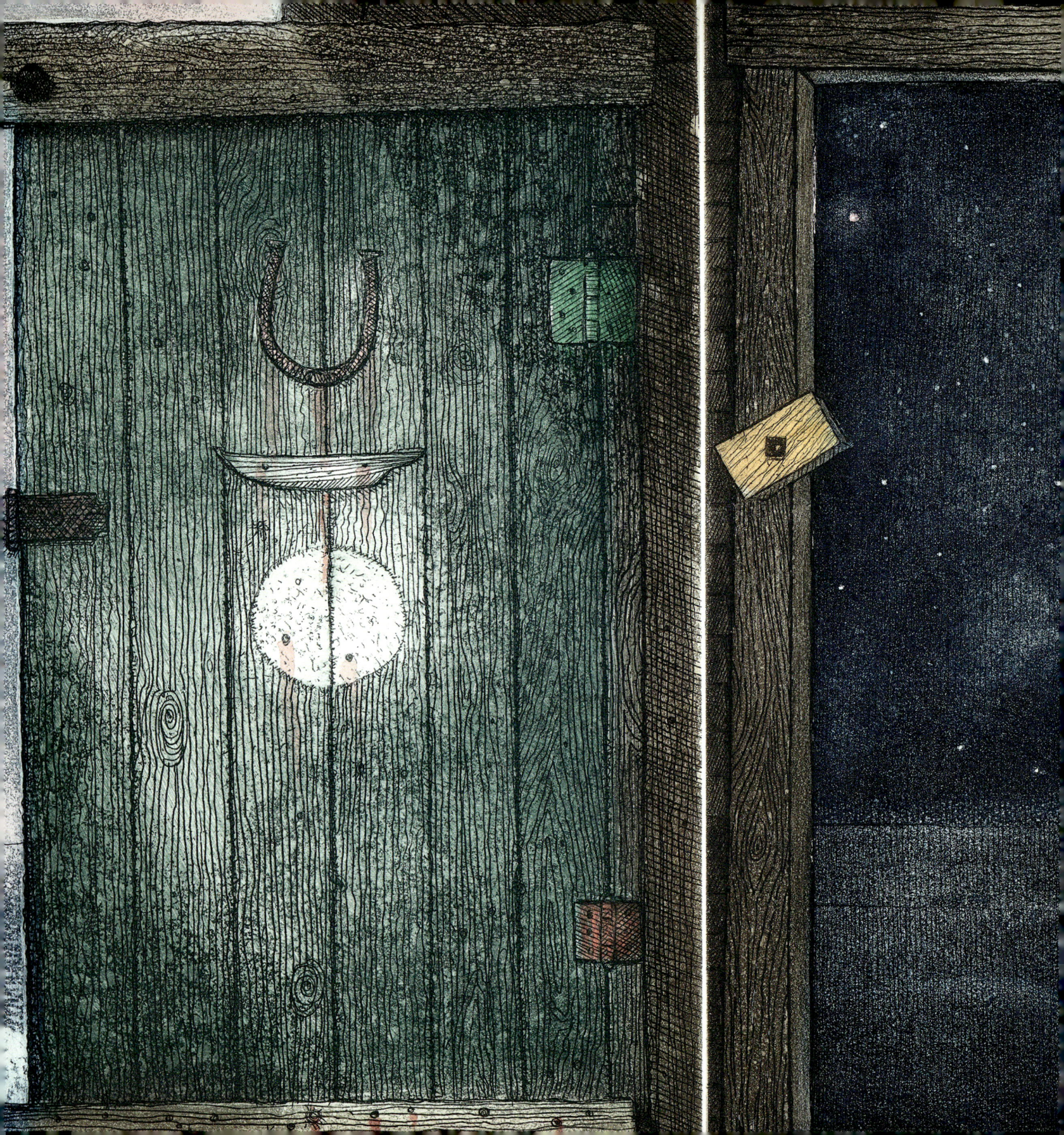

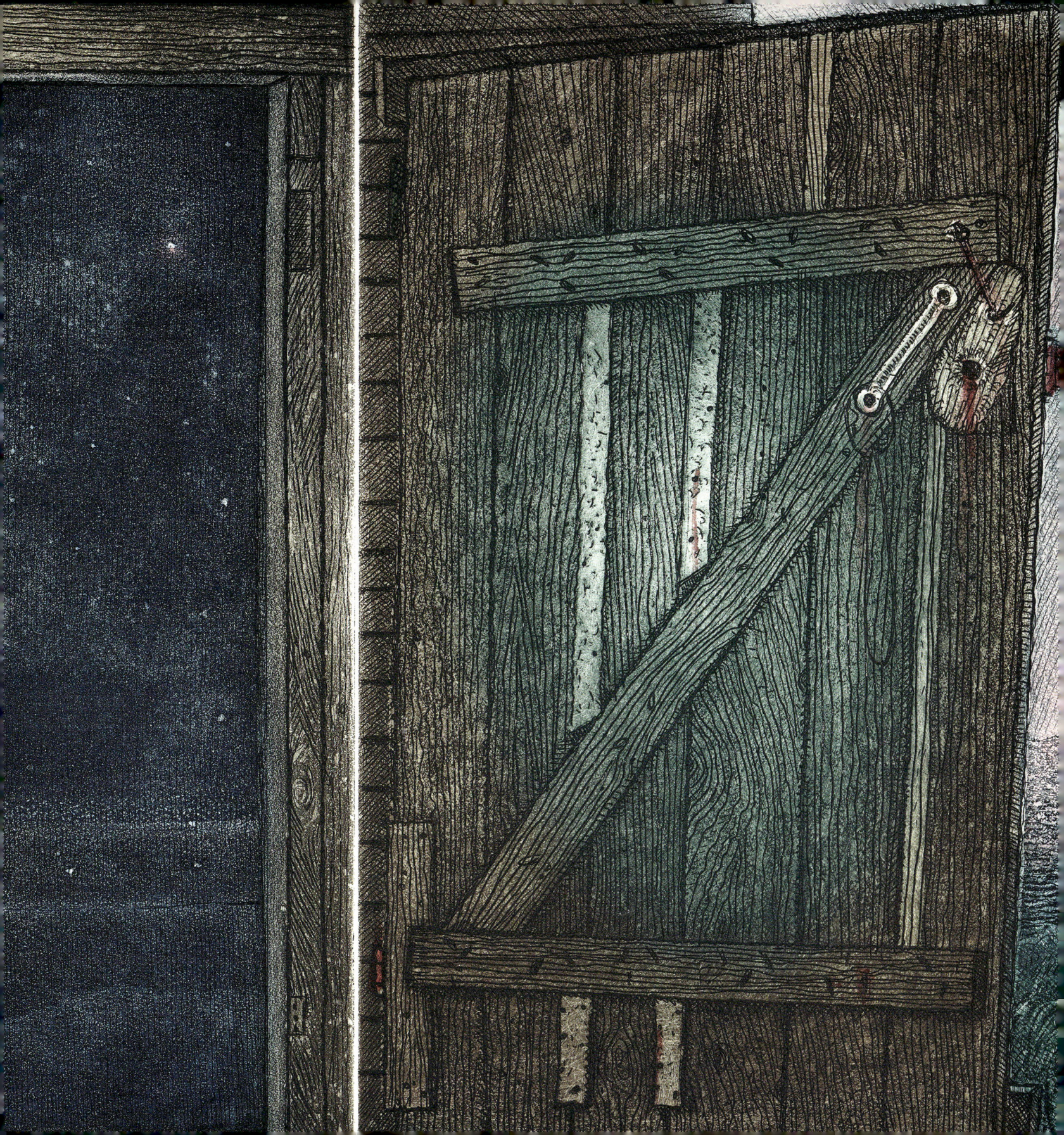

List of Works Illustrated

David Blackwood
born November 7, 1941, Wesleyville,
Newfoundland
died July 2, 2022, Port Hope, Ontario

Unless otherwise noted, all works © Estate
of David Blackwood. All works collection of
the Art Gallery of Ontario with images courtesy
of the AGO, photographed by Craig Boyko.

Abbreviations
AP – Artist's proof
H/C – Hors commerce (out of trade)
NE – No edition
WP – Working proof

April Iceberg Off Bragg's Island
1976
etching and aquatint on paper
AP
50.3 × 80.6 cm
Gift of David and Anita Blackwood, 2008
2008/273
Pages 18–19

Aunt Gerti Hann Home in Wesleyville
1987
graphite and coloured pencil on paper
52.3 × 62.2 cm
Promised Gift of David and Anita Blackwood,
Port Hope, Ontario
Page 64

Aunt Gerti Hann Home in Wesleyville
1987
etching, aquatint, and watercolour on paper
AP
40.7 × 50.7 cm
Promised Gift of David and Anita Blackwood,
Port Hope, Ontario
Page 65 & back cover

Aunt Julia Carter, Midwife, Wesleyville
2020
graphite and watercolour on paper
91.9 × 61.2 cm
Promised Gift of David and Anita Blackwood,
Port Hope, Ontario
Page 95

Autobiography
2010
etching and aquatint on paper
edition 25/50
81.3 × 50.8 cm
Promised Gift of David and Anita Blackwood,
Port Hope, Ontario
Pages 78 & 131

Barbour's "Seabird" Leaving Newtown
1998
etching, aquatint, and watercolour on paper
edition 54/75
60.8 × 91 cm
Promised Gift of David and Anita Blackwood,
Port Hope, Ontario
Page 73

Bonfire Night on Greenspond Island
2002
etching, aquatint, and watercolour on paper
edition 49/75
38 × 91.1 cm
Promised Gift of David and Anita Blackwood,
Port Hope, Ontario
Pages 68–69

Cape Spear, Newfoundland
1983
graphite on paper
60.1 × 90 cm
Gift of David and Anita Blackwood, 2018
2021/173
Page 50

Cape Spear, Newfoundland
1983
pen and ink with graphite and
porous-point pen on tracing paper
59.9 × 87 cm
Gift of David and Anita Blackwood, 2018
2021/175
Page 51

Cape Spear, Newfoundland
1983
etching and aquatint on paper
fourth-stage proof
50.7 × 81 cm
Gift of David and Anita Blackwood, 2008
2008/304
Page 53

Mummer Family at the Door
1985
etching and aquatint on paper
AP
91.4 × 61 cm
Promised Gift of David and Anita Blackwood,
Port Hope, Ontario
Page 55 & back endsheet (right)

The Nickerson Passing
2015
etching and aquatint on paper
edition 9/50
16.5 × 17.8 cm
Promised Gift of David and Anita Blackwood,
Port Hope, Ontario
Page 86

The Nickerson Passing on our Starboard Quarter
2019
etching, aquatint, watercolour, and friable
drawing media on paper
edition 10/50
50.6 × 55.8 cm
Promised Gift of David and Anita Blackwood,
Port Hope, Ontario
Page 87

Outward Bound for the Labrador
1985
etching and aquatint on paper
H/C
38.1 × 91.4 cm
Promised Gift of David and Anita Blackwood,
Port Hope, Ontario
Pages 60–61

Passing Under the Rostellan
2013
etching and aquatint on paper
edition 13/50
30.4 × 45.6 cm
Promised Gift of David and Anita Blackwood,
Port Hope, Ontario
Page 83

Passing Under the Rostellan (Rigging Detail)
2013
graphite on paper
20.4 × 50.3 cm
Promised Gift of David and Anita Blackwood,
Port Hope, Ontario
Page 82

Search Party: Lost
1970–2021
etching and aquatint on paper
edition 33/50
80.8 × 50.7 cm
Promised Gift of David and Anita Blackwood,
Port Hope, Ontario
Page 94

Seated Figure Studies
date unknown
graphite on paper
41 × 30.9 cm
Promised Gift of David and Anita Blackwood,
Port Hope, Ontario
Page 90

Self-Portrait [David L. Blackwood]
1981
graphite on paper
94 × 66 cm
Promised Gift of David and Anita Blackwood,
Port Hope, Ontario
Page 49

Self-Portrait [Fragment]
1981
graphite on paper
41 × 25 cm
Promised Gift of David and Anita Blackwood,
Port Hope, Ontario
Page 15

Studies Hands, Heads
2002
pen and ink on paper
30.3 × 37.4 cm
Promised Gift of David and Anita Blackwood,
Port Hope, Ontario
Page 48

Survivors
1961
etching and aquatint on paper
edition 1/10
17.7 × 25.4 cm
Gift of David and Anita Blackwood,
Port Hope, Ontario, 1999
99/884
Page 42

Wedding on Deer Island
2020
graphite on paper
51.4 × 72.6 cm
Promised Gift of David and Anita Blackwood,
Port Hope, Ontario
Page 96

Wedding on Deer Island
2020
graphite and ballpoint ink on tracing paper
34.9 × 52.1 cm
Promised Gift of David and Anita Blackwood,
Port Hope, Ontario
Page 97

Wedding on Deer Island
2020
copperplate
30.4 × 45.5 cm
Edward P. Taylor Library & Archives,
Art Gallery of Ontario
Promised Gift of David and Anita Blackwood,
Port Hope, Ontario
Pages 105, 106–107

Wedding on Deer Island
March 13, 2020
etching, with plate tone, and graphite on paper
WP 1
30.4 × 45.5 cm
Promised Gift of David and Anita Blackwood,
Port Hope, Ontario
Page 98 & front endsheet

Wedding on Deer Island
March 2020
etching, with plate tone, and graphite on paper
WP 2
30.4 × 45.5 cm
Promised Gift of David and Anita Blackwood,
Port Hope, Ontario
Pages 1 & 98

Wedding on Deer Island
March 2020
etching and aquatint on paper
WP 3
30.4 × 45.5 cm
Promised Gift of David and Anita Blackwood,
Port Hope, Ontario
Page 99

Wedding on Deer Island
April 3, 2020
etching and aquatint on paper
WP 4
30.4 × 45.5 cm
Promised Gift of David and Anita Blackwood,
Port Hope, Ontario
Pages 2–3, 99

Wedding on Deer Island
April 15, 2020
etching and aquatint on paper
WP 5
30.4 × 45.5 cm
Promised Gift of David and Anita Blackwood,
Port Hope, Ontario
Pages 4–5, 100

Wedding on Deer Island
April 17, 2020
etching and aquatint on paper
WP 6
30.4 × 45.5 cm
Promised Gift of David and Anita Blackwood,
Port Hope, Ontario
Page 101

Wedding on Deer Island
April 20 & 22, 2020
etching and aquatint on paper
WP 7
30.4 × 45.5 cm
Promised Gift of David and Anita Blackwood,
Port Hope, Ontario
Pages 6–7, 101

Wedding on Deer Island
April 24, 2020
etching and aquatint on paper
WP 8
30.4 × 45.5 cm
Promised Gift of David and Anita Blackwood,
Port Hope, Ontario
Page 102

Wedding on Deer Island
2020
etching and aquatint on paper
WP 9
30.4 × 45.5 cm
Promised Gift of David and Anita Blackwood,
Port Hope, Ontario
Page 102

Wedding on Deer Island
May 24, 2020
etching, aquatint, colour washes,
and white pencil on paper
WP 10
30.4 × 45.5 cm
Promised Gift of David and Anita Blackwood,
Port Hope, Ontario
Pages 8–9, 103

Wedding on Deer Island
2020
etching, aquatint, and watercolour on paper
edition 28/50
30.4 × 45.5 cm
Promised Gift of David and Anita Blackwood,
Port Hope, Ontario
Pages 10–11, 104

Wesleyville: Burning of the Methodist Church
1976
etching and aquatint on paper
AP
55.4 × 70.9 cm
Gift of David and Anita Blackwood,
Port Hope, Ontario, 1999
99/940
Page 93

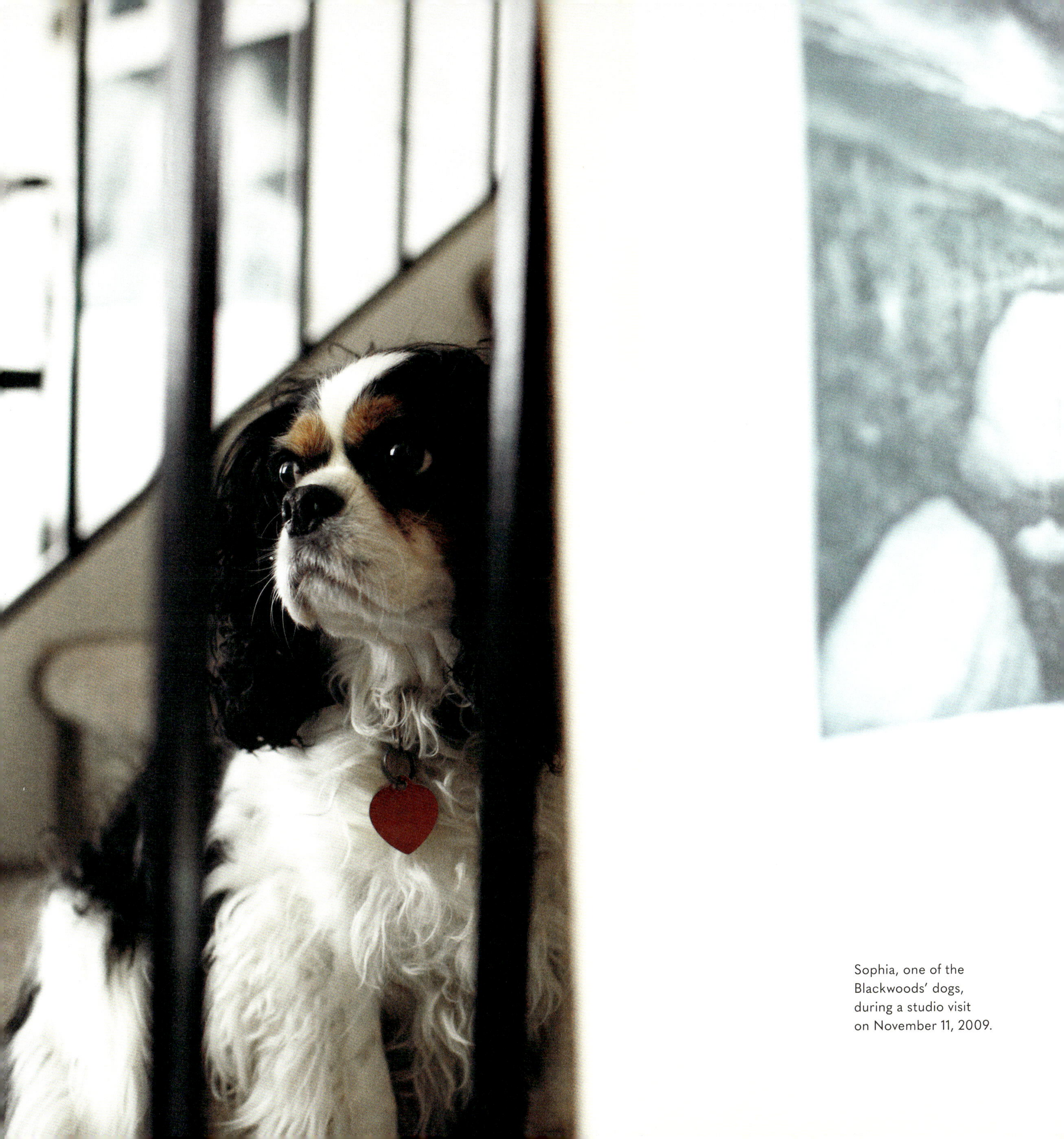

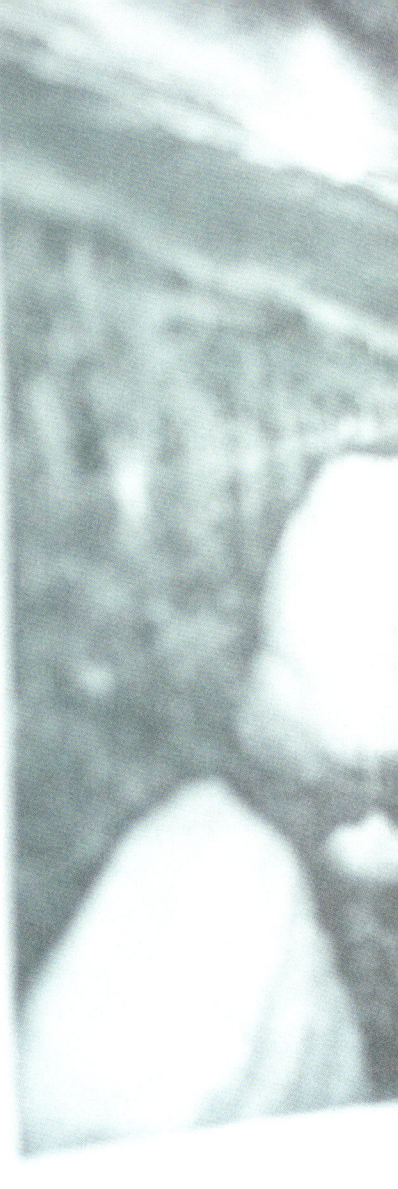

Sophia, one of the
Blackwoods' dogs,
during a studio visit
on November 11, 2009.

Land Acknowledgement

The Art Gallery of Ontario operates on land that is the territory of the Anishinaabe (Mississauga) nation and is also the territory of the Wendat and Haudenosaunee. The Dish with One Spoon Wampum Belt Covenant is an agreement between the Haudenosaunee Confederacy and the Anishinaabe Three Fires Confederacy to peaceably share and care for the resources around the Great Lakes. Toronto is also governed by a treaty between the federal government of Canada and the Mississaugas of the New Credit (Anishinaabe nation). Toronto has always been a trading centre for First Nations.

Goose Lane Editions is located on the unceded territory of the Wəlastəkwiyik whose ancestors along with the Mi'kmaq and Peskotomuhkati Nations signed Peace and Friendship Treaties with the British Crown in the 1700s.

Thank You

Supporting Sponsor

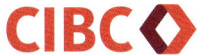

Contributing Sponsor

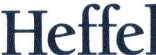

Lead Support

Volunteers of the AGO

Generous Support

Maxine Granovsky Gluskin & Ira Gluskin

In Memory of Martine Vilas and
Gerald Conway of Cleveland, Ohio

Additional Assistance

Elizabeth Tory

This publication is supported by the
Sorel Etrog Publication Fund.

The Art Gallery of Ontario is partially
funded by the Ontario Ministry of Culture.
Additional operating support is received
from the City of Toronto, the Department
of Canadian Heritage, and the Canada
Council for the Arts.

Contemporary programming at the
Art Gallery of Ontario is supported by

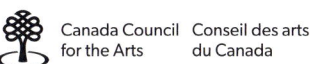

Goose Lane Editions acknowledges the
generous support of the Government of
Canada, the Canada Council for the Arts,
and the Government of New Brunswick.

Publication

Editor: Alexa Greist
Publishing Director: Jim Shedden
Publishing Coordinator: Kathryn Yuen
Content Editor: Nives Hajdin-Rorabeck
Production Editor: Alan Sheppard,
    Goose Lane Editions
Proofreader: David Marsh
Designer: Lara Minja of Lime Design
Photographer: Craig Boyko
Pre-Press: Paul Jerinkitsch
Printing: Type A Print Inc.

Exhibition

Deputy Director & Chief Curator: Julian Cox
Curator: Alexa Greist
Rosamond Ivey Special Collections Archivist &
Head, Library & Archives:
    Amy Marshall Furness
Project Managers: Katarina Veljovic,
    Chloé Wittes
Curatorial Coordinator: Wendy Hebditch
Research & Collections Coordinator,
    Marvin Gelber Print and Drawing
    Study Centre: Emily Miller
Interpretive Planner: Nadia Abraham
Editor: Nives Hajdin-Rorabeck
Production: Evelyn Quinn
Exhibition Designer: Marco Cheuk
Graphic Designer: Aleksandra Grzywaczewska

Exhibitions, Collections, and Conservation

Chief, Exhibitions, Collections &
    Conservation: Jessica Bright
Director, Exhibitions: Laura Comerford
Registration: Donna Austria, Alison Beckett,
    Jerry Drozdowsky, Joel Herman,
    Matthew Janisse, Jason Laudadio,
    Alison Lindsay, Dale Mahar, Doug Moore,
    Sabine Schaefer
Collection Information: Alexander Arslanyan,
    Alexandra Cousins, Tracy Mallon-Jensen,
    Liana Radvak, Olga Zotova
Conservation: Lisa Ellis, Margaret Haupt,
    Brent Roe, Maria Sullivan, Tessa Thomas,
    John Williams

Logistics and Art Services

Director, Logistics and Art Services:
    Iain Hoadley
Manager, Art Services: Craig Whiteside
Curtis Amisich, Paul Ayers, Gregory
    Baszun, Michael Beynon, Scott Cameron,
    Colin Campbell, Corinne Carlson,
    Brian Davis, Alex DiGiacomo, Christian
    Echeverri, Andre Ethier, Randal Fedje,
    Tina Giovinazzo, Ruth Jones, David
    Kinsman, Nanthini Kirupakaran, Paul
    Mathiesen, Phil Scott, Damian Seguin,
    Sasi Sivapalan, Stephanie Vittas, Phil
    Woollam, Darla Yorston, Tanya Zhilinsky

Education & Programming

Richard & Elizabeth Currie Chief,
    Education & Programming:
    Robert Durocher
Charlotte Big Canoe, Maureen DaSilva,
    Nathan Huisman, Jesse King, Natalie
    Lam, Zavette Quadros-Evangelista, Tiana
    Roebuck, Bojana Stancic, Joey Suriano,
    Ida Zongo

Media Production

Chief, Brand & Business Officer: Ros Lawler
Director, Brand, Marketing: Kimber Slater
Associate Director, Brand and Marketing:
    Suman Chahal
Senior Manager, Creative Studio:
    Malene Hjørngaard
Manager, Digital Projects:
    Catherine Thomson
Media: Fraser Wrighte
Photographers: Craig Boyko, Steve Jacobs,
    Ian Lefebvre, Leah Maghanoy, Tracey
    Owusu, Dean Tomlinson, Sean Weaver

Development

Chief Development Officer: Kate Halpenny
Senior Director, Major Gifts and Campaign:
    Andrea Orr
Director, Corporate Partnerships &
    Development Special Events:
    Taryn Sarkozi
Philanthropy: Anastasia Hare, Erin Thadani
Donor Relations: Michelle Greenspoon,
    Matt Semansky

This book was published on the occasion of *David Blackwood: Myth & Legend* organized by the Art Gallery of Ontario, exhibited October 8, 2025, to July 12, 2026.

Published in 2025 by the Art Gallery of Ontario and Goose Lane Editions.

Cover Images

David Blackwood, *January Visit Home* (detail), 1975. Etching and aquatint on paper, NE, 50.5 × 80.7 cm. Art Gallery of Ontario, Gift of David and Anita Blackwood, Port Hope, Ontario, 1999 (99/936). © Estate of David Blackwood. Photo: AGO.

David Blackwood, *Aunt Gerti Hann Home in Wesleyville* (detail), 1987. Etching, aquatint, and watercolour on paper, AP, 40.7 × 50.7 cm. Art Gallery of Ontario, Promised Gift of David and Anita Blackwood, Port Hope, Ontario. © Estate of David Blackwood. Photo: AGO, Craig Boyko.

Printed and bound in Belgium.
Printed on Magno Volume 150gsm (interior) and Wibalin Natural White (cover).

Set in Scala and Quasimoda.

ISBN: 9781773104782

10 9 8 7 6 5 4 3 2 1

Library and Archives Canada Cataloguing in Publication

Title: David Blackwood : myth & legend / edited by Alexa Greist.
Other titles: David Blackwood (2025) | Myth & legend | Myth and legend
Names: Container of (work): Blackwood, David. Works. Selections. | Greist, Alexa, editor | Art Gallery of Ontario, issuing body, host institution.
Description: Catalogue of an exhibition organized by the Art Gallery of Ontario, running October 8, 2025 – July 12, 2026. | Includes bibliographical references.
Identifiers: Canadiana 20250179695 | ISBN 9781773104782 (hardcover)
Subjects: LCSH: Blackwood, David—Exhibitions. | LCSH: Prints, Canadian—Newfoundland and Labrador—20th century—Exhibitions. | LCGFT: Exhibition catalogs.
Classification: LCC NE2013.5.B63 A4 2025 | DDC 769.92—dc23

Art Gallery of Ontario
317 Dundas Street West
Toronto, Ontario
M5T 1G4
Canada
ago.ca

Goose Lane Editions
500 Beaverbrook Court, Suite 330
Fredericton, New Brunswick
E3B 5X4
Canada
gooselane.com

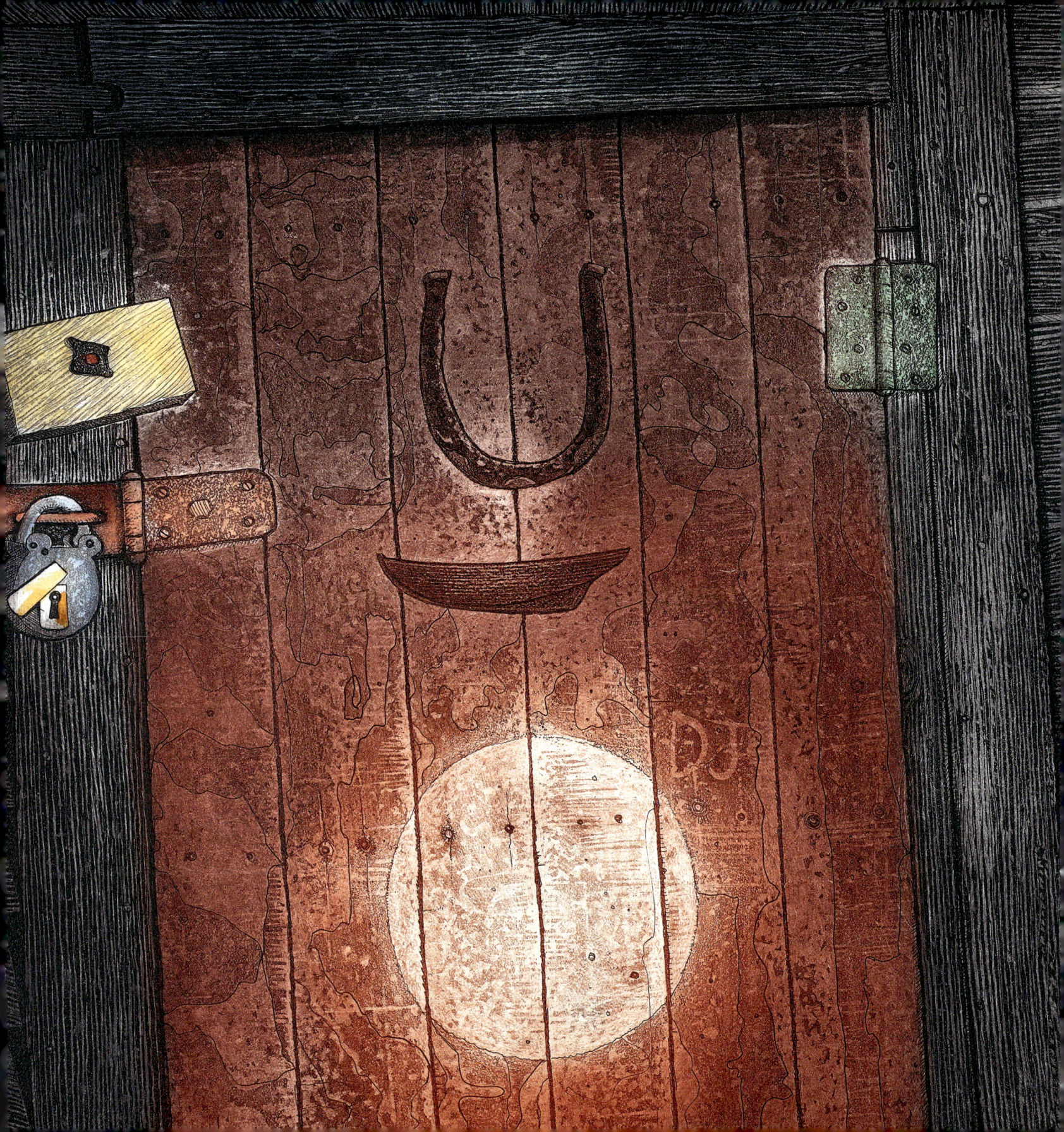

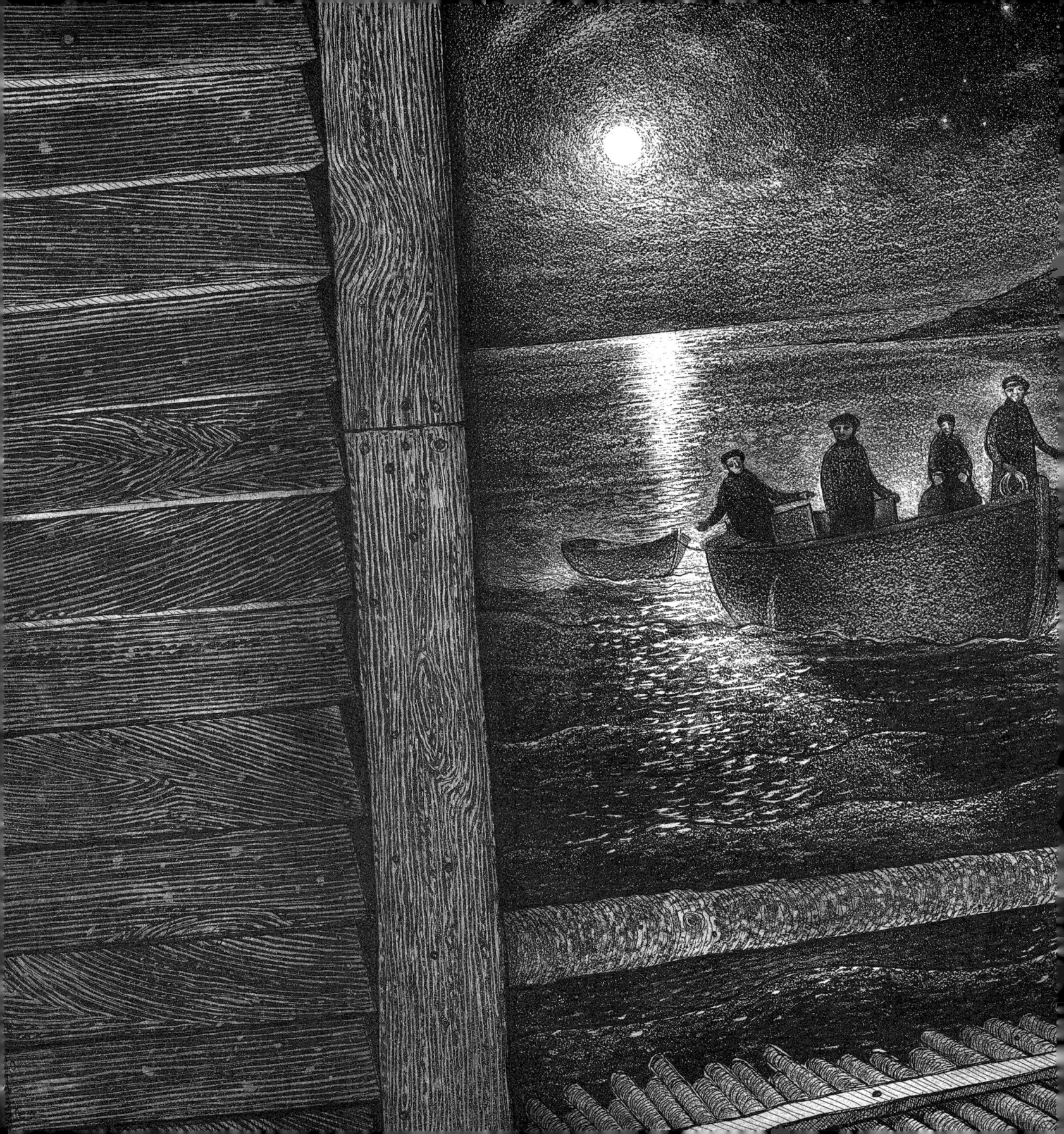

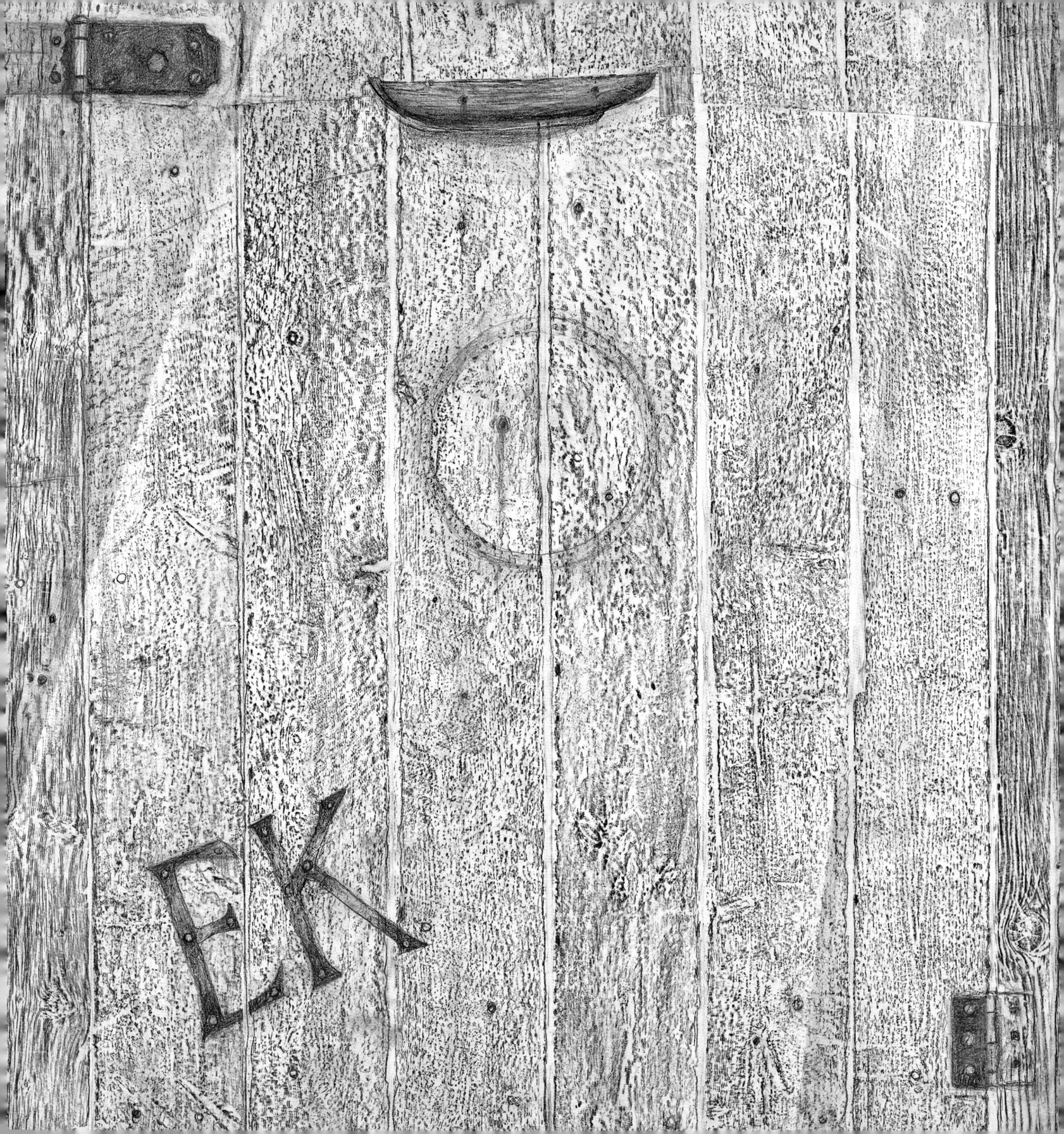